THE ANCIENT AMERICAN WORLD

TEACHING GUIDE

OXFORD
UNIVERSITY PRESS

OXFORD
UNIVERSITY PRESS

Oxford University Press, Inc., publishes works that
further Oxford University's objective of excellence
in research, scholarship, and education.

Oxford   New York
Auckland   Cape Town   Dar es Salaam   Hong Kong   Karachi
Kuala Lumpur   Madrid   Melbourne   Mexico City   Nairobi
New Delhi   Shanghai   Taipei   Toronto

With offices in
Argentina   Austria   Brazil   Chile   Czech Republic   France   Greece
Guatemala   Hungary   Italy   Japan   Poland   Portugal   Singapore
South Korea   Switzerland   Thailand   Turkey   Ukraine   Vietnam

Copyright © 2005 by Oxford University Press, Inc.

Published by Oxford University Press, Inc.
198 Madison Avenue, New York, NY 10016
www.oup.com

Oxford is a registered trademark of Oxford University Press
All rights reserved. No part of this publication may be reproduced,
stored in a retrieval system, or transmitted in any form or by any means,
electronic, mechanical, photocopying, recording, or otherwise,
without the prior permission of Oxford University Press.

Writer: Susan Moger
Editor: Robert Weisser
Project Editor: Lelia Mander
Project Director: Jacqueline A. Ball
Education Consultant: Diane L. Brooks, Ed.D.
Design: designlabnyc

Casper Grathwohl, Publisher

ISBN-13: 978-0-19-522287-6 (California edition)   ISBN-13: 978-0-19-517900-2

Printed in the United States of America
on acid-free paper

CONTENTS

Note to the Teacher	5
The World in Ancient Times Program Using the Teaching Guide and Student Study Guide	6
Improving Literacy with *The World in Ancient Times*	16
Teaching Strategies for *The Ancient American World*	
Unit 1 Mesoamerica—Early Civilizations (Introduction, Chapters 1–2)	20
Unit 2 Mesoamerican Cities (Chapters 3–4)	32
Unit 3 The Maya (Chapters 5–8)	44
Unit 4 The Aztec Empire (Chapters 9–11)	64
Unit 5 War of the Worlds (Chapters 12–13)	80
Unit 6 The Andean World (Chapters 14–16)	92
Unit 7 Highland and Coastal Empires before the Inca (Chapters 17–19)	108
Unit 8 The Inca Empire (Chapters 20–21, Epilogue)	124
Wrap-Up Test	136
Graphic Organizers	138
Rubrics	146
Answer Key	150

HISTORY FROM OXFORD UNIVERSITY PRESS

"A thoroughly researched political and cultural history... makes for a solid resource for any collection."
– School Library Journal

THE WORLD IN ANCIENT TIMES
RONALD MELLOR AND AMANDA H. PODANY, EDS.
THE EARLY HUMAN WORLD
THE ANCIENT NEAR EASTERN WORLD
THE ANCIENT EGYPTIAN WORLD
THE ANCIENT SOUTH ASIAN WORLD
THE ANCIENT CHINESE WORLD
THE ANCIENT GREEK WORLD
THE ANCIENT ROMAN WORLD
THE ANCIENT AMERICAN WORLD

"Bringing history out of the Dark Ages!"

THE MEDIEVAL AND EARLY MODERN WORLD
BONNIE G. SMITH, ED.
THE EUROPEAN WORLD, 400-1450
THE AFRICAN AND MIDDLE EASTERN WORLD, 600-1500
THE ASIAN WORLD, 600-1500
AN AGE OF EMPIRES, 1200-1750
AN AGE OF VOYAGES, 1350-1600
AN AGE OF SCIENCE AND REVOLUTIONS, 1600-1800

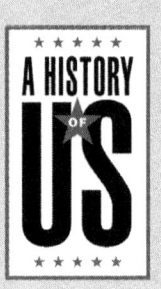

"The liveliest, most realistic, most well-received American history series ever written for children."
– Los Angeles Times

A HISTORY OF US
JOY HAKIM
THE FIRST AMERICANS
MAKING THIRTEEEN COLONIES
FROM COLONIES TO COUNTRY
THE NEW NATION
LIBERTY FOR ALL?
WAR, TERRIBLE WAR
RECONSTRUCTING AMERICA
AN AGE OF EXTREMES
WAR, PEACE, AND ALL THAT JAZZ
ALL THE PEOPLE

FOR MORE INFORMATION, VISIT US AT WWW.OUP.COM

New from Oxford University Press
Reading History, by Janet Allen
ISBN 0-19-516595-0 hc 0-19-516596-9 pb

"*Reading History* is a great idea. I highly recommend this book."
–Dennis Denenberg, *Professor of Elementary and Early Childhood Education, Millersville University*

NOTE TO THE TEACHER

Dear Educator

You probably love history. You read historical novels, watch documentaries, and enjoy (and, as a history teacher, no doubt criticize) Hollywood's attempts to recreate the past. So why don't most kids love history too? We think it might be because of the tone of the history books they are assigned. Many textbook authors seem to assume that the sole goal of teaching history is to make sure the students memorize innumerable facts. So, innumerable facts are crammed onto the pages, facts without context, as thrilling to read as names in a phone book.

Real history, however, is not just facts; it's the story of real people who cared deeply about the events and controversies of their times. And learning real history is essential. It helps children to understand the events that brought the world to where they find it now. It helps them distrust stereotypes of other cultures. It helps them read critically. (It also helps them succeed in standardized assessments of their reading skills.) We, like you, find history positively addicting. Students can feel the same way. (Can you imagine a child reading a history book with a flashlight after lights out, just because it is so interesting?)

The World in Ancient Times books reveal ancient history to be a great story—a whole bunch of great stories—some of which have been known for centuries, but some of which are just being discovered. Each book in the series is written by a team of two writers: a scholar who is working in the field of ancient history and knows what is new and exciting, and a well-known children's book author who knows how to communicate these ideas to kids. The teams have come up with books that are historically accurate and up to date as well as beautifully written. They also feature magnificent illustrations of real artifacts, archaeological sites, and works of art, along with maps and timelines to allow readers to get a sense of where events are set in place and time. Etymologies from the *Oxford English Dictionary*, noted in the margins, help to expand students' vocabulary by identifying the ancient roots, along with the meanings, of English words.

The authors of our books use vivid language to describe what we know and to present the evidence for *how* we know what we know. We let the readers puzzle right along with the historians and archaeologists. The evidence comes in the form of primary sources, not only in the illustrations but especially in the documents written in ancient times, which are quoted extensively.

You can integrate these primary sources into lessons with your students. When they read a document or look at an artifact or building in the illustrations they can pose questions and make hypotheses about the culture it came from. Why was a king shown as much larger than his attendants in an Egyptian relief sculpture? Why was Pliny unsure about what to do with accused Christians in his letter to the emperor? In this way, students can think like historians.

The series provides a complete narrative for a yearlong course on ancient history. You might choose to have your students read all eight narrative books as they learn about each of the civilizations in turn (or fewer than eight, depending on the ancient civilizations covered in your school's curriculum). Or you might choose to highlight certain chapters in each of the books, and use the others for extended activities or research projects. Since each chapter is written to stand on its own, the students will not be confused if you don't assign all of them. The *Primary Sources and Reference Volume* provides longer primary sources than are available in the other books, allowing students to make their own interpretations and comparisons across cultures.

The ancient world was the stage on which many institutions that we think of as modern were first played out: law, cities, legitimate government, technology, and so on. The major world religions all had their origins long ago, before 600 CE, as did many of the great cities of the world. *The World in Ancient Times* presents this ancient past in a new way—new not just to young adults, but to any audience. The scholarship is top-notch and the telling will catch you up in the thrill of exploration and discovery.

Amanda H. Podany and Ronald Mellor
General Editors, *The World in Ancient Times*

THE WORLD IN ANCIENT TIMES PROGRAM

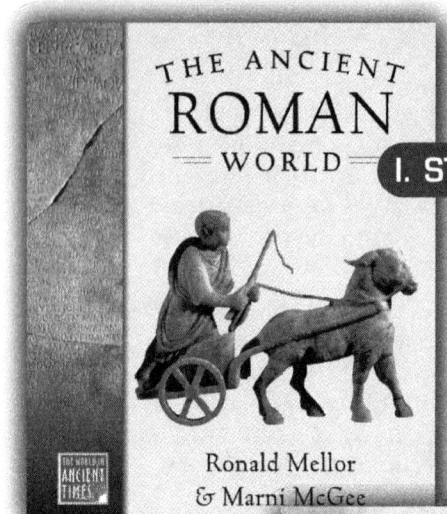

I. STUDENT EDITION

- Engaging, friendly narrative
- A wide range of primary sources in every chapter
- The authority of Oxford scholarship
- Period illustrations and specially commissioned maps

II. TEACHING GUIDE

- Wide range of activities and classroom approaches
- Strategies for universal access and improving literacy (ELL, struggling readers, advanced learners)
- Multiple assessment tools

III. STUDENT STUDY GUIDE

- Exercises correlated to Student Edition and Teaching Guide
- Portfolio approach
- Activities for every level of learning
- Literacy through reading and writing

PRIMARY SOURCES AND REFERENCE VOLUME

- Broad selection of primary sources in each subject area
- Ideal resource for in-class exercises and unit projects

TEACHING GUIDE: KEY FEATURES

The Teaching Guides organize each *The World in Ancient Times* book into units, usually of three or four chapters each. The chapters in each unit cover a key span of time or have a common theme, such as a civilization's origins, government, religion, economy, and daily life.

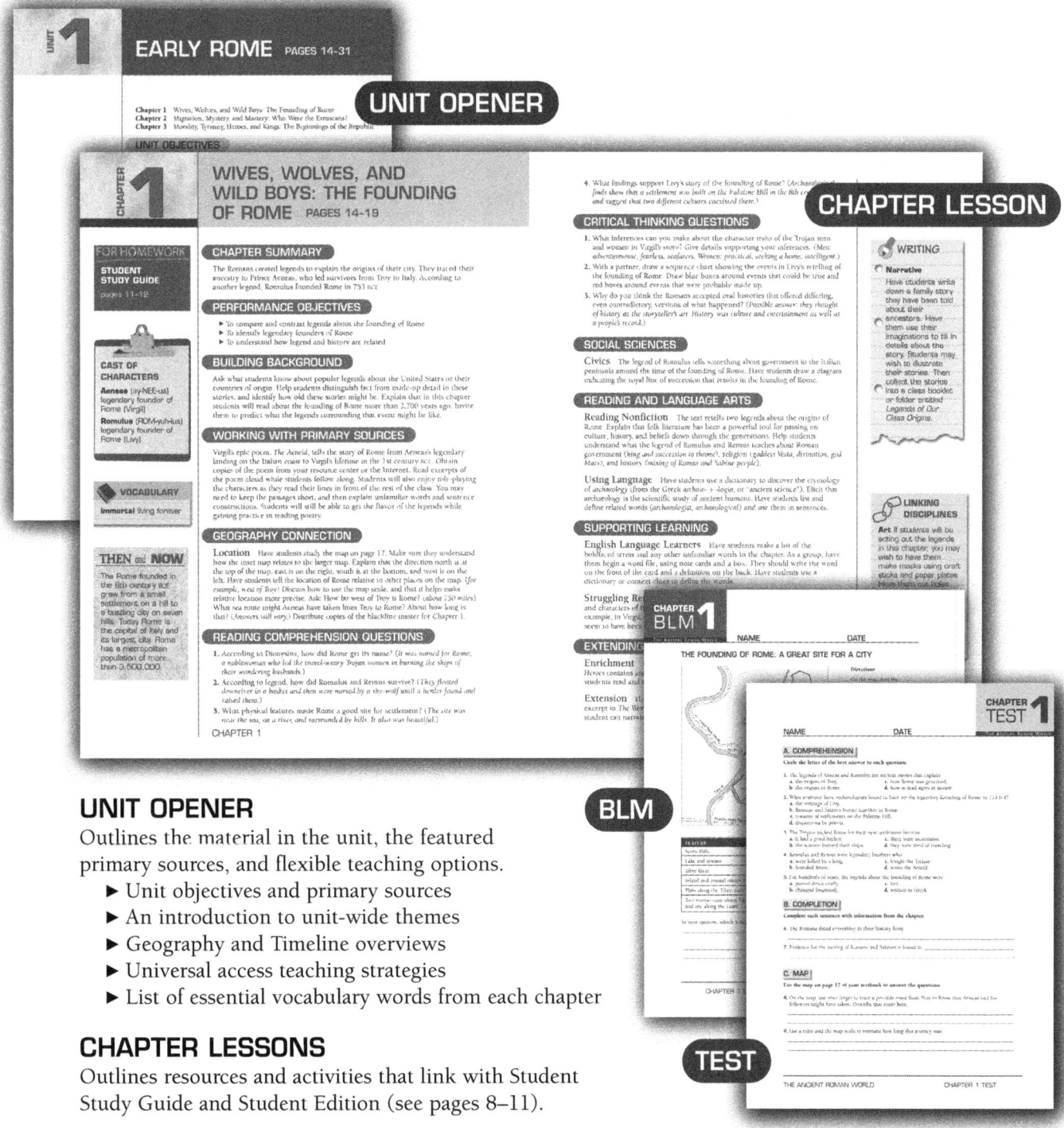

UNIT OPENER
Outlines the material in the unit, the featured primary sources, and flexible teaching options.
- Unit objectives and primary sources
- An introduction to unit-wide themes
- Geography and Timeline overviews
- Universal access teaching strategies
- List of essential vocabulary words from each chapter

CHAPTER LESSONS
Outlines resources and activities that link with Student Study Guide and Student Edition (see pages 8–11).

TESTS AND BLACKLINE MASTERS (BLMS)
Reproducible tests and exercises for assessment, homework, or classroom projects

7

TEACHING GUIDE: CHAPTER LESSONS

Organized so that you can easily find the information you need.

CHAPTER SUMMARY AND PERFORMANCE OBJECTIVES
The Chapter Summary gives an overview of the information in the chapter. The Performance Objectives are the three or four important goals students should achieve in the chapter. Accomplishing these goals will help students master the information in the book.

BUILDING BACKGROUND
This section connects students to the chapter they are about to read. Students may be asked to use what they know to make predictions about the text, preview the images in the chapter, or connect modern life with the ancient subject matter.

WORKING WITH PRIMARY SOURCES
A major feature of *The World in Ancient Times* is having students read about history through the words and images of the people who lived it. Each book includes excerpts from the best sources from these ancient civilizations, giving the narrative an immediacy that is difficult to match in secondary sources. Students can read further in these sources on their own or in small groups using the accompanying *The World in Ancient Times Primary Sources and Reference Volume*. The Teaching Guide recommends activities so students of all skill levels can appreciate the ways people from the past saw themselves, their ideas and values, and their fears and dreams.

CHAPTER 1
WIVES, WOLVES, AND WILD BOYS: THE FOUNDING OF ROME PAGES 14–19

FOR HOMEWORK
STUDENT STUDY GUIDE
pages 11–12

CAST OF CHARACTERS
Aeneas (ay-NEE-us) legendary founder of Rome (Virgil)
Romulus (ROM-yuh-lus) legendary founder of Rome (Livy)

VOCABULARY
immortal living forever

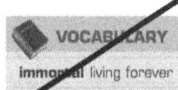

THEN and NOW
The Rome founded in the 8th century BCE grew from a small settlement on a hill to a bustling city on seven hills. Today Rome is the capital of Italy and its largest city. Rome has a metropolitan population of more than 3,500,000.

CHAPTER SUMMARY
The Romans created legends to explain the origins of their city. They traced their ancestry to Prince Aeneas, who led survivors from Troy to Italy. According to another legend, Romulus founded Rome in 753 BCE.

PERFORMANCE OBJECTIVES
- To compare and contrast legends about the founding of Rome
- To identify legendary founders of Rome
- To understand how legend and history are related

BUILDING BACKGROUND
Ask what students know about popular legends about the United States or their countries of origin. Help students distinguish fact from made-up detail in these stories, and identify how old these stories might be. Explain that in this chapter students will read about the founding of Rome more than 2,700 years ago. Invite them to predict what the legends surrounding that event might be like.

WORKING WITH PRIMARY SOURCES
Virgil's epic poem, *The Aeneid*, tells the story of Rome from Aeneas's legendary landing on the Italian coast to Virgil's lifetime in the 1st century BCE. Obtain copies of the poem from your resource center or the Internet. Read excerpts of the poem aloud while students follow along. Students will also enjoy role-playing the characters as they read their lines in front of the rest of the class. You may need to keep the passages short, and then explain unfamiliar words and sentence constructions. Students will still be able to get the flavor of the legends while gaining practice in reading poetry.

GEOGRAPHY CONNECTION
Location Have students study the map on page 17. Make sure they understand how the inset map relates to the larger map. Explain that the direction north is at the top of the map, east is on the right, south is at the bottom, and west is on the left. Have students tell the location of Rome relative to other places on the map. (*for example, west of Troy*) Discuss how to use the map scale, and that it helps make relative location more precise. Ask: How far west of Troy is Rome? (*about 750 miles*) What sea route might Aeneas have taken from Troy to Rome? About how long is that? (*Answers will vary.*) Distribute copies of the blackline master for Chapter 1.

READING COMPREHENSION QUESTIONS
1. According to Dionysius, how did Rome get its name? (*It was named for Roma, a noblewoman who led the travel-weary Trojan women in burning the ships of their wandering husbands.*)
2. According to legend, how did Romulus and Remus survive? (*They floated downriver in a basket and then were nursed by a she-wolf until a herder found and raised them.*)
3. What physical features made Rome a good site for settlement? (*The site was near the sea, on a river, and surrounded by hills. It also was beautiful.*)

CHAPTER 1

GEOGRAPHY CONNECTION
Each chapter has a Geography Connection to strengthen students' map skills as well as their understanding of how geography affects human civilization. One of the five themes of geography (Location, Interaction, Movement, Place, and Regions) is highlighted in each chapter. Map skills such as reading physical, political, and historical maps; using latitude and longitude to find locations; and using the features of a map (mileage scale, legend) are taught throughout the book and reinforced in blackline masters.

READING COMPREHENSION AND CRITICAL THINKING QUESTIONS

The reading comprehension questions are general enough to allow free-flowing class or small group discussion, yet specific enough to be used for oral or written assessment of students' grasp of the important information. The critical thinking questions are intended to engage students in a deeper analysis of the text and can also be used for oral or written assessment.

SOCIAL SCIENCES ACTIVITIES

Students can use these activities to connect the subject matter in the Student Edition with other areas in the social sciences: economics, civics, and science, technology, and society.

READING AND LANGUAGE ARTS

These activities serve a twofold purpose: Some are designed to facilitate the development of nonfiction reading strategies. Others can be used to help students' appreciation of fiction and poetry, as well as nonfiction, by dealing with concepts such as word choice, description, and figurative language.

---

4. What findings support Livy's story of the founding of Rome? (*Archaeological finds show that a settlement was built on the Palatine Hill in the 8th century BCE and suggest that two different cultures coexisted there.*)

CRITICAL THINKING QUESTIONS

1. What inferences can you make about the character traits of the Trojan men and women in Virgil's story? Give details supporting your inferences. (*Men: adventuresome, fearless, seafarers. Women: practical, seeking a home, intelligent.*)
2. With a partner, draw a sequence chart showing the events in Livy's retelling of the founding of Rome. Draw blue boxes around events that could be true and red boxes around events that were probably made up.
3. Why do you think the Romans accepted oral histories that offered differing, even contradictory, versions of what happened? (*Possible answer: they thought of history as the storyteller's art. History was culture and entertainment as well as a people's record.*)

SOCIAL SCIENCES

Civics The legend of Romulus tells something about government in the Italian peninsula around the time of the founding of Rome. Have students draw a diagram indicating the royal line of succession that results in the founding of Rome.

READING AND LANGUAGE ARTS

Reading Nonfiction The text retells two legends about the origins of Rome. Explain that folk literature has been a powerful tool for passing on culture, history, and beliefs down through the generations. Help students understand what the legend of Romulus and Remus teaches about Roman government (*king and succession to throne*), religion (*goddess Vesta, divination, god Mars*), and history (*mixing of Roman and Sabine people*).

Using Language Have students use a dictionary to discover the etymology of *archaeology* (from the Greek *archaio-* + *-logia*, or "ancient science"). Elicit that archaeology is the scientific study of ancient humans. Have students list and define related words (*archaeologist, archaeological*) and use them in sentences.

SUPPORTING LEARNING

English Language Learners Have students make a list of the boldfaced terms and any other unfamiliar words in the chapter. As a group, have them begin a word file, using note cards and a box. They should write the word on the front of the card and a definition on the back. Have students use a dictionary or context clues to define the words.

Struggling Readers Have students make a chart comparing the events and characters of the two legends. Then help students draw conclusions: for example, in Virgil, the founders of Rome came from Troy; in Livy, the founders seem to have been living in Italy already.

EXTENDING LEARNING

Enrichment Edith Hamilton's book *Mythology: Timeless Tales of Gods and Heroes* contains another myth about the founding of Rome by Aeneas. Have students read and summarize this myth for the class.

Extension Have student groups act out scenes from *The Aeneid*, from the excerpt in *The World in Ancient Times Primary Sources and Reference Volume*. One student can narrate while the others take the parts of the characters involved.

THE ANCIENT ROMAN WORLD

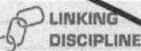

WRITING

Narrative
Have students write down a family story they have been told about their ancestors. Have them use their imaginations to fill in details about the story. Students may wish to illustrate their stories. Then collect the stories into a class booklet or folder entitled *Legends of Our Class Origins*.

LINKING DISCIPLINES

Art If students will be acting out the legends in this chapter, you may wish to have them make masks using craft sticks and paper plates. Have them cut holes for eyes and mouth. They can model their characters' features after the pictures of Roman men and women in Chapters 1–3.

SUPPORTING LEARNING AND EXTENDING LEARNING

Each chapter gives suggestions for students of varying abilities and learning styles; for example, advanced learners, below-level readers, auditory/visual/tactile learners, and English language learners. These may be individual, partner, or group activities, and may or may not require your ongoing supervision.
(For more on Supporting or Extending Learning sections, see pages 16–19.)

TEACHING GUIDE: CHAPTER SIDEBARS

Icons quickly help to identify key concepts, facts, activities, and assessment activities in the sidebars.

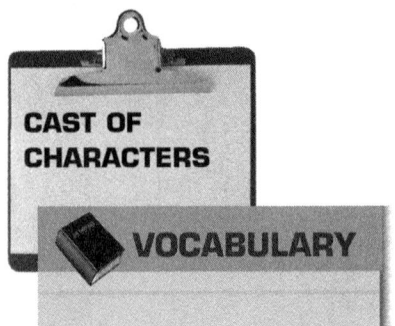

▶ **Cast of Characters/Vocabulary**
These sidebars point out and identify bolded, curriculum-specific vocabulary words and significant personalities in the chapter. Pronunciation guides are included where necessary. Additional important vocabulary words are listed in each unit opener.

▶ **Writing**
Each chapter has a suggestion for a specific writing assignment. You can make these assignments as you see fit—to help students meet state requirements in writing as well as to help individual students improve their skills. Areas of writing covered include the following:

Description	Personal writing (journal/diary)
Narration	News article (print and electronic)
Explanation	Dialogue
Persuasion	Interview
Composition	Poetry

▶ **Then and Now**
This feature provides interesting facts and ideas about the ancient civilization and relates it to the modern world. This may be an aspect of government that we still use today, word origins of common modern expressions, physical reminders of the past that are still evident, and other features. You can use this item simply to promote interest in the subject matter or as a springboard to other research.

▶ **Linking Disciplines**
This feature offers opportunities to investigate other subject areas that relate to the material in the Student Edition: math, science, arts, and health. Specific areas of these subjects are emphasized: **Math** (arithmetic, algebra, geometry, data, statistics); **Science** (life science, earth science, physical science); **Arts** (music, arts, dance, drama, architecture); **Health** (personal health, world health).

▶ **For Homework**
A quick glance links you to additional activities in the Student Study Guide that can be assigned as homework.

ASSESSMENT

The World in Ancient Times program intentionally omits from the Student Edition the kinds of section, chapter, and unit questions that are used to review and assess learning in standard textbooks. It is the purpose of the series to engage readers in learning—and loving—history written as good literature. Rather than interrupting student reading, and enjoyment, all assessment instruments for the series have been placed in the Teaching Guides.

▶ **CHAPTER TESTS**
A reproducible chapter test follows each chapter in this Teaching Guide. These tests will help you assess students' mastery of the content standards addressed in each chapter. These tests measure a variety of cognitive and analytical skills, particularly comprehension, critical thinking, and expository writing, through multiple choice, short answer, and essay questions.
An answer key for the chapter tests is provided at the end of the Teaching Guide.

▶ **WRAP-UP TEST**
After the last chapter test you will find a wrap-up test consisting of 10 essay questions that evaluate students' ability to synthesize and express what they've learned about the ancient civilization under study.

▶ **RUBRICS**
The rubrics at the back of this Teaching Guide will help you assess students' written work, oral presentations, and group projects. They include a Scoring Rubric, based on the California State Public School standards for good writing and effective cooperative learning. In addition, a simplified hand-out is provided, plus a form for evaluating group projects and a Library/Media Center Research Log to help students focus and evaluate their research. Students can also evaluate their own work using these rubrics.

▶ **BLACKLINE MASTERS (BLMs)**
A blackline master follows each chapter in the Teaching Guide. These BLMs are reproducible pages for you to use as in-class activities or homework exercises. They can also be used for assessment as needed.

▶ **ADDITIONAL ASSESSMENT ACTIVITIES**
Each unit opener includes suggestions for using one or more unit projects for assessment. These points, and the rubrics provided, will help you evaluate how your students are progressing towards meeting the unit objectives.

USING THE STUDENT STUDY GUIDE FOR ASSESSMENT

▶ Study Guide Activities
Assignments in the Student Study Guide correspond with those in the Teaching Guide. If needed, these Student Study Guide activities can be used for assessment.

▶ Portfolio Approach
Student Study Guide pages can be removed from the workbook and turned in for grading. When the pages are returned, they can be part of the students' individual history journals. Have students keep a 3-ring binder portfolio of Study Guide pages, alongside writing projects and other activities.

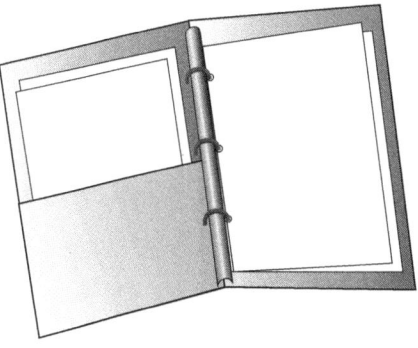

STUDENT STUDY GUIDE: KEY FEATURES

The Student Study Guide works as both standalone instructional material and as a support to the Student Edition and this Teaching Guide. Certain activities encourage informal small-group or family participation. These features make it an effective teaching tool:

Flexibility

You can use the Study Guide in the classroom, with individuals or small groups, or send it home for homework. You can distribute the entire guide to students; however, the pages are perforated so you can remove and distribute only the pertinent lessons.

A page on reports and special projects in the front of the Study Guide directs students to the Further Reading resource in the student edition. This feature gives students general guidance on doing research and devising independent study projects of their own.

FACSIMILE SPREAD
The Study Guide begins with a facsimile spread from the Student Edition. This spread gives reading strategies and highlights key features: captions, primary sources, sidebars, headings, etymologies. The spread supplies the contextualization students need to fully understand the material.

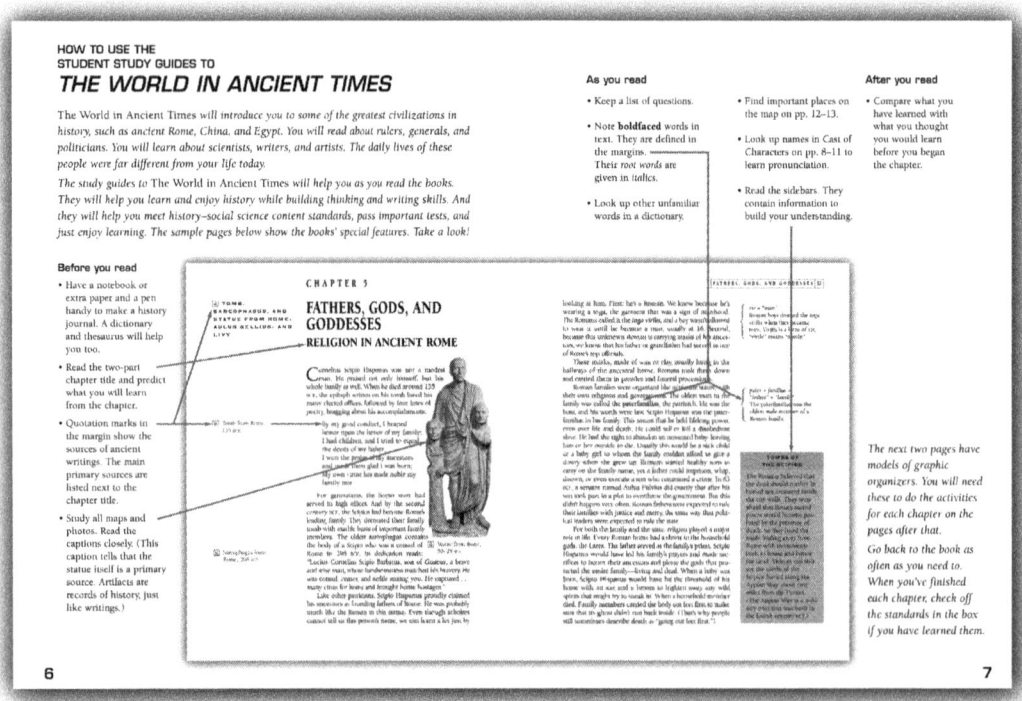

Portfolio Approach

The Study Guide pages are three-hole-punched so they can be integrated with notebook paper in a looseleaf binder. This history journal or portfolio can become both a record of content mastery and an outlet for each student's unique creative expression. Responding to prompts, students can write poetry or songs, plays and character sketches, create storyboards or cartoons, or construct multi-layered timelines.

The portfolio approach gives students unlimited opportunities for practice in areas that need strengthening. Students cam share their journals and compare their work. And the Study Guide pages in the portfolio make a valuable assessment tool for you. It is an ongoing record of performance that can be reviewed and graded periodically.

> **GRAPHIC ORGANIZERS**
> This feature contains reduced models of seven graphic organizers referenced frequently in the guide. Using these devices will help students organize the material so it is meaningful to them. (Full-size reproducibles of each graphic organizer are provided at the back of this Teaching Guide.) These graphic organizers include: outline, main idea map, K-W-L chart (What I Know, What I Want to Know, What I Learned), Venn diagram, timeline, sequence of events chart, and T-chart.

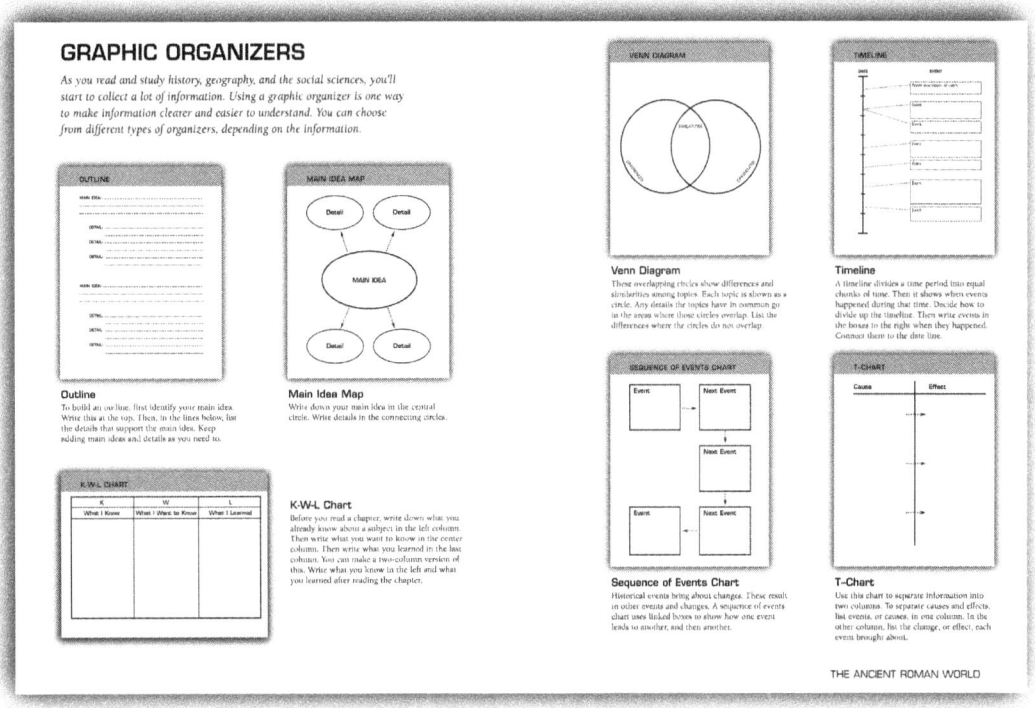

STUDENT STUDY GUIDE: CHAPTER LESSONS

Each chapter lesson is designed to draw students into the subject matter. Recurring features and exercises challenge their knowledge and allow them to practice valuable analysis skills. Activities in the Teaching Guide and Student Study Guide complement but do not duplicate each other. Together they offer a wide range of class work, group projects, and opportunities for further study and assessment that can be tailored to all ability levels.

CHAPTER SUMMARY briefly reviews big ideas from the chapter.

ACCESS invites students into the content by building background, tapping prior knowledge, or visual note-taking.

ADDITIONAL VOCABULARY Additional vocabulary words important to accessing student book content are listed on page 10 of every Student Study Guide.

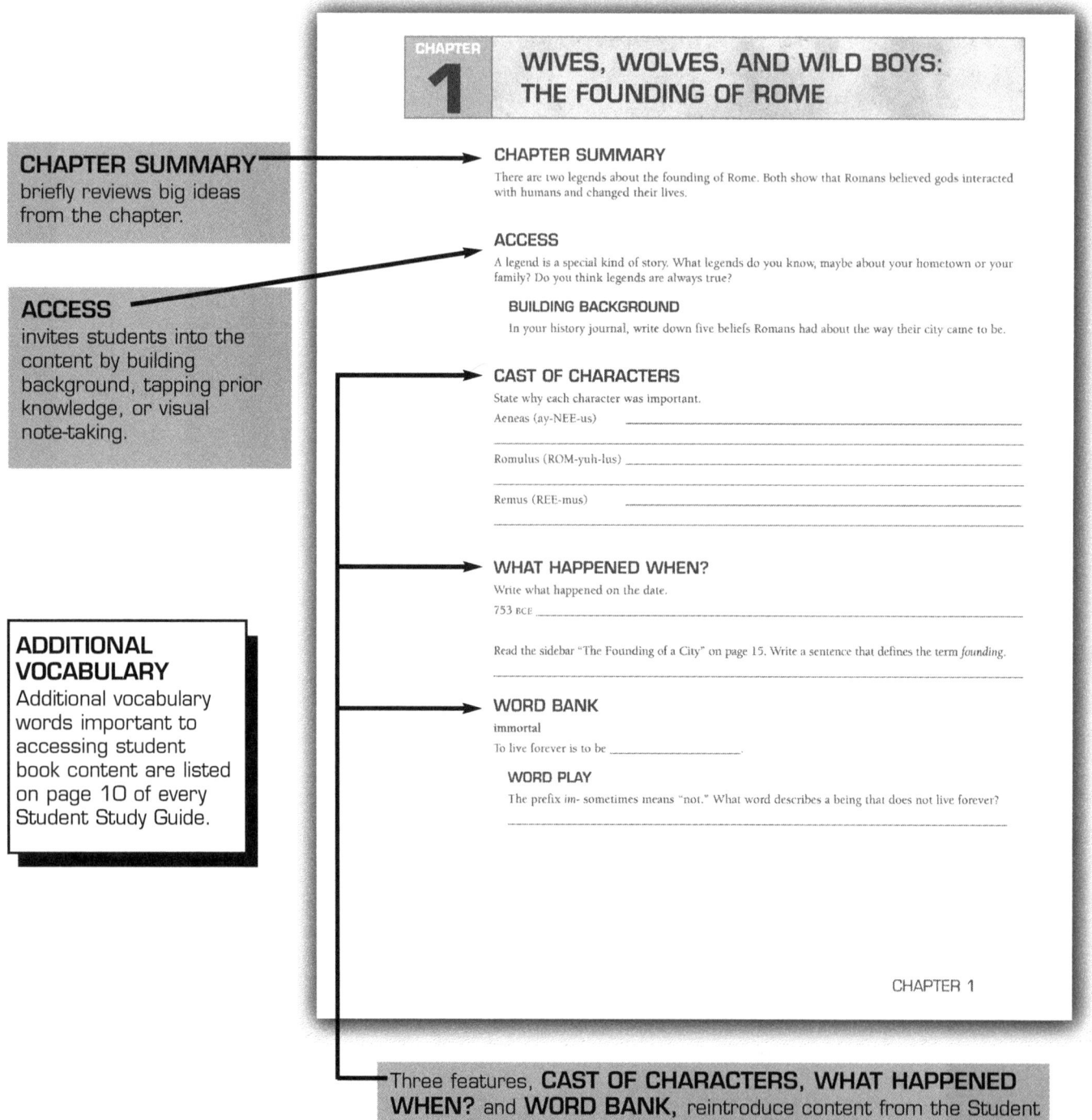

Three features, **CAST OF CHARACTERS**, **WHAT HAPPENED WHEN?** and **WORD BANK**, reintroduce content from the Student Edition on key personalities, dates, and vocabulary words. The Teaching Guide also reinforces this information chapter-by-chapter in the VOCABULARY and CAST OF CHARACTERS sidebars.

CRITICAL THINKING
CAUSE AND EFFECT

Draw a line from each cause and connect it to the result, or effect. (There is one extra effect.)

CAUSE	EFFECT
1. Amulius feared he would be overthrown,	a. they floated down the river and were saved by a she-wolf.
2. Rhea Silvia broke her vows,	b. the Romans and Sabines went to war.
3. A servant couldn't kill the babies,	c. Romulus killed Remus.
4. Remus made fun of Romulus,	d. Romans and Sabines called a truce.
5. Romulus's men kidnapped Sabine women,	e. Romulus and Remus were born.
6. The Sabine women ran onto the battlefield,	f. he forced Rhea Silvia to join the Vestal Virgins.
	g. Remus killed Romulus.

WITH A PARENT OR PARTNER

When you have completed the chart, read aloud each cause-and-effect pairing to a parent or partner. Use the word "so" to connect each cause with each effect.

WRITE ABOUT IT

The Trojan women were *appalled* that Aeneas and the Trojan men were planning another journey after they reached the mouth of the Tiber River. To be *appalled* means to be

a) happy.
b) excited.
c) shocked.

Circle your answer.

In your history journal, write a short dialogue or a descriptive scene between the Trojan men and women about making this second journey. Why were the women appalled? How did the men respond?

WORKING WITH PRIMARY SOURCES

The image at left is an ancient Roman coin. It shows an image of a Roman god. Think about what we can learn about ancient cultures through artifacts like this one. Answer the following questions in your history journal.

1. Why do you think the figure is wearing an olive wreath?
2. Why would the Romans put a god on their coins?
3. What famous people do we use on coins today? (It's okay to take a peek at your pocket change!)
4. If people found your coins hundreds of years from now, what conclusions might they draw about your culture?
5. Think up a design for your own coin and draw it in your history journal.

THE ANCIENT ROMAN WORLD

CRITICAL THINKING exercises draw on such thinking skills as establishing cause and effect, making inferences, drawing conclusions, determining sequence of events, comparing and contrasting, identifying main ideas and details, and other analytical process.

WRITE ABOUT IT gives students writing suggestions drawn from the material. A writing assignment may stem from a vocabulary word, a historical event, or a reading of a primary source. The assignment can take any number of forms: newspaper article, letter, short essay, a scene with dialogue, a diary entry.

WORKING WITH PRIMARY SOURCES invites students to read primary sources closely. Exercises include answering comprehension questions, evaluating point of view, and writing and other forms of creative expression, including music, art, and design. "In Your Own Words" writing activities ask students to paraphrase a primary source.

IMPROVING LITERACY WITH THE WORLD IN ANCIENT TIMES

The books in this series are written in a lively, narrative style to inspire a love of reading history–social science. English language learners and struggling readers are given special consideration within the program's exercises and activities. And students who love to read and learn will also benefit from the program's rich and varied material. Following are strategies to make sure each and every student gets the most out of the subjects you will teach through *The World in Ancient Times*.

ENGLISH LANGUAGE LEARNERS

For English learners to achieve academic success, the instructional considerations for teachers include two mandates:

- Help them attain grade level, content area knowledge, and academic language.
- Provide for the development of English language proficiency.

To accomplish these goals, you should plan lessons that reflect the student's level of English proficiency. Students progress through five developmental levels as they increase in language proficiency:

Beginning and Early Intermediate (*grade level material will be mostly incomprehensible, students need a great deal of teacher support*)

Intermediate (*grade level work will be a challenge*)

Early Advanced and Advanced (*close to grade level reading and writing, students continue to need support*)

The books in this program are written at the intermediate level. However, you can still use the lesson plans for students of different levels by using the strategies below:

Tap Prior Knowledge
What students know about the topic will help determine your next steps for instruction. Using K-W-L charts, brainstorming, and making lists are ways to find out what they know. English learners bring a rich cultural diversity into the classroom. By sharing what they know, students can connect their knowledge and experiences to the course.

Set the Context
Use different tools to make new information understandable. These can be images, artifacts, maps, timelines, illustrations, charts, videos, or graphic organizers. Techniques such as role-playing and story-boarding can also be helpful. Speak in shorter sentences, with careful enunciation, expanded explanations, repetitions, and paraphrasing. Use fewer idiomatic expressions.

Show—Don't Just Tell
English learners often get lost as they listen to directions, explanations, lectures, and discussions. By showing students what is expected, you can help them participate more fully in classroom activities. Students need to be shown how to use the graphic organizers in this guide and the mini versions in the student study guide, as well as other blackline masters for note-taking and practice. An overhead transparency with whole or small groups is also effective.

Use the Text
Because of unfamiliar words, students will need help. Teach them to preview the chapter using text features (headings, bold print, sidebars, italics). See the suggestions in the facsimile of the Student Edition, shown on pages 6–7 of the Student Study Guide. Show students organizing structures such as cause and effect or comparing and contrasting. Have students read to each other in pairs. Encourage them to share their history journals with each other. Use Read Aloud/Think Aloud, perhaps with an overhead transparency. Help them create word banks, charts, and graphic organizers. Discuss the main idea after reading.

Check for Understanding
Rather than simply ask students if they understand, stop frequently and ask them to paraphrase or expand on what you just said. Such techniques will give you a much clearer assessment of their understanding.

Provide for Interaction
As students interact with the information and speak their thoughts, their content knowledge and academic language skills improve. Increase interaction in the classroom through cooperative learning, small group work, and partner share. By working and talking with others, students can practice asking and answering questions.

Use Appropriate Assessment
When modifying the instruction, you will also need to modify the assessment. Multiple choice, true and false, and other criterion reference tests are suitable, but consider changing test format and structure. English learners are constantly improving their language proficiency in their oral and written responses, but they are often grammatically incorrect. Remember to be thoughtful and fair about giving students credit for their content knowledge and use of academic language, even if their English isn't perfect.

STRUGGLING READERS

Some students struggle to understand the information presented in a textbook. The following strategies for content-area reading can help students improve their ability to make comparisons, sequence events, determine importance, summarize, evaluate, synthesize, analyze, and solve problems.

Build Knowledge of Genre
Both the fiction and narrative nonfiction genres are incorporated into *The World in Ancient Times*. This combination of genres makes the text interesting and engaging. But teachers must be sure students can identify and use the organizational structures of both genres.

Fiction	Nonfiction
Each chapter is a story	Content: historical information
Setting: historical time and place	Organizational structure: cause/effect, sequence of events, problem/solution
Characters: historical figures	Other features: maps, timelines, sidebars, photographs, primary sources
Plot: problems, roadblocks, and resolutions	

In addition, the textbook has a wealth of the text features of nonfiction: bold and italic print, sidebars, headings and subheadings, labels, captions, and "signal words" such as *first*, *next*, and *finally*. Teaching these organizational structures and text features is essential for struggling readers.

Build Background

Having background information about a topic makes reading about it so much easier. When students lack background information, teachers can preteach or "front load" concepts and vocabulary, using a variety of instructional techniques. Conduct a chapter or book walk, looking at titles, headings, and other text features to develop a big picture of the content. Focus on new vocabulary words during the "walk" and create a word bank with illustrations for future reference. Read aloud key passages and discuss the meaning. Focus on the timeline and maps to help students develop a sense of time and place. Show a video, go to a website, and have trade books and magazines on the topic available for student exploration.

Comprehension Strategies

While reading, successful readers are predicting, making connections, monitoring, visualizing, questioning, inferring, and summarizing. Struggling readers have a harder time with these "in the head" processes. The following strategies will help these students construct meaning from the text until they are able to do it on their own.

> **PREDICT:** Before reading, conduct a picture and text feature "tour" of the chapter to make predictions. Ask students if they remember if this has ever happened before, to predict what might happen this time.
>
> **MAKE CONNECTIONS:** Help students relate content to their background (text to text, text to self, and text to the world).
>
> **MONITOR AND CONFIRM:** Encourage students to stop reading when they come across an unknown word, phrase, or concept. In their notebooks, have them make a note of text they don't understand and ask for clarification or figure it out. While this activity slows down reading at first, it is effective in improving skills over time.
>
> **VISUALIZE:** Students benefit from imagining the events described in a story. Sketching scenes, story-boarding, role-playing, and looking for sensory details all help students with this strategy.
>
> **INFER:** Help students look beyond the literal meaning of a text to understand deeper meanings. Graphic organizers and discussions provide opportunities to broaden their understanding. Looking closely at the "why" of historical events helps students infer.
>
> **QUESTION AND DISCUSS:** Have students jot down their questions as they read, and then share them during discussions. Or have students come up with the type of questions they think a teacher would ask. Over time students will develop more complex inferential questions, which lead to group discussions. Questioning and discussing also helps students see ideas from multiple perspectives and draw conclusions, both critical skills for understanding history.

DETERMINE IMPORTANCE: Teach students how to decide what is most important from all the facts and details in nonfiction. After reading for an overall understanding, they can go back to highlight important ideas, words, and phrases. Clues for determining importance include bold or italic print, signal words, and other text features. A graphic organizer such as a main idea map also helps.

Teach and Practice Decoding Strategies

Rather than simply defining an unfamiliar word, teach struggling readers decoding strategies:

- Have them look at the prefix, suffix, and root to help figure out the new word.
- Look for words they know within the word.
- Use the context for clues, and read further or reread.

ADVANCED LEARNERS

Every classroom has students who finish the required assignments and then want additional challenges. Fortunately, the very nature of history and social science offers a wide range of opportunities for students to explore topics in greater depth. Encourage them to come up with their own ideas for an additional assignment. Determine the final product, its presentation, and a timeline for completion.

▶ Research

Students can develop in-depth understanding through seeking information, exploring ideas, asking and answering questions, making judgments, considering points of view, and evaluating actions and events. They will need access to a wide range of resource materials: the Internet, maps, encyclopedias, trade books, magazines, dictionaries, artifacts, newspapers, museum catalogues, brochures, and the library. See the Further Reading section at the end of the Student Edition for good jumping-off points.

▶ Projects

You can encourage students to capitalize on their strengths as learners (visual, verbal, kinesthetic, or musical) or to try a new way of responding. Students can prepare a debate or write a persuasive paper, play, skit, poem, song, dance, game, puzzle, or biography. They can create an alphabet book on the topic, film a video, do a book talk, or illustrate a book. They can render charts, graphs, or other visual representations. Allow for creativity and support students' thinking.

Cheryl A. Caldera, M.A.
Literacy Coach

MESOAMERICA— EARLY CIVILIZATIONS

PAGES 12–30

Introduction What's Under Your Bedroom?
Chapter 1 People of Maize: Early Farmers in the Valley of Oaxaca
Chapter 2 Land of Rubber: The Olmec Civilization

UNIT OBJECTIVES

Unit 1 introduces the geographic location of Mesoamerica and covers Mesoamerican civilizations from farmers in the Valley of Oaxaca through the Olmec, a period from 5000 BCE through 900 BCE. In this unit your students will learn

- ▶ the location of ancient civilizations in Mesoamerica.
- ▶ how archaeologists interpret evidence.
- ▶ the origins of a market economy in the Oaxaca Valley.
- ▶ theories about the colossal stone heads that the Olmec chiseled from basalt.
- ▶ theories about the end of the Olmec civilization.

PRIMARY SOURCES

Unit 1 includes excerpts from the following primary sources:

- ▶ Fray Bernardino de Sahagún, the *Florentine Codex*
- ▶ *Popol Vuh*

Unit 1 also includes photographs of the following artifacts from ancient Mesoamerica, which can be analyzed as primary sources:

- ▶ Remains of house and tools, Mexico
- ▶ Jar with Sky Dragon image, Mexico
- ▶ Olmec rubber ball
- ▶ Remains of Red Palace, San Lorenzo
- ▶ Head of monumental Olmec statue, Mexico
- ▶ Olmec throne
- ▶ Jade figurines, La Venta, Mexico

BIG IDEAS IN UNIT 1

Archaeology, agriculture, and **trade** are the big ideas in Unit 1. The questions asked by archaeologists working in Mesoamerica and the methods they use to answer these questions set the stage for discoveries discussed throughout the textbook. Agricultural abundance in the Oaxaca Valley resulted in the growth of trade and the development of towns and cities. Meanwhile, the Olmec were creating giant stone heads and developing their own culture rooted in agriculture and trade.

GEOGRAPHY CONNECTION

Refer students to the map of ancient Mesoamerica on page 10. Have students identify the following places: the Oaxaca Valley, the Gulf Coast region of Mexico, San Lorenzo, and La Venta. Tell them that this region was the Olmec cultural region. Lead a class discussion about what students think a "cultural region" is. Elicit that it is a region that has one dominant culture.

TIMELINE

5000 BCE	Maize agriculture begins in Mesoamerica
1300 BCE	Village life is well-established in Mesoamerica
1150 BCE	Olmec town of San Lorenzo rises
900 BCE	Tierras Largas house in Oaxaca abandoned; Olmec settlement of San Lorenzo abandoned; Olmec establish La Venta

UNIT PROJECTS

Olmec Archaeology

Have interested students investigate and report on past and present archaeological explorations into the Olmec civilization. Students can find information online at *www.famsi.org/research/pohl/index.html* that will help them prepare a information for a report to the class.

Olmec Mystery

Have a team of students create a presentation about the enormous Olmec heads, focusing on theories about their origin and meaning. Students can use information from books listed on the Further Reading page at the back of their book, such as *Mexico: From the Olmecs to the Aztecs,* 5th ed., rev. and expanded, by Michael D. Coe and Rex Koontz (London: Thames and Hudson, 2002), and from Internet sites listed on the Websites page of their book.

All-American Maize

Have students research and present an illustrated report on the amazing maize. They can find information on maize's origins, an animated trip inside a corn plant, and information about the uses of corn today at Iowa State University's Agronomy Department website at *http://maize.agron.iastate.edu/general.html*.

The Three Sisters

Ask a group of students to find out more about the Three Sisters by visiting *http://horizon.nmsu.edu/ddl/3sisresources.html*. They can expand their research by investigating other sections of the website and preparing a report for the class.

ADDITIONAL ASSESSMENT

For Unit 1, divide the class into groups and have them all undertake the Olmec Mystery project. In particular, note how students' reports explain the theories about why the heads were created and how they fit into the Olmec belief system. Use the scoring rubric at the back of this guide to assess students' work, and have students rate their own work with the self-assessment rubric.

LITERATURE CONNECTION

The great literary work concerning the ancient customs, myths, and beliefs of the Mesoamericans is the *Popol Vuh,* which was written down in the 17th century CE. There are numerous translations of this work. You can download a full text copy of the work at *www.sacred-texts.com/nam/maya/pvgm/*.

There are a number of books that students can enjoy that will broaden their knowledge of early Mesoamerica and increase their understanding of those civilizations. Suggest some of the following to students (keep in mind that historical fiction is not always accurate in its details):

- Kirwan, Anna. *Lady of Palenque: Flower of Bacal* (The Royal Diaries series). New York: Scholastic, 2004. Fiction. ADVANCED. This novel is about the trials and tribulations of a young, educated Maya woman who is betrothed to a king.
- Montejo, Victor. *The Bird Who Cleans the World and Other Mayan Fables.* Curbstone Press, 1992. AVERAGE. This book features Maya stories of creation, nature, relations between peoples, and conflicts.
- Montejo, Victor. *Popol Vuh: A Sacred Book of the Maya.* Toronto: Groundwood Books, 1999. AVERAGE. One of the few Maya documents to survive the Spanish conquest, the Popol Vuh describes the creation of the Maya universe and of humans.
- Peppas, Lynn. *Life in Ancient Mesoamerica* (*Peoples of the Ancient World*). New York: Crabtree Publishing, 2004. Nonfiction. EASY. This book tells about life in ancient Mesoamerica, with many illustrations.

UNIVERSAL ACCESS

The following strategies are designed to cover a range of learning styles and reading, language, and skill levels. This section includes suggestions for differentiating instruction to meet the diverse needs of your students.

Reading Strategies

- To facilitate reading, point out features such as illustrations, information, and definitions in the side columns that students will encounter as they read.
- Have students as a group begin a word file for the book. Provide note cards and a box. Students should write the word on the front of the card and a definition on the back. Students should include the bold-faced terms in the text as well as other unfamiliar words. Have them copy the word lists in their history journals and add to the list throughout the course, so students will have the words easily accessible for reference.
- Have students use the K-W-L chart (see the graphic organizer at the back of this guide) to assist them in their reading. Preview each chapter and have students fill in the first column of the chart with what they *know* about the subject. Have them write what they *want to know* about the subject in the second column. When they are finished with the chapter, have them complete the third column by writing what they *learned*.
- Have students use the main idea map graphic organizer (at the back of this guide) to organize the information about the Olmec civilization, which is considered the mother culture for later Mesoamerican civilizations. As students read, they should group the details into categories such as religion, agriculture, towns, crafts, and so on.

Writing Strategies

- Have partners make a three-column chart with headings for each of the unit's big ideas. Partners should get together after reading each chapter to jot down their observations in each category.
- Have students create a cause and effect chart showing the connection between agricultural surplus and the growth of trade in Mesoamerica.
- Have students write a description of a typical Mesoamerican village from the perspective of one of the residents stepping out of his or her house. Students should include various sensory details as the ancient inhabitant might have experienced them.

Listening and Speaking Strategies

▶ Have a group of students create a panel presentation on the work of archaeologists, in which they script comments on the types of questions archaeologists ask, some of the ways archaeologists answer questions, their training, and the curiosity that drives them. Information can come from the Introduction, Chapters 1 and 2, and the print and Internet resources in the students' book.

▶ Encourage a group to write questions and answers for an interview with the family in the Valley of Oaxaca described in chapter 1, pages 18–21. Questions could concern their household tasks, materials they used for tools, and the impact of droughts and floods on their crops. Answers should be based on information in the chapter.

▶ Have small groups act out activities of the Oaxaca Valley people. For example, one student could read aloud the information about the construction of a terrace on page 20 to the group while another student goes through the motions described.

UNIT VOCABULARY LIST

The following words that appear in Unit 1 are important for your students' understanding of the social studies content as well as for development of literacy. Use these words for vocabulary study or to reinforce language arts skills (e.g., synonyms, compound words, prefixes and suffixes, and related words). The words are listed below in the order in which they appear in the chapters.

Introduction	**Chapter 1**	**Chapter 2**
nomads	moody	colossal
chronicles	worrisome	basalt
	shrivel	plateau
	fickle	debris
	vari-colored	hearths
	spindles	mother culture
	willy-nilly	radiocarbon
	nutritional	levees
	carbohydrates	sacred
	kernels	
	tortilla	
	pot irrigation	
	terrace	
	luxury	
	embroidery	
	barter	

CHAPTER 1

PEOPLE OF MAIZE: EARLY FARMERS IN THE VALLEY OF OAXACA

PAGES 15–21

FOR HOMEWORK
STUDENT STUDY GUIDE
pages 11–12

VOCABULARY

hypothesis "base (for an argument)" in ancient Greek. *Hypothetical* describes something that has been assumed or imagined.

THEN and NOW

The National Museum of the American Indian (NMAI) in Washington, D.C., honors the vibrant cultures of the Americas. The NMAI website (*www.nmai.si.edu*) includes an online exhibition of ancient Mexican art. Have students visit the website and then write a letter to the editor of a local paper recommending the NMAI website and giving examples of what it has to offer.

CHAPTER SUMMARY

Agriculture in the Valley of Oaxaca in Mesoamerica began with the cultivation of maize about 5000 BCE. In this chapter students will learn how droughts and floods affected farmers there and how agricultural plenty led to the growth of trade.

PERFORMANCE OBJECTIVES

▶ To understand the effects of rain and drought on farmers in the Valley of Oaxaca
▶ To describe the home of a farmer in the Oaxaca Valley and the tools he and his family used in daily life
▶ To comprehend how surpluses in agriculture led to the growth of trade in Mesoamerica

BUILDING BACKGROUND

Ask students about their favorite form of corn: for example, corn flakes, popcorn, corn chips, corn on the cob. Point out that corn syrup and cornstarch are found in many foods, so they also eat corn in their favorite candy bar or cookie. Then explain that corn is used in inedible products too, such as rubber, plastics, and fuel. Explain that today's corn has come a long way from its origins as maize, or wild corn, first cultivated 5,000 years ago in Mexico.

WORKING WITH PRIMARY SOURCES

Have students list the primary sources named or artifacts shown in the chapter (*Popol Vuh, Florentine Codex,* jar, remains of hut). Discuss with the class how these primary sources are different from the written sources we have for other ancient civilizations. Encourage students to draw their own conclusions about how we can still learn about most of the Mesoamerican and South American cultures discussed in this book, even though they never developed a system of writing. (*Historians have to depend heavily on archaeological evidence and the accounts of later writers to reconstruct most of the history of ancient America.*)

GEOGRAPHY CONNECTION

Location Copy and distribute the blackline master for Chapter 1, an outline map of Mesoamerica. In studying the map and responding to the questions, students will appreciate the varied geography of Mesoamerica.

READING COMPREHENSION QUESTIONS

1. What is a possible reason that Mesoamerican villagers built their homes in a circle? (*better communication with neighbors*)
2. Archaeologists uncovered tools used by men and women. What were some of the tools and who used them? (*Men: corn-shucker, hammer stone; women: hammer stone, needle, grill*)
3. As people ran from the village during a flood, how did they carry food with them? (*They stored cornmeal in jars; when they ran, they took the jars with them.*)

4. Why were cacao seedpods desirable to ancient Mesoamericans? (*They used the seeds to make a popular chocolate drink.*)

CRITICAL THINKING QUESTIONS

1. In what ways did the rain god control the fate of farmers in Mesoamerica? (*The farmers believed that if the god sent too little rain, the farmers' crops would not grow. If the god sent too much rain, floods would ruin the crops.*)
2. How did archaeologists figure out who used the tools found in the Oaxaca Valley hut? (*The archaeologists used written texts to find out where men and women worked in the home. They also talked to people today who follow the same custom: men work on the left side of the doorway, women work on the right side, and they share some tasks in the middle of the room.*)
3. What did maize and heavy cotton cloaks have in common in ancient Mesoamerica? (*They could be traded for other items.*)
4. Explain the meaning of this statement: "Thanks to a steady food supply, the people of maize were building their first civilization." (*Because they had plenty of food, people in Mesoamerica had time to create luxury items that could then be traded for other desirable items. Trade led to the building of towns and cities and the rise of leaders and rules for behavior.*)

SOCIAL SCIENCES

Science, Technology, and Society The chapter describes various tools used for household tasks in the Oaxaca Valley around 900 BCE. Have students make a two-column chart labeled *Women's Tools* and *Men's Tools*. In the appropriate column have them write a description of tools found in the home. Then have students speculate about tools used today to accomplish the same tasks.

READING AND LANGUAGE ARTS

Reading Nonfiction Work with students to examine the language used on pages 18–21 to involve readers in the scene inside the villager's house. Start by discussing how the use of the second person draws the reader into the description. Then ask students to identify verbs that bring the scene to life. These include *hear, see, scrapes, grinds, cooks, strikes*.

Using Language Remind students of the uses of apostrophes: to form possessives of nouns (*god's, people's*) and to indicate missing letters in contractions. Have students identify apostrophes in this chapter and explain why each was used.

SUPPORTING LEARNING

Struggling Readers Have students read the Introduction and then create a K-W-L chart (see the graphic organizer at the back of this guide) to identify the topics they want to find out more about while reading the book.

EXTENDING LEARNING

Enrichment Have students get more information about the land and climate of the area shown on the map on page 15 (Mexico and Guatemala). Groups can use print or online encyclopedias to learn about the area's volcanic activity, the effect of the mountains and the ocean on the climate, the jungles, the dry highlands, and the navigability of the rivers. Have them display their information on posters.

Extension Have students role-play a scene in which the family described on pages 18–21 decides it is time to leave their home because of rising flood waters.

WRITING

Skit Have students write a script for the flood scene on page 20. The script should have a narrator to "set the scene" and speaking parts for a father, mother, son, and daughter who have to leave their home (and tools) behind to get to safety when floods come.

LINKING DISCIPLINES

Art Have students cut out and color/decorate corn shapes—kernels and cobs—and on each one write a fact about Mesoamerican agriculture. Then have them punch holes in the corn shapes and create a mobile by suspending them from wires.

LONGITUDE AND LATITUDE IN MESOAMERICA

Directions

This map shows the region known as Mesoamerica, one of the world's cradles of civilization. Follow the directions to complete the map.

We use latitude to measure locations on the globe north and south of the equator. Mesoamerica lies between 15° and 40° North latitude. These coordinates measure the position of Mesoamerica north of the equator. Longitude measures distances from east to west.

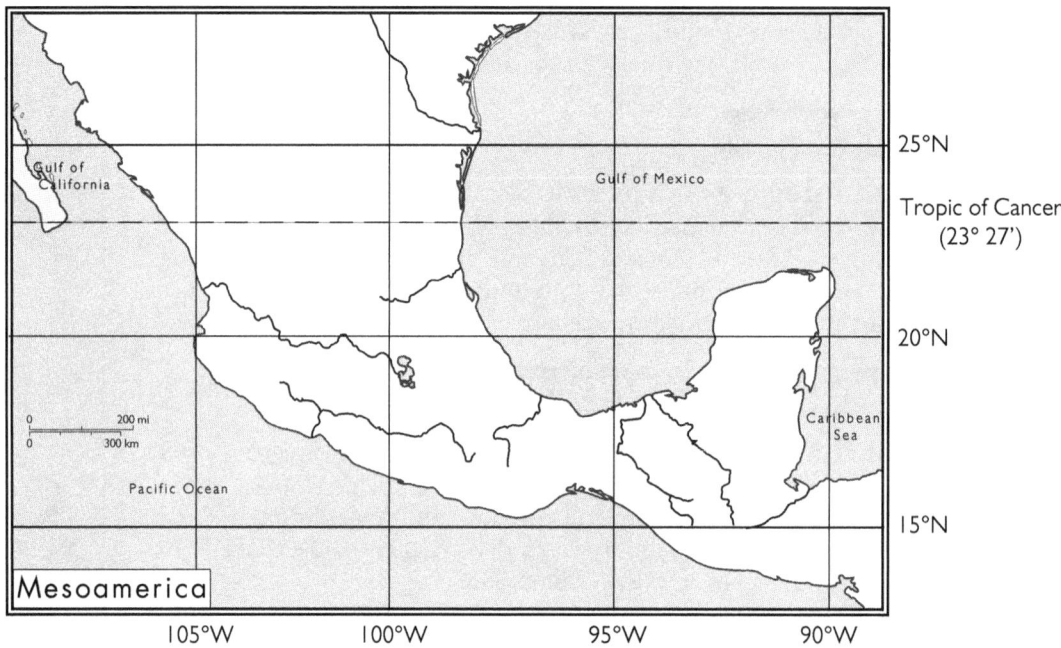

1. Using the inset map on page 15 of your book as a guide, copy and label the major geographic features of the region onto the map on this page. Include mountains, valleys, lakes, and peninsulas.

2. Other regions close to 25° latitude include the Caribbean Ocean near the southern coast of Florida and the Bahamas. Cuba and Jamaica are near 20° latitude. All of these areas, including Mesoamerica, are close to the equator. With this information, describe what kind of climate you would expect to find in Mesoamerica.

3. Longitude and latitude help us locate areas on a map. Use this grid to give approximate coordinates for the following locations:
   a) Lake Texcoco
   b) the mouth of the Rio Grande
   c) the northernmost point of the Yucatan Peninsula

4. Which mountain ranges pass through the Tropic of Cancer?

CHAPTER TEST 1

THE ANCIENT AMERICAN WORLD

NAME _____ DATE _____

A. MULTIPLE CHOICE

Circle the letter of the best answer for each question.

1. Which of the following is **not** a reason that the people of Oaxaca tried to keep the rain god happy?
   a. They needed the god to send enough rain for crops to grow.
   b. They needed the rain to stop before there was flooding.
   c. They wanted to avoid a drought.
   d. They wanted to see the sacred mountains.

2. In the Valley of Oaxaca archaeologists found a pottery bowl with a carving of the rain god on it. Why did people make this carving long ago?
   a. to keep flood waters away
   b. to make the rain god happy
   c. to tell a story about their lives
   d. to keep wild animals away

3. Archaeologists found evidence in the Valley of Oaxaca of which of the following?
   a. a flood that washed away five huts
   b. a giant statue of the rain god
   c. a drought that killed all the people in the village
   d. an ancient zoo

4. Terraces and pot irrigation tell archaeologists that the people of the Valley of Oaxaca were
   a. desperately hungry.
   b. very resourceful.
   c. very wealthy.
   d. extremely lazy.

5. Early Mesoamericans used which of the following the way we use cash?
   a. maize plants
   b. cactus spines
   c. avocado pits
   d. cacao seedpods

B. SHORT ANSWER

Write one or two sentences to answer each question.

6. What tasks did the men and women living in the Valley of Oaxaca perform?

7. Why would a midden be an important site for an archaeologist to study?

8. What information does the *Florentine Codex* tell about ancient Mesoamerican customs?

C. ESSAY

On a separate sheet of paper, write an essay explaining this statement from the textbook: "The geography of Mesoamerica is so varied that no one place could provide everything people needed."

CHAPTER 2

LAND OF RUBBER: THE OLMEC CIVILIZATION

PAGES 22–30

FOR HOMEWORK

STUDENT STUDY GUIDE
pages 13–14

 **VOCABULARY**

olmeca "land of rubber" in the Nahuatl (NAH-what) language. The Olmec lived in a region that produced rubber from the sap of rubber trees.

achiote a tropical shrub; Mesoamericans stir their chocolate drink with achiote root to give it a pleasing musky flavor. They also use powdered achiote to add flavor and a yellow color to foods such as stews.

 **WRITING**

Composition Have students write a diary entry from the point of view of an observer who was with Ann Cyphers when she uncovered the giant head in San Lorenzo in 1994. The entry should describe the excitement of the discovery and include specific details from Chapter 2.

CHAPTER SUMMARY

In this chapter students meet the Olmec, a Mesoamerican people best known for chiseling colossal stone heads from volcanic rock between 1200 and 600 BCE. Students meet the Olmec through Ann Cyphers, an archaeologist who has studied their civilization for many years.

PERFORMANCE OBJECTIVES

▶ To summarize the questions and possible answers about the colossal Olmec stone heads
▶ To describe how ordinary Olmec lived
▶ To understand the methods used by archaeologists

BUILDING BACKGROUND

Ask students what they associate with the word *dig*. Lead students to an understanding that *dig* can be both a verb and a noun and in both forms is associated with the work of archaeologists. Explain that in this chapter students will meet an archaeologist who works in Mesoamerica and whose digging has uncovered information about the Olmec civilization.

WORKING WITH PRIMARY SOURCES

Have students look at the photograph on page 26 of Ann Cyphers with a colossal head of an Olmec king. Ask students how having a person in the picture helps them understand the size of the head. Have them make projections about the size and weight of the head.

GEOGRAPHY CONNECTION

Place Have students locate San Lorenzo on the map of Mesoamerica on page 10. Then have them identify the river near San Lorenzo on the map on page 15. Lead a class discussion on how the river's depositing of rich soil in levees helped the growth of agriculture in the San Lorenzo region.

READING COMPREHENSION QUESTIONS

1. How did the Olmec in San Lorenzo change the geography of the place in which they lived? (*They built it up into a man-made mountain, 150 feet high and three-quarters of a mile long.*)
2. What was archaeologist Ann Cyphers's major interest in San Lorenzo? (*She wanted to find out how ordinary Olmec people lived.*)
3. What discoveries led to an appreciation of the Olmec civilization? (*the first discoveries of the colossal stone heads in the Gulf Coast area of Mexico*)
4. How did the Olmec of San Lorenzo become rich? (*Fertile soil permitted them to grow surplus maize. Having access to a river for travel, they became rich by trading with other Mesoamericans.*)

CRITICAL THINKING QUESTIONS

1. What does Cyphers mean when she says that Olmec people had "home offices"? (*She found evidence of stoneworking in homes that showed people worked, lived, and ate in the same place—a home office of ancient times.*)
2. Basalt chips, deer bones, charcoal—what might this evidence suggest to archaeologists working in Mesoamerica? (*basalt chips—colossal heads were probably carved there; deer bones—this was a garbage pit, so people lived nearby; charcoal—this indicated the site of a fire, possibly for cooking*)
3. How did radiocarbon dating settle the question of whether the Olmec or Maya civilization came first? (*Charcoal from an Olmec site was dated by measuring the amount of radioactive carbon left inside, and that date was compared to the date of charcoal taken from a Maya site.*)
4. What are two theories about why San Lorenzo was abandoned? (*invasion by another Olmec group, such as people from La Venta; volcanic eruptions that changed the courses of San Lorenzo's rivers, interrupting trade, reducing the wealth of San Lorenzo, and leading to a revolt*)

SOCIAL SCIENCES

Economics Discuss with students the economic implications for the Olmec of growing two maize crops per year.

READING AND LANGUAGE ARTS

Reading Nonfiction Have students read aloud the Archaeologist at Work feature on pages 24–25. Discuss students' reactions to the interview. Then ask them to evaluate what the interview adds to the book and why it might have been placed in Chapter 2.

Using Language Have students investigate the definitions and origins of these words found in the chapter: *plateau, colossal, home office, hunch*. They should present the results of their research to the class.

SUPPORTING LEARNING

English Language Learners Have students identify the adjectives used to describe the Olmec stone heads: *colossal, giant, huge, important*. Have students add synonyms to the list and then define each word and use it in an original sentence.

Struggling Readers Have students use the main idea map graphic organizer (see the back of this guide) to help them understand the significance of the colossal Olmec heads. They can write *Colossal Heads* in the central circle, and the headings *Material, Movement, Meaning,* and *Discovery* in the surrounding circles. Students can then add details from the chapter to complete the map.

EXTENDING LEARNING

Enrichment Students can read more theories about how the Olmec moved the colossal heads at *www.bbc.co.uk/history/programmes/secrets/secrets_olmec.shtml*. Students should write their opinion about which theory is best and why.

Extension Have students create and perform a skit based on the description of Ann Cyphers's workers' discovery of a colossal head (pages 26–27).

THEN and NOW

In northwestern Mexico an ancient Olmec ball game, *ulama de cadera*, or hip *ulama*, is still played using only the hips. The more than 3,000-year-old game is being studied by a professor of art history from California State University at Los Angeles and his colleague, an archaeologist. They want to investigate the role of women in the game in ancient times and to learn more about the religious significance of the game. Refer students to an account of an Aztec ball game from the *Florentine Codex* in *The World in Ancient Times Primary Sources and Reference Volume*.

LINKING DISCIPLINES

Science Distribute copies of the blackline master for Chapter 2. Review students' responses to make sure they are able to distinguish between organic and inorganic archaeological evidence.

THE ANCIENT AMERICAN WORLD

NAME _____ DATE _____

RADIOCARBON DATING

Directions

Read the paragraphs below and then complete the chart. For each item in the first column, decide whether it was once part of a living thing—animal or plant. Then place a check in the correct column to show how to determine its age. Finally, complete the writing assignment.

All living things contain carbon—both normal and radioactive. The ratio of normal carbon to radioactive carbon is the same in all living things while they are alive. After a plant or animal dies, the normal carbon remains, but the radioactive carbon decays at a steady rate. After 5,568 years, half of it is gone. In another 5,568 years half of the remaining radioactivity is gone. After about 50,000 years, all the radioactive carbon is gone.

Scientists can use this knowledge to estimate the age of a once-living sample—a piece of bone or a fossilized leaf, for example—up to 50,000 years old. They do this by measuring the ratio of radiocarbon to normal carbon in the sample. Remember, the ratio in living things is always the same. The ratio changes once the plant or animal dies and the radioactive carbon starts to decay. This is called radiocarbon dating. Scientists have to use other methods to find the age of nonliving things.

To Determine the Age of...	Use Radiocarbon Dating	Use Another Method
animal bone		
clay bowl		
stone tool		
charcoal		
gold		
human bone		
basalt chips		
stone beads		
fossilized seeds		

On a separate sheet of paper, write a paragraph explaining why radiocarbon dating is useful to archaeologists.

CHAPTER TEST 2

THE ANCIENT AMERICAN WORLD

NAME _____ DATE _____

A. MULTIPLE CHOICE

Circle the letter of the best answer for each question.

1. Which of the following is **not** one of the questions that scientists and historians ask about the colossal Olmec heads?
   a. How were the stones for the colossal heads moved?
   b. Who does each head represent?
   c. What was the purpose of the giant heads?
   d. What material were they carved from?

2. Researchers believe the colossal Olmec heads may represent
   a. gods.
   b. leaders.
   c. enemies.
   d. myths.

3. When Ann Cyphers uncovered basalt chips at an Olmec site, she decided she had found the site of
   a. an ancient volcano.
   b. an ordinary Olmec home.
   c. an Olmec palace.
   d. a workplace where giant heads were carved.

4. Radiocarbon dating of charcoal proved that the Olmec civilization is
   a. the oldest civilization ever discovered.
   b. older than the Maya civilization.
   c. older than the Valley of Oaxaca.
   d. younger than the Maya civilization.

5. Riverbeds around San Lorenzo reveal that floods
   a. deposited fertile soil in which maize grew well.
   b. wiped out the maize crop every growing season.
   c. hardly ever occurred.
   d. washed away precious soil from farmers' land.

B. SHORT ANSWER

Write one or two sentences to answer each question.

6. How did people in San Lorenzo become rich?
   _____
   _____

7. What was the connection between good harvests and power in the Olmec region?
   _____
   _____

8. Summarize two theories of why San Lorenzo was abandoned around 900 BCE.
   _____
   _____

C. ESSAY

The San Lorenzo plateau is believed to have been an important Olmec site. Write an essay on a separate sheet of paper explaining why archaeologists believe this. Include details from the chapter.

MESOAMERICAN CITIES
PAGES 31–45

Chapter 3 Conquests and Captives: The First Mesoamerican Cities
Chapter 4 Pyramids, Paintings, and Pottery: Teotihuacan, City of the Gods

UNIT OBJECTIVES

Unit 2 covers the rise and fall of three important ancient Mesoamerican cities—Monte Albán, El Mirador, and Teotihuacan—between 500 BCE and 550 CE. In this unit your students will learn

- ▶ how Monte Albán became a flourishing mountaintop city.
- ▶ the obstacles the Maya overcame in building El Mirador, a rainforest city.
- ▶ how Teotihuacan became the largest Mesoamerican city of its day.
- ▶ the significance of the Teotihuacan pyramids, the tallest in Mesoamerica.
- ▶ why Teotihuacan is considered the "eternal city" of Mesoamerica.
- ▶ similarities between these ancient cities and modern cities.

PRIMARY SOURCES

Unit 2 includes pictures of the following artifacts, which can be analyzed as primary sources:
- ▶ Drawings of carved place names
- ▶ Stone portrait of One Earthquake's death
- ▶ Stone burial urn
- ▶ *Danzante* carving, Monte Albán
- ▶ Tigre Pyramid, El Mirador
- ▶ Mural in Tepantitla apartment
- ▶ Sculpture of feathered serpent, Teotihuacan
- ▶ Jaguar figurine

BIG IDEAS IN UNIT 2

Movement and **cities** are the big ideas in Unit 2. People moved to the sacred mountain of Monte Albán and built a city there for religious reasons. They moved away from destructive volcanoes to the desert area where Teotihuacan was built. People moved to the rainforest and built El Mirador. The three sites shared the features of all cities—roads, concentrations of people, markets, sports arenas, houses, gardens, and religious structures. Like cities today, these were lively centers of art and trade. Ask students to describe cities they have visited or know about. Discuss why people move to cities today and what structures dominate modern city skylines.

GEOGRAPHY CONNECTION

Help students locate Monte Albán, El Mirador, and Teotihuacan on the map of ancient Mesoamerica on page 10. As you work through the chapters, have students note differences in the geography of each site and ask them to draw conclusions about how geography affected life in each city.

TIMELINE

500 BCE	One Earthquake sacrificed; Zapotec capital of Monte Albán founded
350 BCE	Rise of El Mirador, first Maya city
250 BCE	El Mirador flourishes
200 BCE	Monte Albán flourishes
1 CE	Teotihuacan founded
400 CE	Population of Teotihuacan reaches 125,000
550 CE	Temples burned in Teotihuacan

UNIT PROJECTS

Research Report

Groups of students can research and report on the current state of the sites of Monte Albán, El Mirador, and Teotihuacan. For Monte Albán and Teotihuacan, a source of information is *www.mesoamerican-archives.com*. For El Mirador, students can find information at *www.globalheritagefund.org/sites/americas/index.html*. (Click on "Guatemala" and then "Mirador Basin.") Students can also find sources of information on the Websites page of their book.

Engineering Marvels

Students can sketch or make models of the following engineering feats described in the unit: terraced fields, Tigre Pyramid, Pyramid of the Sun, raised roads (for travel through a swamp). Consider making a corner of your classroom an Ancient America museum whose exhibits can change throughout the course of study.

Drama

Have a group of students work together to write a script for a play about life in Teotihuacan as seen through the eyes of a pilgrim such as the one described in Chapter 4. Other characters can include city residents who guide the newcomer through Teotihuacan, and traders and pottery makers whom the pilgrim meets in the central market. Allow time for the group to prepare and present their play.

Classroom Rainforest

Students can create a classroom rainforest based on the description on page 36 and on independent research. Stretch lengths of string or clothesline across the room at various heights (to simulate the canopies of the rainforest). Students can attach labeled drawings of trees, birds, and animals found at various levels in the rainforest and indicate how they were used by the people of El Mirador. Students can find general rainforest information on the Internet at *www.rainforesteducation.com*.

ADDITIONAL ASSESSMENT

For Unit 2, divide the class into groups and have them all undertake the Research Report project so you can assess their knowledge of the major early cities of Mesoamerica and their influence on others. Use the scoring rubric at the back of this guide to assess students' work, and have students rate their own work with the self-assessment rubric. Distribute the library/media center research log so students can evaluate their sources as they conduct their research.

LITERATURE CONNECTION

There are numerous books that students can enjoy that will broaden their knowledge of the ancient cities of Mesoamerica. A particularly useful book is listed below:

▶ Arnold, Caroline. *City of the Gods: Mexico's Ancient City of Teotihuacan.* New York: Clarion Books, 1994. Nonfiction. AVERAGE. This guide explores the ruins of the ancient metropolis and ceremonial complex of Teotihuacan in the valley of Mexico and explains what life was like for the people who lived there.

UNIVERSAL ACCESS

The following strategies are designed to cover a range of learning styles and reading, language, and skill levels. This section includes suggestions for differentiating instruction to meet the diverse needs of your students.

Reading Strategies

▶ To spark students' interest, read the title and first paragraph of each chapter aloud. Use the reading as a springboard for predicting what the chapter is about. Record and review students' predictions. When students have finished reading the chapter, ask them to evaluate their predictions.

▶ Before reading a chapter, point out potentially difficult words and ask volunteers to pronounce and define them. Say each word several times and then write it on the board. Help students associate the spoken word with the written word.

▶ Have students use the outline graphic organizer (at the back of this guide) to organize the information about the Olmec civilization, which is considered the mother culture for later Mesoamerican civilizations. As students read, they should group the details into categories such as religion, agriculture, towns, crafts, and so on.

Writing Strategies

▶ Have students create a cause and effect chart based on what may have happened to El Mirador.

▶ Have students make a main idea map (see graphic organizer at the back of this guide), writing *Life in the City* in the central circle. They can fill in the outer circles with details about life in Monte Albán, El Mirador, and Teotihuacan.

▶ Have students write a description of a typical Mesoamerican village from the perspective of one of the residents stepping out of his or her house. Students should include various sensory details as the ancient inhabitant might have experienced them.

Listening and Speaking Strategies

▶ Assign students different sections of Chapter 4 to read aloud. Encourage students to make their voices expressive and to use hand gestures where appropriate.

▶ Challenge groups of students to become specialized tour guides for Monte Albán, El Mirador, and Teotihuacan. Students can do additional research to learn more about their assigned city. Tour guides can make presentations to the class.

▶ Have small groups act out activities of the Oaxaca Valley people. For example, one student could read aloud the information about the construction of a terrace on page 20 to the group while another student goes through the motions described.

UNIT VOCABULARY LIST

The following words that appear in Unit 2 are important for your students' understanding of the social studies content as well as for development of literacy. Use these words for vocabulary study or to reinforce language arts skills (e.g., synonyms, compound words, prefixes and suffixes, and related words). The words are listed below in the order in which they appear in the chapters.

Chapter 3
flaunt
codex
sacrificial
sacrifice
barren
irrigation
aggressive
organic
excrement
bumper
canopy
guttural

Chapter 4
refugee
reservoir
deity
majestic
citadel
hypothetical
pandemonium
ceramic
vandal

CHAPTER 3
CONQUESTS AND CAPTIVES: THE FIRST MESOAMERICAN CITIES
PAGES 31–38

FOR HOMEWORK

STUDENT STUDY GUIDE
pages 15–16

CAST OF CHARACTERS

One Earthquake war captive and sacrificial victim of Zapotec rulers of San José Mogote, Mexico

 WRITING

○ **Personal Writing** Ask students to write a diary entry from the perspective of a young person living in a village that has recently become part of Monte Albán. In the entry, students should explain some of the advantages of being part of the large city. The entry can also include plans to travel to see the sights in the mountaintop city.

CHAPTER SUMMARY

In this chapter students learn about the founding, flourishing, and abandonment of two ancient cities, Monte Albán and El Mirador. While there are similarities between them, their locations and the amount of information known about them differ widely.

PERFORMANCE OBJECTIVES

▶ To understand the religious reasons for the founding of Monte Albán
▶ To describe the conquests that contributed to the expansion of Monte Albán
▶ To appreciate the architectural and engineering accomplishments of Monte Albán and El Mirador

BUILDING BACKGROUND

Ask students how many have ever attended a large sporting event in person. Point out that the enthusiasm for watching ball games is a tradition dating back to Mesoamerica thousands of years ago.

WORKING WITH PRIMARY SOURCES

While students examine the stone portrait of One Earthquake on page 32, ask a volunteer to read the caption aloud. Then have students take turns reading the story of One Earthquake. Define any unfamiliar words and have students use them in original sentences. Storyboard the One Earthquake story and review it after reading the rest of the chapter. Ask: What is One Earthquake's importance to the chapter? Why do you think the authors started a chapter about the growth of cities with this story?

GEOGRAPHY CONNECTION

Location Have students use the map on page 33 to identify the locations of Monte Albán and El Mirador. Ask them to use the map scale to calculate distances between the cities and from the cities to various points on the map. Discuss with the class what effect distance has on societies and their economies.

READING COMPREHENSION QUESTIONS

1. When the Zapotec abandoned their villages to found a city, where did they go and why? (*They went to Monte Albán, a sacred mountain, to please the rain god.*)
2. As the kingdom of Monte Albán grew, where did 20,000 people live? (*on terraces, in the foothills, and at the base of the mountain*)
3. How did the Maya living in El Mirador expand their diet? (*by eating the meat of animals that lived in the rainforest*)
4. People in El Mirador were able to trade with other smaller towns in the rainforest thanks to what engineering accomplishment? (*raised roads built by hand*)

CRITICAL THINKING QUESTIONS

1. What are "beasts of burden" and why is their absence from Monte Albán and El Mirador significant? (*Beasts of burden are animals capable of carrying loads. Because there were no beasts of burden in ancient Mesoamerica, people had to do all the work of carrying and hauling materials to build cities.*)
2. What are some examples of expert Maya engineering and architecture? (*raised roads and fields that solved the problems of travel and farming in swamps; pyramids; large sculptures on buildings*)
3. Compare some of the reasons that archaeologists give to explain why people abandoned Monte Albán and El Mirador. (*Monte Albán: possibly, people were attracted by other towns in the Valley of Oaxaca. El Mirador: possibly, war with neighbors or crop destruction from erosion caused by cutting down too many trees.*)
4. Distribute copies of the blackline master for Chapter 3 and have students complete the activity comparing Monte Albán and El Mirador.

SOCIAL SCIENCES

Science, Technology, and Society Have students investigate and report on the ancient Mesoamerican calendar described on page 31. They can find more sources of information on the Websites page of their book.

READING AND LANGUAGE ARTS

Reading Nonfiction Ask students to look carefully at the graphic aids in the chapter, asking what each one adds to their understanding of the chapter's content. For example, how does the view of the Danta complex at El Mirador on page 37 help them understand the impact of the city on the people of the time?

Using Language Have students note the words used to describe the rainforest on page 36, specifically the adjective–noun combinations (*thick canopy, amazing animals, leafy umbrella,* and *guttural howls*), as well as the example of figurative language (*slice through the mist*). Have students define unfamiliar words. Then ask them to invent original descriptions using an adjective–noun pattern or figurative language.

SUPPORTING LEARNING

Struggling Readers Have students use the sequence of events graphic organizer (see the back of this guide) to understand the stages in the rise and fall Monte Albán and El Mirador.

EXTENDING LEARNING

Enrichment Have interested students report on the Mirador Basin's designation as a Global Heritage Fund site. They can find information online at *www.globalheritagefund.org/sites/americas/index.html* (click on "Guatemala" and then on "Mirador Basin").

Extension Have students create an illustrated chart showing the connection among food, trade, and cities based on information in the chapter.

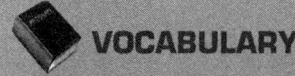

VOCABULARY

danzantes (dahn-SAHN-tehs) "dancers" in Spanish. The figures looked like dancers to early 20th century Mexican archaeologists, who first saw the stones standing upright.

El Mirador "the lookout point" in Spanish. Local workers who first discovered the ancient city looked out from the tops of tall gum trees and saw the tops of pyramids rising through the forest.

macaw very large parrot with a long tail and brightly colored feathers

stucco from an old German word for "crust." The Maya made stucco by burning limestone until it was powder. Then they blended the powder with water and coated the outsides of their buildings with the mixture.

MONTE ALBÁN AND EL MIRADOR

Directions

Use the chart to compare and contrast the cities of Monte Albán and El Mirador. Then complete the writing prompt on a separate sheet of paper.

	Monte Albán	El Mirador	Location (advantages/disadvantages)
Years city was inhabited			
Reason city was built			
Notable architecture			
Building materials used			
Farming techniques			
Number of residents			
Reason city was abandoned			
Sports			
Water source			

Choose one of these cities and write a paragraph explaining the difficulties that had to be overcome in building it.

CHAPTER TEST 3

THE ANCIENT AMERICAN WORLD

A. MULTIPLE CHOICE

Circle the letter of the best answer for each question.

1. The story of One Earthquake is an example of the way Zapotec
   a. cities extended their power.
   b. nobles treated their sons.
   c. leaders used hieroglyphic name tags.
   d. villages resisted being taken over by larger villages.
2. Why did the Zapotec people move to the sacred site of Monte Albán?
   a. to accommodate a large population
   b. to please the sun god
   c. to please the rain god
   d. to be safe from their enemies
3. How do archaeologists know that Monte Albán's rulers were powerful and aggressive?
   a. Their books describe their conquests.
   b. Many statues show their powerful enemies.
   c. Three hundred conquest slabs show defeated enemies.
   d. Stories of the conquests were passed down for generations.
4. What problem did Maya farmers have to overcome at El Mirador?
   a. The ground was too swampy for farming.
   b. There was not enough water for irrigation.
   c. There was too much meat available, and no one wanted to eat maize.
   d. The hillsides were too steep for farming.
5. Which of the following questions still remain about El Mirador's people?
   a. Why did they go to El Mirador?
   b. Why did they build raised roads and fields?
   c. Were they expert architects?
   d. Were they skilled engineers?

B. SHORT ANSWER

Write one or two sentences to answer each question.

6. Why was One Earthquake's portrait carved on a stone at the Zapotec village of San José Mogote?

7. What are the advantages of city life for the Zapotecs of Monte Albán?

8. How did the Maya of El Mirador build their roads?

C. ESSAY

On a separate sheet of paper, write an essay comparing and contrasting the solutions that the people of Monte Albán and El Mirador found for the challenges they faced in the places that they chose for their cities.

CHAPTER 4

PYRAMIDS, PAINTINGS, AND POTTERY: TEOTIHUACAN, CITY OF THE GODS
PAGES 39–45

FOR HOMEWORK
STUDENT STUDY GUIDE
pages 17–18

VOCABULARY

Teotihuacan "teo" + "tihuacan" = "place of the gods" in Nahuatl. This is the Aztec name; we don't know the original name of the city.

pilgrims people who journey from afar to worship at a religious center

- **Letter** Invite students to put themselves in the place of the pilgrim in the chapter. Ask students to pick out three things about Teotihuacan that most impressed them and describe them in a letter to family back home in Monte Albán.

CHAPTER SUMMARY

Teotihuacan was the largest Mesoamerican city of its day. Called the "eternal city" of Mesoamerica, its influence was felt as far as 900 miles away. Fourteen hundred years later people still come to Teotihuacan's Sun Pyramid to celebrate the spring equinox.

PERFORMANCE OBJECTIVES

▶ To understand the reason that Teotihuacan was built
▶ To describe Teotihuacan's art and architecture
▶ To identify the influence of the city on other parts of Mesoamerica

BUILDING BACKGROUND

Explain to students that they will be reading about a city where artists decorated their apartment walls with colorful paintings showing gods and goddesses and city life. Ask students how they decorate their walls at home and what decorating means to them. Look around the classroom and discuss what the wall decorations would suggest to archaeologists of the future.

WORKING WITH PRIMARY SOURCES

Direct students' attention to the Tepantitla mural on pages 40–41 while a volunteer reads the caption aloud. Then read the descriptions of other murals on pages 41–42 to the class. Provide groups with paper and pencils and invite them to sketch a mural representing life in your school. Once they have finalized the sketches, provide students with large sheets of paper and paints (red, green, blue, and yellow—the colors artists used in Teotihuacan) with which to create the final mural. Display the completed mural in the classroom or hallway.

GEOGRAPHY CONNECTION

Location Copy and distribute the blackline master for Chapter 4. Students will be labeling important sites in Teotihuacan based on the picture on page 42 and information in the chapter to get a sense of the size and layout of Teotihuacan.

READING COMPREHENSION QUESTIONS

1. How did volcanoes influence the settlement of Teotihuacan? (*When volcanoes erupted twice in 50 years, wiping out villages for miles around, people looked for a place to live far away from volcanoes.*)
2. Why did people think Teotihuacan was an "ideal spot for a brand new city"? (*The availability of water from springs and from the San Juan River meant year-round irrigation of crops to feed a large population.*)
3. What written evidence have archaeologists found that Teotihuacan influenced Maya areas of Mesoamerica? (*They found hieroglyphic texts about Teotihuacan describing trips made by the Maya to and from the "city of the gods."*)
4. How did some artists use pottery to represent people of importance in the city? (*They made hollow figurines, 5–20 inches tall, and filled these with smaller figures.*)

CRITICAL THINKING QUESTIONS

1. Why did people come to Teotihuacan? (*As the "city of the gods," Teotihuacan attracted people who wanted to pay their respects to the gods. People also went there to trade.*)
2. What is the connection between a steady food supply and the growth of cities? (*People like to have a steady supply of food. As more people move into an area where there is plenty of food, some can afford not to be farmers and instead work on other tasks, like building a city or creating art.*)
3. Copy and distribute the blackline master for Chapter 4 and have students review the important sites of Teotihuacan.

SOCIAL SCIENCES

Economics The Great Compound in Teotihuacan was the focal point for trade; some goods came from as far away as the Pacific Coast. Have students find out more about patterns of trade in Mesoamerica. For example, would seashell jewelry have come all the way from the Pacific Coast to the market at Teotihuacan, or would it have been traded in other places before it reached Teotihuacan? What was the source of the obsidian and jade items found at Teotihuacan? Students can present their answers to the class.

READING AND LANGUAGE ARTS

Reading Nonfiction Have students identify examples of the use of the present tense in describing the pilgrim's tour of Teotihuacan. Discuss the effectiveness this tense in making the scenes more immediate to the reader.

Using Language Point out the following descriptive words and colloquial expressions used in the chapter: *blew its top; bonanza; piggyback; eagle's eye view; torched.* Have students discuss each one and then define and use it in an original sentence.

SUPPORTING LEARNING

English Language Learners Have partners read together the description of the pottery workshop on page 44, identifying unfamiliar words, defining them, and using them in original sentences.

Struggling Readers Have students use the cause and effect graphic organizer (see the T-chart at the back of this guide) to better understand Teotihuacan. Have them list the following *causes* and then add the *effects*: Volcanoes destroy villages; crops grow year-round; apartment compounds are built; traders come from far away; temples are destroyed.

EXTENDING LEARNING

Enrichment Students can prepare an illustrated presentation on Teotihuacan using photographs and further information available at *www.mesoamerican-archives.com*.

Extension Invite students to create a skit based on the description of the Great Compound on page 44. Students can create props representing the goods available there. A narrator can set the scene, while other students portray shoppers and traders. The lead role will be the pilgrim, whose lines can express wonder and excitement at seeing Teotihuacan for the first time.

THEN and NOW

Then and Now
Scientists hope that subatomic particles from cosmic rays will help them locate a burial chamber inside the Pyramid of the Sun. The particles, called muons, leave many traces as they pass through solid objects but fewer traces in empty spaces. Scientists hope to pinpoint empty spaces inside the pyramid. These can then be excavated to search for the tombs of Teotihuacan's rulers.

LINKING DISCIPLINES

Art Have students find images of the feathered serpent online and make a presentation about its significance in ancient Mesoamerica. One useful site is *www.utexas.edu/cofa/a_ah/dir/precol/teotihuacan.htm*.

THE ANCIENT AMERICAN WORLD

NAME   DATE

THE WONDER OF TEOTIHUACAN

Directions
Complete the chart by describing the different features of Teotihuacan. Use details from the chapter. Then imagine you are the hypothetical pilgrim mentioned in the chapter. On a separate sheet of paper, write your reaction to your tour of the city, including the feature that you found most impressive.

Feature of Teotihuacan	Description
Apartment compounds	
Moon Pyramid	
Avenue of the Dead	
Sun Pryamid	
Citadel	
Great Compound	
Pottery workshop	

CHAPTER TEST 4

THE ANCIENT AMERICAN WORLD

A. MULTIPLE CHOICE

Circle the letter of the best answer for each question.

1. Which of the following was **not** a reason for building a city near Fat Mountain?
   a. Springs provided water.
   b. It was far from volcanoes.
   c. The San Juan River provided water.
   d. Pyramids had been built there earlier.

2. Teotihuacan was known as the city of the
   a. rainforest.
   b. gods.
   c. desert.
   d. ball games.

3. Archaeologists have found information about life in Teotihuacan in
   a. murals painted by artists.
   b. graffiti travelers carved on walls.
   c. letters travelers wrote.
   d. ceramic figurines made by artists.

4. The two-mile-long Street of the Dead was lined on both sides by
   a. large markets.
   b. palaces and temples.
   c. small pyramids.
   d. ball courts and theaters.

5. Women played a key role in making Teotihuacan a great trading center because they alone
   a. made sacrifices to the gods.
   b. were the city's bankers.
   c. made millions of ceramic figurines.
   d. traveled far and wide as traders.

B. SHORT ANSWER

Write one or two sentences to answer each question.

6. What attracted so many people to come to live at Teotihuacan?

7. Why wouldn't the tale of the sacrifice of 200 warriors during the building of the Citadel bother a pilgrim to Teotihuacan?

8. What activities went on in the Great Compound at Teotihuacan?

C. ESSAY

Write an essay on a separate sheet of paper describing the major architectural wonders of the city of Teotihuacan.

UNIT 3: THE MAYA

PAGES 46–71

Chapter 5	K'uk' Mo' Takes a Hike: Written History Takes a Leap
Chapter 6	The Boy-King of Bone: An Explosion of Maya Hieroglyphs
Chapter 7	Fear and Fire: The Fall of Maya Kingdoms
Chapter 8	Cotton, Copper, and Canoes: The Rise of the Putún Maya at Chichén Itzá

UNIT OBJECTIVES

Unit 3 covers the period from 426 CE through 900 CE and focuses on the civilization of the Maya. In this unit your students will learn

- how Maya hieroglyphs were used and where they are found today.
- information about Maya dynastic rule.
- theories about the end of Maya civilization.
- how and why the city of Chichén Itzá became a center of trade for the Putún.
- the importance of the feathered serpent in ancient Mesoamerica.

PRIMARY SOURCES

Unit 3 includes excerpts from the following primary sources:

- *Popol Vuh*
- *Dresden Codex*
- Bishop Diego de Landa, *Relación de las Cosas de Yucatán*
- Fray Bernardino de Sahagún, *Florentine Codex*
- Ferdinand Columbus, *The Life of the Admiral*

Unit 3 also includes photographs of the following artifacts, which can be analyzed as primary sources:

- Inscriptions and glyphs on Altar Q, Copán, Honduras
- Sculpture of K'uk' Mo' on Altar Q
- Stela 63, Copán, Honduras
- Emblem glyphs for Bone and Calakmul
- Hieroglyphic stairway
- Temple of Inscriptions
- Glyphs on Temple of Inscriptions
- Oval Tablet of Palenque
- Jade mosaic mask in Pakal's tomb
- Pakal's tomb
- Clay figurines, Aguateca
- Scribal house, Aguateca
- Seashell ornament, Aguateca
- Hollowed stones, Aguateca
- Carving from the Temple of the Warriors, Chichén Itzá
- Battle mural, Chichén Itzá
- Engraved gold disk, Chichén Itzá
- Sculpture of Kukulcan
- Temple of the Warriors

BIG IDEAS IN UNIT 3

Writing, power, and **trade** are the big ideas in Unit 3. What we know of Maya writing comes from thousands of hieroglyphs carved in stone and the few fragile pages of the few remaining books, written on deerskin or bark and bound in wood. Using a sophisticated writing system, Maya kings were able to promote their sacred connections and in some cases secure and retain power. Power shifts within Maya kingdoms were common; thus a 400-year dynasty was a notable achievement. In the end, as one group of Maya lost power (in some cases because of disruptions in trade routes) and abandoned their cities, another group, the Putún Maya, rose to prominence. Their seafaring and trading skills resulted in a powerful trade network with Chichén Itzá at its hub.

GEOGRAPHY CONNECTION

On the map of ancient Mesoamerica on page 10, have students locate the cities described in these chapters—Teotihuacan, Copán, Bone (Palenque), and Chichén Itzá. Students can use a topographic map for better understanding of the lowland and highland regions mentioned in these chapters. Students can also use an interactive map of the Maya world at *www.pbs.org/wgbh/nova/maya/world.html*. They can report on their trip in an oral or written presentation.

TIMELINE

426 CE	K'uk' Mo' travels from Teotihuacan to Copán
612 CE	Lady Sak K'uk' becomes Queen of Palenque
615 CE	Pakal becomes King of Palenque
763 CE	Altar Q dedicated by Copán's last ruler
800–900 CE	Aguateca invaded; other lowland cities abandoned; Putún Maya seafaring merchants gain power

UNIT PROJECTS

Stela!

Have students record their names and facts about themselves on a four-sided cardboard stela such as the one that Learned One erected for his father K'uk' Mo' (Chapter 5). Students can create their names in Maya hieroglyphs at *www.halfmoon.org/names.html* and attach the hieroglyphs to the stela. Display the stela in a classroom museum of ancient Mesoamerica.

Maya Cities Tour

Have students work in groups to locate and present information about the following cities: Palenque, Copán, Aguateca, Chichén Itzá. Each group should identify its city on a map of ancient Mesoamerica and provide facts about architecture, population, and key events in the city's history. The Resources section of the student book suggests books and websites related to the Maya.

Putún Maya Trading Cards

Have students organize a demonstration of Putún Maya trade as described in Chapter 8. They can label large index cards to represent items such as embroidered cloaks, pottery bowls, cacao pods, jade, spiny oyster shells, blocks of salt, obsidian knives, and copper hatchets. Students can illustrate their cards with images from the Peabody Museum collection (*www.peabody.harvard.edu/col/browse.cfm?ListKey =228*) or those found on other sites listed on the Websites page of their book. These trading cards can also become part of the classroom museum.

THE ANCIENT AMERICAN WORLD

Glyph Gazette

Encourage a group of students to prepare and present interviews in which reporters for the Maya *Glyph Gazette* interview K'uk' Mo' about his long hike; the king's scribe, Bol, about the night Aguateca was burned; or the crew of a Putún Maya dugout canoe about the strange people and ship they met off the coast of Honduras.

ADDITIONAL ASSESSMENT

For Unit 3, divide the class into groups and have them all undertake the Maya Cities Tour project so you can assess their knowledge of the rise and fall of the early Maya kingdoms and the rejuvenation of the Maya civilization led by the Putún Maya. Use the scoring rubric at the back of this guide to assess students' work, and have students rate their own work with the self-assessment rubric.

LITERATURE CONNECTION

There are numerous books that students can enjoy that will broaden their knowledge of the Maya civilization. Suggest some of the following to students:

- Linares, Frederico Navarrete. *A Day with a Maya*. Minneapolis: Lerner Publishing, 1999. Fiction. AVERAGE. This book narrates a day in the life of an imaginary Maya artisan.
- Mann, Elizabeth. *Tikal: The Center of the Maya World*. Mikaya Press, 2002. Nonfiction. ADVANCED. An illustrated history describes the Maya city of Tikal on the Yucatan Peninsula.
- Palacios, Argentina. *The Hummingbird King: A Guatemalan Legend*. New York: Troll Communications, 1993. Fiction. EASY. This book gives the legend of a Mayan prince protected by a hummingbird feather, his jealous uncle who destroys him, and the Maya belief that the good prince still protected them after his death.

UNIVERSAL ACCESS

The following strategies are designed to cover a range of learning styles and reading, language, and skill levels. This section includes suggestions for differentiating instruction to meet the diverse needs of your students.

Reading Strategies

- To facilitate reading, point out features such as illustrations, information, and definitions in the side columns that students will encounter as they read.
- Call on students to read sections of the chapters aloud. Encourage students to make their voices expressive and to use hand gestures where appropriate. Fit the reading passage to the abilities of each student.
- Help students organize their understanding of the material by creating an annotated timeline of the people and events in each chapter.

Writing Strategies

- Have partners make a three-column chart with headings for each of the unit's big ideas. Partners should get together after reading each chapter to jot down their observations in each category.
- Encourage students to write an essay about the importance of Maya writing. Encourage them to specify how writing was used to honor the Copán dynasty or to help with the "extreme makeover" of Lady Sak K'uk'. Have students orally summarize their conclusions for the class.
- Each chapter describes places in ancient Mesoamerica. Have students write brief descriptions of a key feature of each place and its significance.

Listening and Speaking Strategies

▶ As you read portions of the chapters, call on volunteers to describe what they think the scenes looked like; for example, the scene of the boy-king of Bone being crowned, people escaping from the burning city of Aguateca, or Putún Maya arriving in Chichén Itzá.

▶ Have students make masks of the personalities in this unit—K'uk' Mo', Learned One, Lady Sak K'uk', Pakal, Bol, Ferdinand Columbus—using markers, paper plates, and craft sticks. Call on volunteers to come to the front of the class and share facts about their chosen personalities while holding their masks in front of their faces.

UNIT VOCABULARY LIST

The following words that appear in Unit 3 are important for your students' understanding of the social studies content as well as for development of literacy. Use these words for vocabulary study or to reinforce language arts skills (e.g., synonyms, compound words, prefixes and suffixes, and related words). The words are listed below in the order in which they appear in the chapters.

Chapter 5	**Chapter 6**	**Chapter 7**	**Chapter 8**
table-altar	self-appointed	chasm	galley
promotion	computation	crackle	awning
reckon	fateful	thatch	mantle
resistance	prophecy		relief
stela	sarcophagus		efficient
insignia	mosaic		navigate
dynasty			cenote
epigrapher			architectural
genealogy			

CHAPTER 5
K'UK' MO' TAKES A HIKE: WRITTEN HISTORY TAKES A LEAP

PAGES 46–52

FOR HOMEWORK
STUDENT STUDY GUIDE
pages 19–20

CAST OF CHARACTERS

K'inich Yax K'uk' Mo' (KUH-een-eech yahsh KUH-oo-kuh MO-uh) first king of Copán; originally named K'uk' Mo' Ajaw, "quetzal macaw lord" in Mayan

epigraphy (epi + graphia) "upon" + "writing" in ancient Greek. An epigrapher studies ancient inscriptions on stone, pottery, and other artifacts.

Popol Vuh "The Book of the Community" in Mayan

CHAPTER SUMMARY

Maya hieroglyphs—signs standing for syllables and words—allowed the Maya to leave a complex written record that sets them apart from other cultures in the Americas. As more Maya hieroglyphs are interpreted by scientists, more details of their history become clear. The 400-year reign of a dynasty founded by K'uk' Mo' was discovered through painstaking interpretation of hieroglyphs and remains.

PERFORMANCE OBJECTIVES

▶ To understand the significance of Maya hieroglyphs in understanding historical events
▶ To comprehend how a Maya dynasty of rulers was founded in Copán
▶ To compare Maya numbers to Arabic numerals and perform calculations

BUILDING BACKGROUND

Ask students to describe the written words they have seen thus far today. These might include road signs, instant messages, newspaper headlines, text on cereal boxes, textbook content, or homework assignments. Explain that in ancient Mesoamerica, the Maya invented a complex writing system. Today archaeologists and other scholars search for and interpret Maya words "written in stone." Of the books "published" by the Maya, only a few scraps remain.

WORKING WITH PRIMARY SOURCES

Have students read excerpts from the *Popol Vuh*, the Maya creation story, in *The World in Ancient Times Primary Sources and Reference Volume*, or online at www.jaguar-sun.com/popolvuh.html. Have volunteers prepare a choral reading to present to the class.

GEOGRAPHY CONNECTION

Place Have students refer to the map of ancient Mesoamerica on page 10 to locate Teotihuacan and Copán. Students can use the map scale to estimate the distance that K'uk' Mo' traveled.

READING COMPREHENSION QUESTIONS

1. How do we know about the hike and reign of K'uk' Mo'? (*glyphs carved into Altar Q and Hieroglyphic Stairway in Copán*)
2. Why do scholars think K'uk' Mo' went to Teotihuacan? (*He went for a ritual related to being or becoming a king; afterward, his title changed from "Lord" to "Great Sun."*)
3. K'uk' Mo' wanted to pass on his kingship to a son. He got his wish. For how many years did K'uk' Mo's dynasty last, and how many kings ruled? (*It lasted more than 400 years, and there were 16 kings.*)
4. What is one reason that Maya priests kept track of stars and planets? (*They believed stars and planets were related to gods who controlled events on earth.*)

CRITICAL THINKING QUESTIONS

1. K'uk' Mo' had a broken right arm that did not heal properly. Why might this have been an advantage in battle? (*He would have held a spear in his left hand, at an unexpected angle, which could have given him an advantage in battle.*)
2. What structures did K'uk' Mo' have built? How did they "earn the loyalty of his subjects"? (*The temple in the style of Teotihuacan pyramids would have impressed people. The ball court would have pleased both players and spectators.*)
3. How did archaeologists identify the skeleton buried under Altar Q? (*They matched the royal title carved on Altar Q, "K'inich Yax K'uk' Mo'," with items shown on a headdress and carvings on oyster shells buried near the skeleton.*)
4. Why is a book like the Maya *Popol Vuh* important? (*It provides historians with information about Maya religious beliefs as well as the family history of one royal Maya family.*)

SOCIAL SCIENCES

Civics Discuss examples of dynasties such as the royal dynasties in England and the generations of powerful political leaders from single families in the United States. Discuss the benefits and drawbacks of having several successive leaders from the same family.

READING AND LANGUAGE ARTS

Reading Nonfiction Point out to students that the story of the epigrapher David Stuart's discovery of the identity of the "lord" of Altar Q is a "story within a story." Have students identify where the Stuart story begins and ends and explain why it is useful to the chapter.

Using Language Have students read aloud the sidebar How to Tell a Stone Story on page 50. Have them identify the verbs for each step in the process of making Altar Q (*put, smoothed, drawn, engraved, smoothed, chiseled*). What would be another way to show these steps on a page? (*number them; use bullets*)

SUPPORTING LEARNING

English Language Learners Encourage students to work in a small group to retell the story of K'uk' Mo's journey and the significance of his change in name.

Struggling Readers Have students use the outline graphic organizer (see the back of this guide) to identify the topics in the chapter's two parts—the story of K'uk' Mo' and the story of David Stuart and Altar Q.

EXTENDING LEARNING

Enrichment Advanced students can find out more about the Maya Calendar at the following websites: *www.halfmoon.org/calendar.html* and *www.mayacalendar.com*. Then students can report their findings to the class.

Extension Have groups of students access video views of Altar Q at *www.peabody.harvard.edu/Copan/qtvr.html* (a page on a website recommended on the Websites page of their book) and describe their impressions of the views they can then share with the class.

LINKING DISCIPLINES

Math Copy and distribute the blackline master for Chapter 5. Students will interpret simple examples of the Maya number system, respond to questions, and then perform simple calculations using Maya numbers.

WRITING

Narrative Using the three-sentence excerpt from a family history in the *Popol Vuh* (page 52) as a model, have students describe the history of a family—their own or an imaginary one—in a narrative.

THE ANCIENT AMERICAN WORLD

MAYA MATH

Directions
Read the information and complete the "translation" of Maya numbers to Arabic numbers. Then follow the directions for the Challenge.

Symbols
Maya math used only three symbols: a dot, a bar, and a shell (symbol for zero) to represent numbers. The chart below shows the Maya numbers 0–10. Use the pattern to fill in the Maya numbers 11–14.

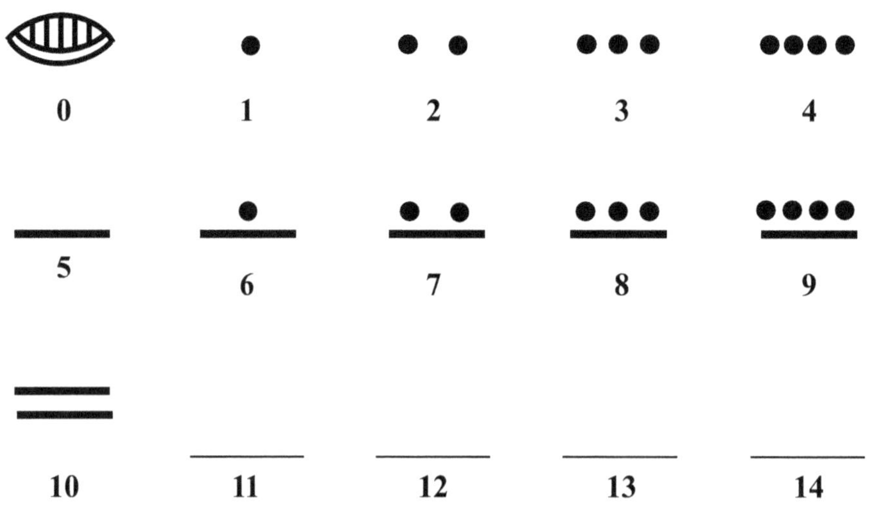

0	1	2	3	4
5	6	7	8	9
10	11	12	13	14

Place Values
The Maya wrote numbers vertically and used a base-20 system. That means the value of each place in a number could be from 0 to 19 (instead of 0 to 9, like in our system). Instead of 1s, 10s, and 100s places, the Maya had 1s, 20s, and 400s places. Look at the Maya number in the place-value chart below. Compute what number it equals in our system.

Place Value	Maya Numeral	Arabic Numeral
400s	•	
20s	•	
1s	 •• over ≡	

NAME   **DATE**

THE ANCIENT AMERICAN WORLD

A. MULTIPLE CHOICE

Circle the letter of the best answer for each question.

1. The longest surviving text in ancient America was written in hieroglyphics in which of the following places?
   a. Pyramid of the Sun
   b. Altar Q
   c. Hieroglyphic Stairway
   d. Tree Root House

2. The hieroglyphics on Altar Q explain
   a. the dynasty founded by K'uk' Mo'.
   b. how the hieroglyphics were carved.
   c. why K'uk' Mo' went to Teotihuacan.
   d. how the Maya calendar works.

3. The Maya recorded their history in books made of which of the following materials?
   a. birch bark
   b. cloth
   c. silk
   d. deerskin or fig-tree bark

4. The Maya thought that when this planet reappeared in the sky it was a good time for war.
   a. Venus
   b. Mercury
   c. Mars
   d. Pluto

5. *Popol Vuh* is important to historians because it explains
   a. how the gods created the world and people.
   b. why K'uk' Mo' traveled to Teotihuacan.
   c. how to write hieroglyphs.
   d. who is buried at Altar Q.

B. SHORT ANSWER

Write one or two sentences to answer each question.

6. Explain why K'uk' Mo' went to Teotihuacan.

7. Why was astronomy important to the Maya?

8. What information does the *Popol Vuh* give about the Maya?

C. ESSAY

Write an essay on a separate sheet of paper summarizing the events in Copán during the rule of the dynasty founded by K'inich Yax K'uk' Mo'.

THE ANCIENT AMERICAN WORLD   CHAPTER 5 TEST   **51**

THE BOY-KING OF BONE: AN EXPLOSION OF MAYA HIEROGLYPHS

PAGES 53–58

STUDENT STUDY GUIDE
pages 21–22

CAST OF CHARACTERS

Lady S'ak K'uk' (SAHK kuh-OOK) queen of Palenque; mother of Pakal I; name means "resplendent quetzal"

K'inich Janaab' Pakal I (KUH-een-eech OO-nahb PAH-kahl) Maya ruler of Palenque; his name means "Great Sun Shield"

- **News Article** Have students write a news article describing the coronation of the 12-year-old King Pakal I. In their articles students could quote comments from residents of Bone on the three years of Lady Sak K'uk's rule. Some might praise her for stepping up to rule; others might be dismissive of a female ruler.

CHAPTER SUMMARY

In this chapter students learn about two Maya rulers of Bone (Palenque). Lady Sak K'uk' ruled for three years before crowning her 12-year-old son, Pakal. As king, Pakal raised his mother's status by likening her to the goddess of creation. To accomplish this, Pakal used hieroglyphics carved in stone to convince people of his mother's godlike status.

PERFORMANCE OBJECTIVES

- To describe Maya intercity warfare using the conflict between Bone and Calakmul as an example
- To summarize the contributions of Lady Sak K'uk' and Pakal to Bone
- To understand the power of hieroglyphs carved in stone

BUILDING BACKGROUND

Ask students about their favorite sports teams' mascots. Suggest they suppose that every time their team loses, its mascot is replaced by the winning team's mascot. Discuss how they would feel at a game where only symbols for the rival team were displayed. Explain that defeated Maya cities gave up their special emblems when conquered by a rival and were then forced to display the conqueror's emblems.

WORKING WITH PRIMARY SOURCES

Scholars working at Palenque have uncovered many sites covered with glyphs. Have students examine a paraphrase of recently discovered glyphs at *www.mesoweb.com/palenque/monuments/T19PW/paraphrase.html*, a page on a site recommended on the Websites page of the students' book.

GEOGRAPHY CONNECTION

Place Have students locate Bone (Palenque) on the map of ancient Mesoamerica on page 10. Ask them to research the topography of Bone and compare it to descriptions of the terrain in the chapter. Another description of the city can be found at *www.mayaruins.com*, a site listed on the Websites page of students' book.

READING COMPREHENSION QUESTIONS

1. When a Maya city was "axed," what happened? What happened when Bone was axed a second time? (*"Axed" means it was attacked by another city and statues of its gods were destroyed. After the second axing, Bone could no longer carve or display its emblem.*)
2. Why was the queen, Lady Sak K'uk', worried when she named her son king? (*She thought the people of Bone might object because only male rulers were supposed to name a king.*)
3. If she had lived that long, what later events would have told her she had succeeded in keeping kingship in the family? (*After Pakal I died, one of his sons and then the other became king of Bone.*)

4. What building contains one of the longest written histories in Mesoamerica? (*the Temple of Inscriptions*)

CRITICAL THINKING QUESTIONS

1. How did his schooling prepare Pakal to be king? (*As a noble Maya child, he was taught to read and write hieroglyphs and to use the Maya calendar to make prophesies. He was also trained by priests to lead an "upright life." These are skills and qualities he needed as king.*)
2. How did Pakal convince people his mother was a not like a "run-of-the-mill" goddess but like the First Mother? (*He wrote about her in stone inscriptions that link her name with the city and with the First Mother, goddess of creation.*)
3. How did Pakal's campaign to elevate his mother to the status of First Mother help his own sons? (*Pakal convinced people that he and his sons were related to an important goddess and therefore had the right to rule.*)
4. What do the authors mean when they say Pakal and his mother "live on in spirit forever"? (*The authors mean that because the inscriptions about them are still read today, they are remembered.*)

SOCIAL SCIENCES

Science, Technology, and Society Invite a group of students to investigate aqueducts built to control water in Palenque. Students can download detailed information from the Palenque Project website: *www.mesoweb.com/palenque/dig/report/mapping/media/Water_Management.pdf*.

READING AND LANGUAGE ARTS

Reading Nonfiction Have students identify the rhetorical questions posed by the authors on pages 54, 55, and 56. Then discuss the function of these rhetorical questions—to arouse interest, organize information, and introduce topics.

Using Language Point out some of the idiomatic expressions used in the chapter, such as *two-time losers, run-of-the-mill, alive and kicking, extreme makeover, ripe old age,* and *no questions asked*. Discuss the meanings of these expressions and have students use them in original sentences.

SUPPORTING LEARNING

Struggling Readers To help students understand how the chapter is organized, have them complete the outline graphic organizer (see the back of this guide).

EXTENDING LEARNING

Enrichment Have a small group give an illustrated presentation to the class about buildings constructed by Pakal. Group members should answer these questions: What important structures did he build? What did they look like? What was their purpose? Students can find information and images at *www.mayaruins.com*.

Extension Distribute the blackline master for Chapter 6 and encourage students to create interesting pieces to use in playing the Maya game of *bul*. Supply four flat corn kernels with one side colored black to a pair of students and have them demonstrate how the game is played. (If corn is not available, use a number cube, with the 6 meaning "roll again.") Students can play the game online at *www.halfmoon.org/bul.html*.

THEN and NOW

Palenque is one of Mexico's most popular archaeological sites, with hundreds of structures as yet uncovered. Palenque was put on the "tourist map" in the 1840s with the publication of a bestseller, *Incidents of Travel in Central America, Chiapas and Yucatan* by John Lloyd Stephens and the illustrator Frederick Catherwood.

LINKING DISCIPLINES

Art On a sheet of paper have students draw or describe a scene they would carve in stone to commemorate an important event in their lives, as Pakal commemorated receiving the crown from his mother.

THE MAYA GAME OF BUL

Directions

In wars between Maya cities, winners took the conquered city's emblem glyph and replaced it with theirs. That happened in Bone before Pakal I became king. Warring cities also captured each other's warriors and took them back as slaves. The Maya board game *bul* echoed Maya war aims. The point of the game was to capture the other player's pieces and transport them out of the game.

Use the diagram below as the *bul* board. The directions that follow are for two players, but any even number of players can play. (For an online version of the game, see *www.halfmoon.org/bul.html*.)

You will need:
A copy of this "board"
5 playing pieces—buttons, coins, seeds—for each player
4 flat corn kernels with a black mark on one side

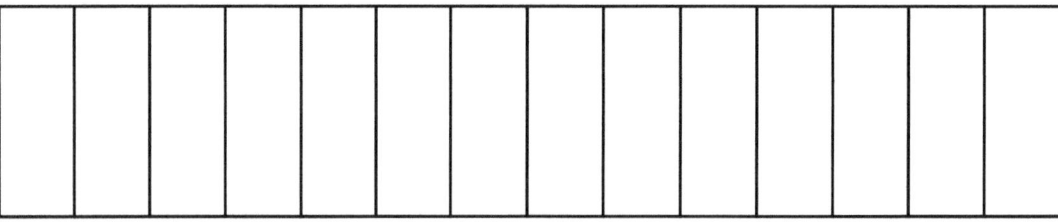

To Play

Each player in turn tosses the corn grains and counts the number of black spots showing. Then the player moves forward that number of spaces. If no spots are showing, the player can move 5 spaces. When a piece reaches the end of the board, it returns to its starting box and begins again.

A player captures the opponent's piece by landing on the space occupied by the opponent's piece. When a piece is captured, the conqueror reverses direction to drag the captive back to his or her end of the board. The captive piece is out of the game, and the player whose piece was captured enters a new piece into the game. Play continues until all of one player's pieces have been captured.

CHAPTER TEST 6

THE ANCIENT AMERICAN WORLD

A. MULTIPLE CHOICE

Circle the letter of the best answer for each question.

1. Which of the following events in Bone was **not** a result of warfare with Calakmul?
   a. Lady Sak K'uk' was taken captive.
   b. Bone was not allowed to display its emblem glyph.
   c. Sculptures of Bone's gods were destroyed.
   d. A monument engraved with Calakmul's glyph was put up in Bone.

2. Twelve-year-old Pakal became king because he was
   a. elected.
   b. named successor by the former king.
   c. named successor by his mother, the queen.
   d. married to a queen.

3. Subjects that noble Maya children studied included reading, writing, and
   a. calendar calculation.
   b. flower cultivation.
   c. stone carving.
   d. cooking.

4. To insure that his sons would be accepted as royalty, Pakal convinced the people of Bone that
   a. his sons were important gods.
   b. his mother was like the goddess of creation.
   c. he was an important god.
   d. his wife was First Mother.

5. Today one of the most complete histories of ancient Mesoamerica can be found in the Palenque
   a. mountains.
   b. aqueducts.
   c. Royal Palace.
   d. Temple of Inscriptions.

B. SHORT ANSWER

Write one or two sentences to answer each question.

6. Why wasn't Lady Sak K'uk' accepted as the ruler of Bone when her husband the king died?

7. What do scholars think was Lady Sak K'uk's major concern after she crowned her son king?

8. How did the structures built by Pakal I at Bone differ from other such buildings in Mesoamerica?

C. ESSAY

Write an essay on a separate sheet of paper summarizing how Lady Sak K'uk' was transformed from human queen to goddess.

FEAR AND FIRE: THE FALL OF MAYA KINGDOMS

PAGES 59–63

STUDENT STUDY GUIDE
pages 23–24

WRITING

Diary Entry Have students write a diary entry for a person living in a Maya city facing life without chocolate because of trade disruptions. The diary entry should indicate the writer's decision to move out of the city.

Health The chapter describes the anthropologist Rebecca Storey's research that led her to the conclusion that the anemia suffered by people living in Copán was caused by infectious disease. Have interested students investigate print or online resources to identify the link between the infectious diseases and anemia and then report their findings to the class.

CHAPTER SUMMARY

Between 800 and 900 CE, most southern Maya cities were abandoned one by one. In this chapter the authors discuss scholars' theories about why this may have happened, ranging from illness, drought, and disruptions in trade to warfare among cities.

PERFORMANCE OBJECTIVES

▶ To summarize what happened in the Maya city of Aguateca in the early 800s
▶ To explain theories about the abandonment of Maya cities between 800 and 900 CE
▶ To understand the continuity of Maya culture

BUILDING BACKGROUND

Ask students what image the term *ghost town* brings to mind. Most students will associate the term with empty, battered buildings standing among tumbleweeds in the American West. Now ask them to imagine what happens to an abandoned town or city in the jungle. Students should realize that jungle plants and vines cover the ruins and make them hard to find and uncover. Explain that this is what happened to Maya cities that were abandoned in the 9th century CE.

WORKING WITH PRIMARY SOURCES

Have students look at the picture of the figurine on page 59 and read the caption aloud. Ask: What can scholars learn from this figurine and similar ones? Why are they a valuable source of information about Aguateca?

GEOGRAPHY CONNECTION

Regions Make available to students a topographical map of Mesoamerica so they can identify the terrain of the cities mentioned in the chapter—Aguateca, Palenque, Copán, and Teotihuacan. One useful site is *http://go.hrw.com/atlas/ norm_htm/namerica.htm*.

READING COMPREHENSION QUESTIONS

1. When did people first ask why the Maya left beautiful places like Copán and Palenque? (*in the 19th century, when travelers first stumbled across city ruins covered by centuries of jungle growth*)
2. What have experts concluded about the collapse of the Maya kingdoms? (*that there are many reasons for the kingdoms' collapse, and the reasons differ from place to place*)
3. How did alliances between Maya cities contribute to their defeat? (*If one member of the alliance was defeated, its ally was probably defeated, too.*)
4. What happened to Maya culture after the kingdoms disappeared? (*It continued and lives on today in the language, religious customs, and art of the Maya.*)

CRITICAL THINKING QUESTIONS

1. What evidence is there that the attack on Aguateca surprised Bol the Scribe and other residents? (*Tools and other valuable objects were left behind, as if some of the people had left in haste.*)
2. How can the skeletons of residents of Copán help explain why the people left that city? (*The anthropologist Rebecca Storey discovered that the skeletons showed people had anemia, which can result from infectious disease. Widespread disease in Copán may have caused some people to die and others to leave the city and never return.*)
3. What might the destruction of Aguateca and Teotihuacan, 300 years apart, have in common? (*The attackers who destroyed each city were trying to end its power as a sacred place.*)

SOCIAL SCIENCES

Civics On pages 62–63 the authors describe some of the reasons that Maya cities made alliances and some of the consequences of doing so. For example, an alliance of two cities could result in a double victory or in a double defeat. Brainstorm with students the present-day allies of the United States. Ask: Who are our allies? Why do we need them?

READING AND LANGUAGE ARTS

Reading Nonfiction Have students examine the first three paragraphs of the chapter and distinguish fact from speculation. Point out the words and phrases that indicate a statement is speculation, such as *perhaps, it's likely,* and *must have been.* Have students note other examples of speculation as they read the chapter.

Using Language Ask students to identify the adjectives used to describe the frightening attack on Aguateca as Bol might have experienced it. These include *victorious, bitter, flaming, hollowed-out, shell, precious,* and *greenstone.* Define the words and have students use them in original sentences.

SUPPORTING LEARNING

Struggling Readers Have students complete the cause and effect graphic organizer (see the T-chart at the back of this guide) to visualize the connections between events—drought, disease, disrupted trade—and the fall of the Maya kingdoms in the 9th century CE.

EXTENDING LEARNING

Enrichment Have students investigate the Maya today, following up on information given at the end of the chapter, and report to the class about where modern Maya live and work.

Extension Students can dig for clues about the fall of the Maya city Copán on *www.learner.org/exhibits/collapse/copan/index.php*. Invite interested students to follow the directions on the website for answering these questions: Why did Copán collapse? Was the end a gradual decline or a rapid fall? Students can present their findings to the class.

CAST OF CHARACTERS

Bol (BOWL) Maya scribe of Aguateca

THEN and NOW

Researchers reported on Aguateca in the May 2003 issue of *National Geographic.* In a feature titled "On Assignment," the researchers describe their excitement in examining items left behind in the homes of ordinary people in Aguateca. They describe "going back in time" to "discover what the materials from everyday houses could tell us about the people [who lived there]." Have students write a paragraph describing what the contents of their home or classroom would reveal about their lives to future researchers.

THE ANCIENT AMERICAN WORLD

NAME   **DATE**

CHARTING THE FALL OF MAYA KINGDOMS

Directions
Fill the blank circles with reasons for the fall of the Maya kingdoms explained in Chapter 7. Briefly describe each reason in its own circle. Then, using complete sentences, summarize how scholars today explain the fall of the Maya kingdoms.

(Fall of Maya Kingdoms)

_____
_____
_____
_____
_____

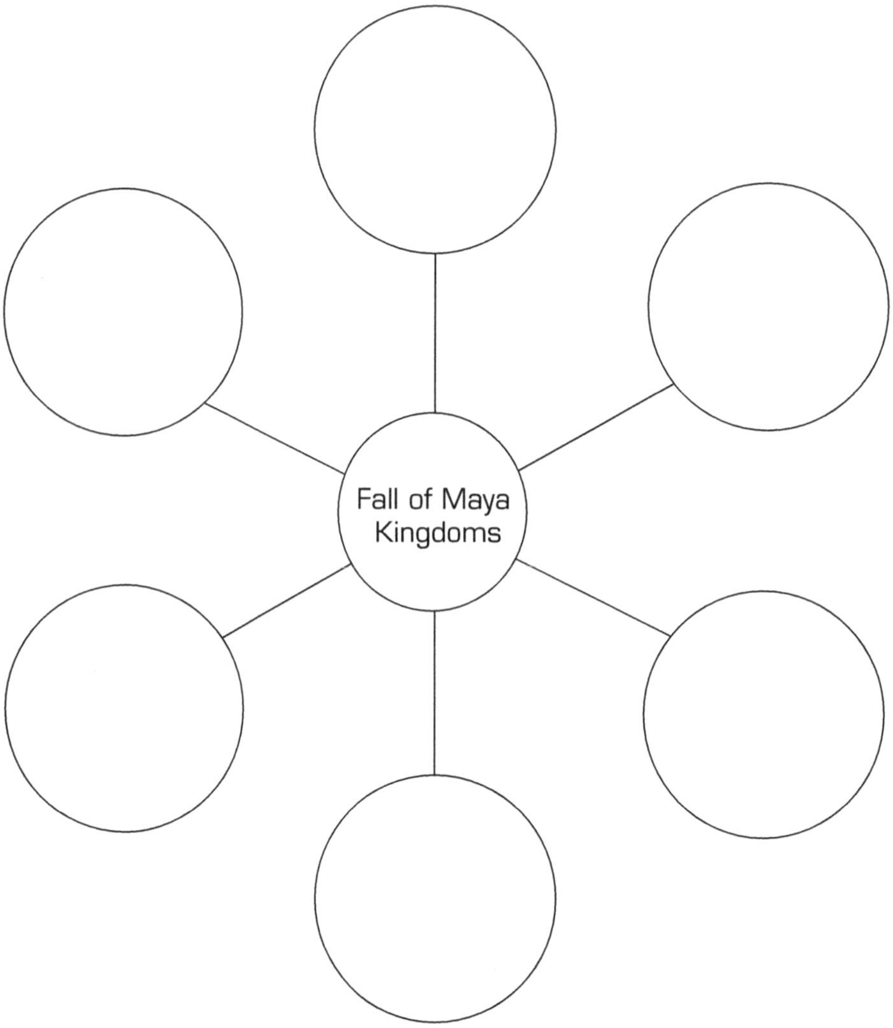

CHAPTER TEST 7

THE ANCIENT AMERICAN WORLD

A. MULTIPLE CHOICE

Circle the letter of the best answer for each question.

1. What was **not** one of Bol's duties as scribe to the king of Aguateca?
   a. writing poems
   b. hunting and fishing
   c. writing treaties
   d. carving and engraving

2. What was the main disadvantage of an alliance between two Maya cities?
   a. They could trade only with each other.
   b. If one was attacked and defeated, the other would be defeated as well.
   c. They were ruled by a single king.
   d. They might run out of chocolate and salt.

3. Which of the following is **not** a theory about why so many Maya kingdoms disappeared between 800 and 900 CE?
   a. disease
   b. drought or loss of farmland
   c. warriors from central Mexico
   d. European invaders

4. Where did the Maya go when they left their cities in the 9th century CE?
   a. to the seacoast of Mesoamerica
   b. to the forests of Mesoamerica
   c. to the forests of North America
   d. to cities in South America

5. How many Maya people live in Mesoamerica today?
   a. 60 million
   b. 6 million
   c. 600,000
   d. 60,000

B. SHORT ANSWER

Write one or two sentences to answer each question.

6. Why would invaders have wanted to destroy the palace at Aquateca?

7. Why would the common people of Aquateca have abandoned their homes gradually?

8. Why does anthropologist Rebecca Storey believe that an infectious disease led to widespread anemia in Copán?

C. ESSAY

The text says, "Finally, it seems, the Maya couldn't stand the uncertainty of life in southern lowland cities." On a separate sheet of paper, write an essay explaining what made life "uncertain" for the Maya in these cities, and how these factors led the Maya to abandon the cities for "a simpler, more peaceful life" in the forests.

CHAPTER 8

COTTON, COPPER, AND CANOES: THE RISE OF THE PUTÚN MAYA AT CHICHÉN ITZÁ

PAGES 64–71

STUDENT STUDY GUIDE pages 25–26

CAST OF CHARACTERS

Quetzalcoatl (ket-zahl-CO-aht) an important Mesoamerican god; means "Feathered Serpent" in Nahuatl

- **Description** Ask students to read the sidebar How to Hug a Shore on page 69. Then have them write a paragraph describing something they know how to do, such as sending a text message, controlling a skateboard, playing a musical instrument, or making a free throw in basketball. Ask students to include in their descriptions information about avoiding a common mistake.

CHAPTER SUMMARY

The Putún Maya were seafaring traders who moved into the Yucatán Peninsula when warfare interrupted trade there. They controlled peninsula seaports and expanded control to the northern lowland city of Chichén Itzá, turning it into a wealthy trading center. They also imposed worship of the Feathered Serpent god.

PERFORMANCE OBJECTIVES

- To explain how the Putún Maya expanded their control of trade in the Yucatán Peninsula
- To describe Chichén Itzá under the Putún Maya, including the Feathered Serpent pyramid
- To give examples of how the Putún Maya trade web worked

BUILDING BACKGROUND

Have students describe a mall they have visited and identify some of the items sold there. Discuss why malls appeal to shoppers and what the alternatives are. Explain that Chichén Itzá in ancient Mesoamerica was a city that acted as a mega-mall—a place where goods from all over the region could be found.

WORKING WITH PRIMARY SOURCES

Have students read aloud the excerpt from Ferdinand Columbus's book about his father on page 64. Challenge students to find out what Columbus's four ships looked like and how they compared in size to the enormous dugout canoe described in the excerpt. Students can draw a storyboard showing Columbus encountering the rowers in the dugout canoe.

GEOGRAPHY CONNECTION

Movement Have students study the map on page 66 and trace the trade routes. Help them recognize why Chichén Itzá was so important to trade on the Yucatán Peninsula.

READING COMPREHENSION QUESTIONS

1. What "discovery" did Columbus's men make off the coast of Honduras that was actually hundreds of years old? (*a dugout canoe made from the trunk of a large tree*)
2. What events helped the Putún Maya get control of seaports on the Yucatán peninsula during the 9th century CE? (*Cities were at war and trade was interrupted; this opened the way for the Putún to step in and take control of the seaports.*)
3. How did the Putún gain control of Chichén Itzá? (*by warfare*)
4. What did the Putún give Chichén Itzá? (*They made it a great center of trade and brought the Feathered Serpent to the city.*)

CRITICAL THINKING QUESTIONS

1. What made Chichén Itzá an attractive target for the Putún to control? (*The city's central location made it an ideal site that connected with cities around the Yucatán Peninsula, so that the Putún could consolidate trade in the area.*)
2. What evidence is there that people of Chichén Itzá hung onto their rain god even after the Putún replaced him with the Feathered Serpent god? (*Offerings to the rain god from thousands of pilgrims have been found in a* cenote, *a natural rock well, in Chichén Itzá.*)
3. What are some of the signs that people in Chichén Itzá accepted the Feathered Serpent as a god? (*They built a magnificent pyramid in such a way that the Feathered Serpent could reveal himself by casting a shadow twice a year.*)

SOCIAL SCIENCES

Economics Distribute the blackline master for Chapter 8 and have students complete the chart and map, using information from the chapter. Discuss students' responses to the writing prompt.

READING AND LANGUAGE ARTS

Reading Nonfiction Ask students to analyze the information presented in maps, illustrations, and photographs in this chapter. Help them develop questions for assessing the value of a graphic aid. Ask: What other type of graphic aid would help present information about this topic?

Using Language Help students identify use of figurative language in the chapter, for example, *thumb-shaped Yucatán Peninsula; necklace of cities around the Yucatán Peninsula;* and *spun their web of trade.* Encourage them to use figurative language in original sentences.

SUPPORTING LEARNING

English Language Learners Discuss the idiomatic phrases used in the chapter: *offer that highland traders couldn't refuse; landed in the Putún's lap; sold on the idea; smooth talking.* Have students use one or more of the idioms in original sentences.

Struggling Readers Have students complete a sequence of events graphic organizer (see the back of this guide) to understand the growth of Chichén Itzá and Putún influence on the Yucatán Peninsula and beyond.

EXTENDING LEARNING

Enrichment Have a group of students research how a Putún Maya dugout canoe was built. Ask students to report on the type of trees and techniques used for the canoes. If possible, have students collect images of the canoes and include them in a captioned exhibit for the classroom museum.

Extension Have students create and perform a skit in which Putún traders interact with people in different places, trading such items as orange bowls, cloaks, and blocks of salt. Students can write parts for a narrator, the traders, canoe paddlers, and porters.

LINKING DISCIPLINES

Art Have students find images of the Feathered Serpent (Kukulcan or Quetzalcoatl) and create a captioned display for the classroom museum. Online sources include the Peabody Museum, Maya Vase Database, and Mesoweb, all listed on the Websites page of the students' book.

THEN and NOW

According to an online guide, the acoustics of the ball court at Chichén Itzá are amazing. Standing at one end of the 168-meter-long court, you can hear someone speaking at the other end. In another part of the court, if you clap your hands the echo will repeat seven times.

THE ANCIENT AMERICAN WORLD

CHAPTER 8 BLM

PUTÚN MAYA TRADE

Directions
Complete the chart with information from the chapter, using the first line as a sample. Then write the place names listed below in their correct locations on the map. On a separate sheet of paper, write a paragraph explaining why Chichén Itzá was a good location for seafaring traders to set up a marketplace.

Item	From/To	Transported By	Traded For
orange bowls	Tabasco/ Chichén Itzá	Slaves inland	Embroidered cloaks

Yucatán Peninsula
Chichén Itzá
Highlands
Pacific Ocean
Isla Cerritos
Tabasco
Caribbean Sea
Cozumel

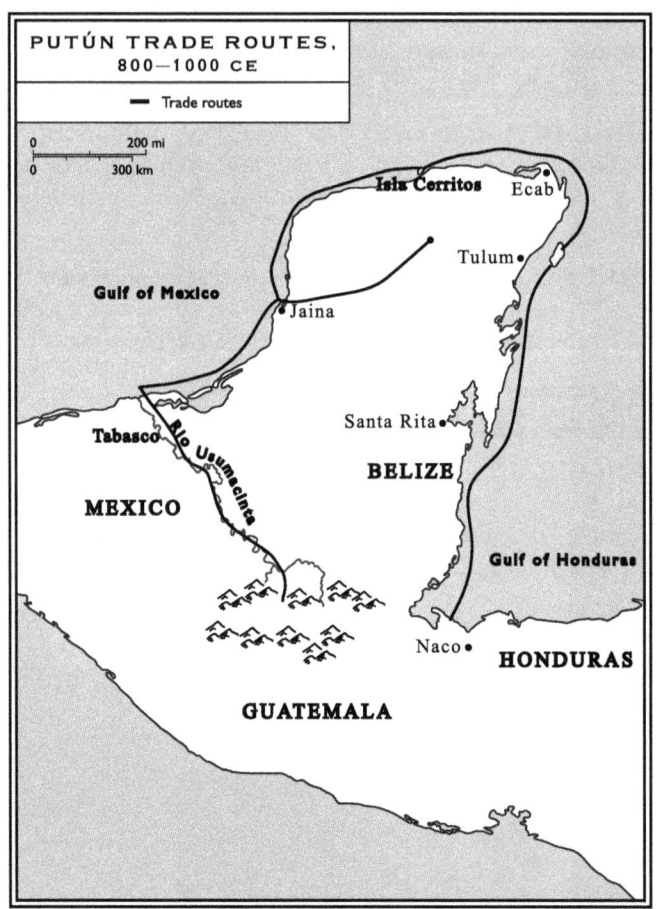

CHAPTER TEST 8

THE ANCIENT AMERICAN WORLD

NAME _____ DATE _____

A. MULTIPLE CHOICE

Circle the letter of the best answer for each question.

1. Which of the following was **not** a characteristic of the Putún Maya?
   a. farmers
   b. watermen
   c. warriors
   d. traders

2. "Circle of trade" means that goods from one place can be traded for something of value
   a. in another place, leading to other trades.
   b. in only one other place.
   c. in a trading center like Chichén Itzá.
   d. on an island.

3. When the Putún were traveling by dugout canoe, they usually
   a. stayed in deep water.
   b. traveled only by night.
   c. used only a few paddlers.
   d. hugged the shore.

4. Where in Chichén Itzá was the Feathered Serpent god found?
   a. only on the pyramid and only at certain times of year
   b. on the pyramid, on columns, and in stairways and temple doorways
   c. only on the ball court walls
   d. only in the *cenote*

5. The Feathered Serpent god was a sign of which of the following in Mesoamerica?
   a. sun and rain
   b. winter and summer
   c. power and command
   d. planting and harvesting

B. SHORT ANSWER

Write one or two sentences to answer each question.

6. Why were the Putún Maya able to take control of coastal cities in the Yucatan Peninsula?

7. How did the Putún Maya gain control of Chichén Itzá?

8. How does the Feathered Serpent god reveal himself twice a year at Chichén Itzá?

C. ESSAY

On a separate sheet of paper, write an essay summarizing how the Putún Maya trade web worked. Include specific details from the chapter.

THE AZTEC EMPIRE
PAGES 72–89

Chapter 9   The Feathered Serpent Rides Again: The City of Tula
Chapter 10   Triple Whammy: Forging the Aztec Empire
Chapter 11   Flowers and Song: The Lives of Aztec Families

UNIT OBJECTIVES

Unit 4 covers the period in history from 900 CE through 1502 CE, encompassing the stories of two groups—the Toltecs, followers of the godlike Topiltzin Quetzalcoatl (TQ), whose city of Tula collapsed around 1150; and the Mexica, whose city Tenochtitlan became the seat of the Aztec Empire under Itzcoatl in the 1400s. In this unit your students will learn
the role of TQ in Toltec belief.

- the difference between historical facts and myths.
- myths about the origins of the Mexica and their city, Tenochtitlan.
- Itzcoatl's role in expanding the Mexica's power in the Valley of Mexico.
- what life was like for ordinary Mexica in the Aztec Empire.

PRIMARY SOURCES

Unit 4 includes excerpts from the following primary sources:

- Fray Bernadino de Sahagún, *Florentine Codex*
- Nahuatl poem
- Fray Diego Durán, *The History of the Indies of New Spain*

Unit 4 also includes pictures of the following artifacts, which can be analyzed as primary sources:

- Painting of Topiltzin Quetzalcoatl
- Clay and mother of pearl sculpture, Tula
- Columns in Tula Grande
- Aztec eagle carving
- Diego Rivera, painting of Tenochtitlan
- Portrait of Huitzilopochtli
- Terracotta statue of an Aztec Eagle Warrior
- Illustration from Codex Mendoza
- Aztec calendar stone

BIG IDEAS IN UNIT 4

Myth, power, and **lifestyle** are the big ideas presented in Unit 4. The unit discusses Toltec and Mexica legends and how they reflect historical reality. It also describes times of great change—the fall of one city, Tula, and the meteoric rise of another, Tenochtitlan, the hub of the Aztec Empire. The unit reveals not only the power of myth but also the power of a ruthless leader, Itzcoatl, who affected the lives and lifestyle of ordinary people in his empire.

Introduce these ideas by eliciting examples of Americans' historical myths and discussing their usefulness. Ask: What do myths provide to people? Why are people upset when historical fact contradicts myth? In these chapters students will learn about the myths and realities of two very different groups, the Toltecs and the Mexica.

GEOGRAPHY CONNECTION

In this time period, the Aztec Empire grew. Have students look at a map showing the extent of the Aztec Empire in relation to the rest of Mesoamerica. A map is available at *http://ecuip.lib.uchicago.edu/diglib/science/cultural_astronomy/cultures_aztec_images-1.html*. Have students use the map scale to estimate the length of the empire from east to west and north to south, then discuss with them the challenges of ruling such a large area.

TIMELINE

700–900 CE	Toltecs build Tula Chico
900 CE	Tula Chico burns
950 CE	Tula Grande is built
1150 CE	Tula Grande is major Mesoamerican city
1200 CE	Tula Grande residents move to Valley of Mexico
1438 CE	Itzcoatl establishes Aztec Triple Alliance
1502 CE	Moctezuma II inaugurated

UNIT PROJECTS

Tula and Tenochtitlan

The unit contains information about these Toltec and Aztec cities. Invite groups of students to choose one of the cities and become experts in its history, art, and cultural significance. The Tula group will include information about the great city of Teotihuacan because Tula echoed its art and architecture.

Toltec Influence in North America

Assign one group of students the role of reporters time-traveling to North America in the 12th century CE to observe Toltec-inspired temple mounds and plazas similar to ones in Tula. Students can include information about where the remains of these mounds can be seen today.

Aztec Boot Camp

Have another group create presentations about Aztec warriors, including information about weapons, armor, transportation, fighting techniques, military societies, and warriors' status.

Women in the Aztec Empire

Have another group of students investigate women's legal rights and economic status in the Aztec Empire and the attributes of an ideal Aztec mother. The group's report to the class can take the form of a panel in which students in the role of Aztec women answer questions in character.

Aztec Diplomacy

Have groups of students use an encyclopedia and other resources from the library/media center to gather additional information about the Triple Alliance of Tenochtitlan, Texcoco, and Tlacopan discussed in Chapter 10. Students should make a timeline of events leading up to the revolt of the three cities against Tepanec and a listing of the leaders involved, and should draw conclusions about why the cities rebelled.

ADDITIONAL ASSESSMENT

For Unit 4, divide the class into groups and have them all undertake the Tula and Tenochtitlan project so you can assess their knowledge of the beliefs, culture, and lifestyle of the Mesoamerican people from 700 CE to the Spanish conquest in

1521. Use the scoring rubric at the back of this guide to assess students' work, and have students rate their own work with the self-assessment rubric. Distribute the library/media center research log so students can evaluate their sources as they conduct their research.

LITERATURE CONNECTION

There are numerous books that students can enjoy that will broaden their knowledge of the Toltec and Aztec civilizations. Suggest some of the following to students:

- Ackroyd, Peter. *Cities of Blood.* New York: DK Publishing, 2004. Nonfiction. ADVANCED. The book takes readers inside the amazing traditions and gory rituals of the Olmec, Maya, and Aztecs of pre-Columbian civilization.
- MacDonald, Fiona. *How Would You Survive as an Aztec?* New York: Franklin Watts, 1997. Nonfiction. AVERAGE. The book attempts to close the gap between an ancient civilization and the reader. General categories of historical anthropology are made specific: "What would you eat and drink?" "What would you wear?"
- McDermott, Gerald. *Musicians of the Sun.* New York: Simon & Schuster, 1997. Fiction. EASY. A retelling of an Aztec myth fragment in which the deity Tezcatlipoca, Lord of the Night, sends Wind to bring the musicians of the Sun to Earth, thus making all things joyful and colorful.
- McManus, Kay. *Land of the Five Suns: Looking at Aztec Myths and Legends.* New York: NTC/Contemporary Publishing, 1997. Fiction. AVERAGE. Stone Turtle uses creation myths and tales of Aztec gods to distract his younger brother. This story is set in the early 1500s, just as Spaniards and Aztecs were encountering one another for the first time.
- Peppas, Lynn. *Life in Ancient Mesoamerica (Peoples of the Ancient World).* New York: Crabtree Publishing, 2004. Nonfiction. EASY. This source tells about life in the Aztec and Maya world.

UNIVERSAL ACCESS

The following strategies are designed to cover a range of learning styles and reading, language, and skill levels. This section includes suggestions for differentiating instruction to meet the diverse needs of your students.

Reading Strategies

- Have students read aloud the sections of Chapter 9 about the mythical history of Tula. They should use the hand motions and expressions of a person who believes the myth.
- Have students use a K-W-L chart to assist them in their reading about the Aztecs. Preview Chapters 10 and 11 and have students fill in the first column of the chart with what they *know* about the subject. Have them write what they *want to know* about the subject in the second column. When they are finished with the chapters, have them complete the third column by writing what they *learned.*
- Instead of having a chronological organization, Chapter 11 deals with several subtopics under the general topic family life. Have students create main idea statements for each subtopic. Then have them point out details or examples that support the main ideas.
- Preview the pictures in the unit so students have an idea of the grandeur and complexity of the Toltec and Aztec civilizations before they begin to read the chapters.

Writing Strategies

- Have students write a paragraph explaining a myth's purpose and then create one explaining a facet of American life.

- Ask students to write a short essay explaining in what way the class structure devised by Itzcoatl resembled a pyramid. Students can provide supporting details from the chapter.
- Have students complete a two-column chart comparing and contrasting the education of boys and girls in the Aztec Empire.
- Have students complete a chart comparing the city of Tula with its predecessor at Teotihuacan (Chapter 4). Students should include details not only about the similar architecture, but also about the kinds of people (artists, craftspeople) who were attracted to the city.

Listening and Speaking Strategies

- Have groups of three students read this unit, one chapter per student. Each group member should take notes on the reading. Group members should come together to tell each other what they learned about TQ, Itzcoatl, and daily life in the Aztec Empire.
- Have students present first-person reports of the following events: TQ saying farewell to his followers on the shore of the Atlantic; the wandering Mexica at last finding the symbol that showed where they should build a city; and Itzcoatl burning books that told the history of the Mexica. In their reports students should convey a sense of mood and place.
- After students read a chapter, have them each write two questions about important ideas explained in the chapter. Call on volunteers to stand and read a question to the class, and then ask other volunteers to answer the question. (This could also be a small-group activity.)

UNIT VOCABULARY LIST

The following words that appear in Unit 4 are important for your students' understanding of the social studies content as well as for development of literacy. Use these words for vocabulary study or to reinforce language arts skills (e.g., synonyms, compound words, prefixes and suffixes, and related words). The words are listed below in the order in which they appear in the chapters.

Chapter 9	Chapter 10	Chapter 11
version	persist	humiliation
neighborhood	vassal	pierce
plumage	upstart	preparatory
penance	lackey	seminary
paradise	fatal	forbidden
wily	snub	rigorous
procession	spoils	summon
	enclosure	essential
	propaganda	inauguration
	multiple	gala
	inconvenient	
	undercover	
	exploit	

CHAPTER 9
THE FEATHERED SERPENT RIDES AGAIN: THE CITY OF TULA

PAGES 72–77

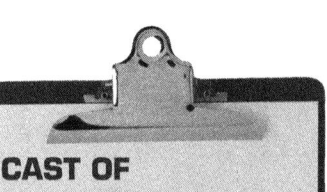

STUDENT STUDY GUIDE
pages 27–28

CAST OF CHARACTERS

Quetzalcoatl (ket-zahl-CO-aht) important Mesoamerican god; also a great Toltec ruler about 750 to 800 CE; means "Feathered Serpent" in Nahuatl

Smoking Mirror "first among all the gods" in Mesoamerica; followers defeated Quetzalcoatl in Tula in about 850

Topiltzin Quetzalcoatl (toe-PEEL-tzeen ket-zahl-CO-aht) "Our Prince" + "Feathered Serpent"

CHAPTER SUMMARY

The king or wizard Topiltzin Quetzalcoatl (TQ) and the city of Tula are wreathed in Toltec myths. The chapter presents mythical information as well as facts and points out historical questions that still persist. One fact is not in doubt—in many respects Tula echoed the past glories of the earlier city of Teotihuacan.

PERFORMANCE OBJECTIVES

▶ To distinguish fact from myth about TQ
▶ To understand the significance of the legends about TQ
▶ To summarize how Tula resembled Teotihuacan

BUILDING BACKGROUND

Ask students to describe Atlantis, Camelot, or some other mythical place. Then discuss what would happen if archaeologists solved the mystery of the existence of those places. Ask: Would people want factual proof of the existence of Atlantis and Camelot, or would they prefer to keep them myths? Explain that in this chapter students will read myths and facts about the Toltec city of Tula.

WORKING WITH PRIMARY SOURCES

Have student volunteers read aloud the section of the chapter about TQ's farewell to Tula, including the Nahuatl poem on page 75. Invite students to respond with journal entries about their own feelings about a place that means a lot to them.

GEOGRAPHY CONNECTION

Place You can find a topographical map of Mexico showing ancient sites such as Tula at *http://homepage.mac.com/i/hpti/1/wimg/Shared/SlideShow/SlideShow.html?lang=en*. Have students study the map and draw conclusions about life at the high altitudes of Tula.

READING COMPREHENSION QUESTIONS

1. What statements about Tula are myths? (*giant ears of maize, choirs of birds, cotton sprouting in colors, everyone was rich*)
2. Why was Tula called "the civilized place"? (*because of its beautiful art*)
3. According to legend, after the followers of Smoking Mirror drove TQ out of Tula, what happened to TQ's followers? (*They buried their wealth, and whole families went with him to the Atlantic coast and observed his departure.*)
4. What are some of the ways that Tula Grande copied Teotihuacan? (*It had two pyramids that were placed at 90-degree angles like those at Teotihuacan, and the shell goggles of the Storm God appeared in the art; Tula homes had patios and porches similar to those at Teotihuacan.*)

CRITICAL THINKING QUESTIONS

1. Looking beyond the legends, what are some facts about Tula Chico? (*The Feathered Serpent was very important to the people of Tula. Skilled craftsmen made beautiful images, and architects built a great temple in the main plaza. Tula covered two square miles and was a fashionable and comfortable place to live. It burned down around 900 CE.*)
2. Why do you think Fray Bernardino de Sahagún wanted to write down the legends about TQ and Tula? (*to understand the people of Mesoamerica better and to leave a record of their old stories*)
3. What evidence is there that TQ was important to the Toltecs? (*Feathered Serpent image found on column; legends about TQ; legends about the faithfulness of his followers*)
4. Distribute copies of the blackline master for Chapter 9. In completing the chart, students will distinguish fact from myth and identify the ways that Tula Grande echoed Teotihuacan.

SOCIAL SCIENCES

Science, Technology, and Society Have students read Sahagún's quote about Toltec craftsmanship on page 74. Then ask a group of students to learn more about Toltec use of gold, jade (greenstone), and feathers and report their findings to the class.

READING AND LANGUAGE ARTS

Reading Nonfiction Have students read the first six and the last two sentences of the chapter. Discuss the effectiveness of starting the chapter with questions and then stating that they do not have definite answers. Ask for students' responses to the foreshadowing of the last two sentences of the chapter.

Using Language Direct students' attention to the material in quotation marks. Have them identify why some legends' content is in quotations and some is not. Find examples of ellipses and discuss what they indicate within a quoted passage. Have students copy parts of a paragraph from the text, using quotes and ellipses correctly.

SUPPORTING LEARNING

English Language Learners Students can meet in small groups to talk about the myths and legends in the chapter. Discuss the possible origins of the widespread myth that 19th-century America had "streets paved with gold."

Struggling Readers Have students complete the main idea map (see the graphic organizer at the back of this guide), writing *TQ* in the center and surrounding it with details about him from the chapter.

EXTENDING LEARNING

Enrichment Have a group of students find out more about the possible Toltec influence in North America, specifically the temple mounds and plazas in the present-day states of Alabama, Georgia, Illinois, and Tennessee. Students can create an illustrated presentation for the class and explain where mounds can still be seen.

Extension Have a group of students select passages from the chapter that describe Tula and the fate of TQ (pages 72–75). They can prepare by defining and learning the correct pronunciation of unfamiliar words and then read with expression.

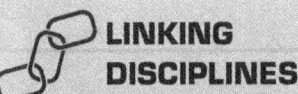

THEN and NOW

Forty miles northwest of Mexico City, near the modern town of Tula de Allende, the ruins of Tula can be seen today. Giant stone warriors loom over the ruins of the temples where the Toltecs placed them.

LINKING DISCIPLINES

Art Invite students to draw a color picture of one of TQ's homes described on page 73. In a label for their drawing, students can explain which house they chose and write a brief statement about why they made that choice.

WRITING

- **Poetry** Have students write a poem in the style of the poem on page 75. They can continue the story of TQ or write about a happier time during his rule of Tula.

THE ANCIENT AMERICAN WORLD

NAME   DATE

UNDERSTANDING TULA

Directions
Read each statement about Tula. Make a check mark in the appropriate column to indicate whether the statement is a fact or a myth. In the last column, write *Yes* or *No* to indicate whether a fact shows that people in Tula copied the art and architecture of Teotihuacan. Finally, write a paragraph on a separate sheet of paper explaining the difference between life in Tula Chico and in Tula Grande.

Statement About Tula	Tula Fact	Tula Myth	Did Tula Copy Teotihuacan?
The craftsmen were highly skilled and famous.			
Maize grew so big that people could hardly carry it.			
A carving of a warrior showed him wearing shell goggles.			
Two pyramids were built at 90-degree angles.			
Houses had porches and patios.			
Red, yellow, and brown cotton plants grew in the fields.			
All the residents were rich.			
Quetzalcoatl invented Toltec crafts.			
Cacao plants were so plentiful that everyone drank cocoa.			

CHAPTER TEST 9

NAME   **DATE**

THE ANCIENT AMERICAN WORLD

A. MULTIPLE CHOICE

Circle the letter of the best answer for each question.

1. Which of the following is **not** part of the legend about Tula under the rule of TQ?
    a. Ears of maize were so big that people could not carry them.
    b. Cotton sprouted in a variety of colors.
    c. Only rich people could drink cocoa.
    d. Choirs of singing birds cheered everyone up.

2. We know details of myths about Tula and TQ because in the 16th century
    a. the Toltecs wrote them in a large book.
    b. TQ dictated them to Bernardino de Sahagún.
    c. a Mesoamerican dictated them to Bernardino de Sahagún.
    d. a Mesoamerican wrote them down in the 16th century.

3. As a god and ruler of Tula, TQ was considered
    a. wise.   c. warlike.
    b. cruel.   d. lazy.

4. In the legend, TQ was driven out of Tula by his own priests, who switched loyalty to Smoking Mirror, the god of
    a. rain.   c. the sun.
    b. peace.   d. war.

5. After Tula collapsed around 1150 CE, the Toltecs went
    a. east to the Atlantic Ocean.   c. west to the Pacific Ocean.
    b. south to the valley of Mexico.   d. north to what became the United States.

B. SHORT ANSWER

Write one or two sentences to answer each question.

6. What values were important to TQ, the legendary ruler of Tula?

7. How did the society who lived in Tula Grande differ from the society who lived in Tula Chico?

8. How did the Toltecs maintain their identity after the collapse of Tula?

C. ESSAY

Write an essay on a separate sheet of paper explaining how this statement applies to the Toltecs: "When storytellers pass a tale down through the centuries, facts can turn into fantasy." Use details from the chapter to support your main idea.

CHAPTER 10

TRIPLE WHAMMY: FORGING THE AZTEC EMPIRE

PAGES 78–83

FOR HOMEWORK

STUDENT STUDY GUIDE
pages 29–30

CAST OF CHARACTERS

Itzcoatl (EETZ-ko-aht) Aztec emperor who forged the Triple Alliance Empire

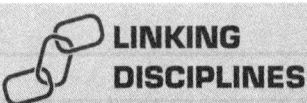

LINKING DISCIPLINES

Art Have students read the explanation of how the Mexica built improved *chinampas* (page 81) and then have them illustrate a scene showing the final results, based on the descriptions in the passage. They can also refer to the photograph on page 80.

CHAPTER SUMMARY

The chapter traces the history of the Mexica (later Aztec), from their origins in Aztlán in northeastern Mexico to Tenochtitlan on Lake Texcoco in the Valley of Mexico. Here the Mexica forged the alliances that brought them power and an empire. The chapter examines how the Aztec emperor, Itzcoatl, increased his power and expanded the empire.

PERFORMANCE OBJECTIVES

- To describe how the Mexica came to build the city of Tenochtitlan
- To identify the reasons for, and success of, the Triple Alliance
- To summarize how Emperor Itzcoatl consolidated his wealth and power and expanded the Aztec Empire

BUILDING BACKGROUND

Ask students to define *underdog* and give examples from movies or TV shows of an underdog who succeeds. Discuss why we applaud the success of people or groups that start out with two strikes against them. Explain that this chapter tells the story of a group of people, the Mexica, who were scorned but whose descendants founded the mighty Aztec Empire.

WORKING WITH PRIMARY SOURCES

Read aloud the sidebar Memories and Manuscripts on page 79. Discuss why Diego Durán's 16th-century interviews with elderly people are still read by historians today. Suggest that students interview their elderly relatives or friends about the past. Establish a list of topics—such as holiday traditions, school memories, clothing styles, favorite music—and guidelines for courteous interviewing. Have students share their interviews with the class.

GEOGRAPHY CONNECTION

Place Make available a map of ancient Mesoamerica showing the extent of the Aztec Empire. Students can identify the Valley of Mexico and the area around Lake Texcoco. Students can use the map scale to estimate the size of the Aztec Empire.

READING COMPREHENSION QUESTIONS

1. According to myth, why did the Mexica settle in the Valley of Mexico near Lake Texcoco? (*That is where they found a cactus with a bird on top as the god Mexi had prophesied.*)
2. Why did the Mexica in Tenochtitlan join with two neighboring cities in the Triple Alliance? (*to combat harsh treatment by the tyrants who ruled the Tepanecs*)
3. Why did Itzcoatl restructure society, create a new religion, and rewrite Mexica history? (*He wanted to make sure that he and his nobles did not have to share their riches with non-royal Mexica, and he wanted total control of the commoners, the lowest class.*)

4. How did Itzcoatl's rewritten Mexica history differ from the original? (*He used the history to explain why only the king and royal families should possess wealth.*)
5. Distribute copies of the blackline master for Chapter 10. The sequence chart will reinforce students' understanding of the events covered in the chapter.

CRITICAL THINKING QUESTIONS

1. In what way were the Mexica underdogs when they first came to the Mexico Valley? (*The Mexica were looked down on as barbarians by royal families in the region who claimed to be descended from the Toltec.*)
2. Explain how the Triple Alliance was the key to the Aztec Empire. (*After defeating the Tepanec tyrants, the three allies divided the spoils and agreed to wage war on other cities, with the city whose warriors led in battle receiving the largest share. The Mexica fought the hardest and soon became the most powerful of the three allies. Their holdings became known as the Aztec Empire.*)

SOCIAL SCIENCES

Civics Invite students to create a graphic representation of the layered society that Itzcoatl created as part of his personal triple whammy. The text refers to the society as a pyramid, but students can create their own graphic, showing the relative positions of emperor, nobles, and commoners. Then have students write in their own words some of the privileges and restrictions that applied to each layer of society.

READING AND LANGUAGE ARTS

Reading Nonfiction Before they read the chapter, have students consider the title and subtitle and define the words *triple* and *whammy*. Then ask students to predict what they think the chapter will cover.

Using Language Point out the similes on page 83: "a message as clear as the water in Lake Texcoco" and "Like a mighty tree." Define *simile* and have students find other examples as they read. Encourage students to write similes of their own to share with the class.

SUPPORTING LEARNING

English Language Learners Define *ally* and *alliance* (nouns) and the related *ally* (verb). Encourage students to use these words in original sentences to show that they understand their meanings. Point out that the suffix *-ance* can be added to verbs like *ally* and *defy* to create nouns—*alliance* and *defiance*.

Struggling Readers Distribute the outline graphic organizer (see the back of this guide) and have students outline the section of the chapter about Itzcoatl's personal triple whammy (pages 81–83).

EXTENDING LEARNING

Enrichment Have students report on the archaeological excavation of the sacred center of the Aztec Empire, the Templo Mayor in Mexico City. Students can find information about the Museo del Templo Mayor at *http://archaeology.asu.edu/tm/index2.php*.

Extension Invite a group of students to create a skit showing Itzcoatl increasing his riches and extending his empire (page 83). Groups can write and perform the following parts: the narrator, Itzcoatl, an Aztec merchant (spy), the king of a prosperous kingdom, and armed warriors.

WRITING

Diary Entry Have students write a diary entry from the point of view of a Texcoco resident who has hidden a Mexica history to prevent it from being burned. In the entry the writer should explain why he or she took the risk of preserving the "real" history.

Aztlán "island in the middle of a lake" in Nahuatl; *Aztlán* led to *Aztec*, a catch-all term referring to many groups who lived in the empire, including the Mexica.

THE ANCIENT AMERICAN WORLD

NAME   **DATE**

CHARTING THE RISE OF THE AZTEC EMPIRE

Directions
Copy each event in the box in the correct space on the timeline. Write the dates on the date line and draw lines to connect each date to each event.

> Triple Alliance defeats Tepanec tyrants.
> Aztec Empire spreads throughout most of Mesoamerica.
> Mexica found Tenochtitlan.
> Tenochtitlan becomes vassal of Tepanec kingdom.
> Spanish conquerors arrive.
> Aztec Empire begins.
> Itzcoatl rewrites history, makes laws favoring king and nobles, and starts a new religion.
> Tenochtitlan, Texcoco, and Tlacopan form Triple Alliance.
> The god Mexi tells people of Aztlán to leave their homeland.

TIMELINE

DATE   **EVENT**

CHAPTER TEST 10

THE ANCIENT AMERICAN WORLD

A. MULTIPLE CHOICE

Circle the letter of the best answer for each question.

1. Which of the following was **not** a mythical prophecy about the Mexica?
   a. They would build a city where they saw a bird on top of a cactus.
   b. They would leave their homeland.
   c. An emperor would come along and rewrite their history.
   d. Their city would rule over others.

2. The Mexica were finally accepted when they began
   a. marrying into royal families of neighboring cities.
   b. conquering their neighbors.
   c. trading with their neighbors.
   d. making human sacrifices to the gods.

3. The Mexica expanded into the *chinampas* region south of Tenochtitlan to
   a. raise food for their large families.
   b. demand tribute from the people who lived there.
   c. drain the lakes.
   d. raise food for the army.

4. Itzcoatl rewrote the history of the Mexica in order to
   a. make himself a hero.
   b. explain why only the king and nobles should have wealth.
   c. discredit neighboring kingdoms.
   d. honor his poor Mexica ancestors who founded Tenochtitlan.

5. The Aztec Empire extended throughout
   a. North and South America.
   b. the Valley of Mexico.
   c. most of Mesoamerica.
   d. South America.

B. SHORT ANSWER

Write one or two sentences to answer each question.

6. What were the origins of the Mexica people?

7. How did the Mexica come to dominate the other members of the Triple Alliance?

8. How did the myth of Hummingbird on the Left promote human sacrifice?

C. ESSAY

Write an essay on a separate sheet of paper explaining the three-step process by which Itzcoatl and his nobles maintained control of their power and wealth.

THE ANCIENT AMERICAN WORLD   CHAPTER 10 TEST   **75**

CHAPTER 11

FLOWERS AND SONG: THE LIVES OF AZTEC FAMILIES

PAGES 84–89

FOR HOMEWORK

STUDENT STUDY GUIDE

pages 31–32

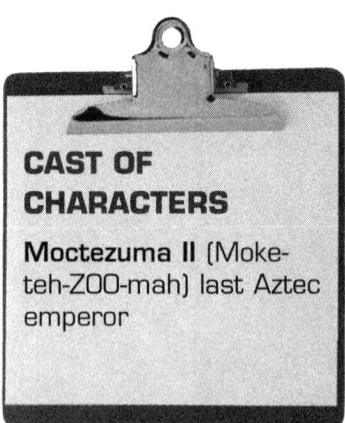

CAST OF CHARACTERS

Moctezuma II (Moke-teh-ZOO-mah) last Aztec emperor

 WRITING

- **Interview** Have students imagine that they can interview one of the family members described in the chapter.
- Students can write the interview in a Q & A format, using complete sentences.

CHAPTER SUMMARY

The chapter examines daily life in the Aztec Empire by observing a hypothetical Mexica family living in Tenochtitlan. The descriptions of the lives of the family members provide insights into education, religion, the army, and the position of women in the Aztec Empire.

PERFORMANCE OBJECTIVES

▶ To describe family life in Tenochtitlan
▶ To explain the training of Aztec priests and priestesses
▶ To summarize the rights of women in the Aztec Empire

BUILDING BACKGROUND

Ask students which would give a better sense of life in the United States today—an interview with a celebrity's family or with an ordinary family? Explain that in this chapter they will meet an imaginary family and find out what life was like for ordinary people living in the Aztec Empire.

WORKING WITH PRIMARY SOURCES

Distribute copies of the blackline master for Chapter 11. Explain that the Fifth Sun legend is a retelling of an Aztec legend. Discuss the differences between a retelling of a primary source and a secondary source. When students have completed the blackline master, discuss their answers. Alternatively, call on volunteers to read the story aloud; have students answer the questions orally.

GEOGRAPHY CONNECTION

Location Have students access maps of Tenochtitlan in books or online. Two useful websites are *www.ancientmexico.com/content/map/tenoch.html* and *http://geoimages.berkeley.edu/geoimages/Alonso_Map/NaviAlonso/alonso.html*. On the first website, have students identify canals. Clicking on the edges of the map on the second website reveals drawings of canoes.

READING COMPREHENSION QUESTIONS

1. How do we know about the lives of ordinary people like those described in this chapter? (*from 16th-century scribes who wrote about their lives*)
2. Why did Mexica families think it was important to dedicate babies at the temple? (*to prevent them from dying young; to assure them a path in life*)
3. How does the family in the chapter earn a living? (*The mother sells cloth in the market; the father is in the army but also has a trade.*)
4. What problems in the empire surfaced with the choice of Moctezuma as emperor? (*The Triple Alliance was dominated by Tenochtitlan whose nobles chose Moctezuma as the next emperor. Nobles of the two other cities resented no longer having a say in who the ruler would be and also resented the amount of tribute they had to pay to Tenochtitlan.*)

CRITICAL THINKING QUESTIONS

1. What does the chapter illustrate about the lives of an ordinary Mexica family at this time? (*Possible answers: love for children; the importance of education and of having a path in life; the importance of the army and of being a warrior; the status of women*)
2. In what ways was the upbringing of the children in the chapter similar to yours? (*Possible answer: parents were attentive and loving, there were rules for eating properly, and education was emphasized*)
3. Why do you think the education of a priest was more demanding than that of a warrior? (*The gods were important in every aspect of Mexica life, and priests were intermediaries between the people and the gods.*)

SOCIAL SCIENCES

Civics Read aloud the sidebar Women's Rights on page 88, and talk about the content. Students can compare this information to the history of women's rights in America by visiting *www.legacy98.org/timeline.html*.

READING AND LANGUAGE ARTS

Reading Nonfiction In the chapter's first paragraph the authors talk about "going back in time" to be with ordinary Mexica. In the second paragraph, the authors use two techniques to help readers do that: the second-person voice and the present tense. Read the second paragraph aloud, stopping to point this out to students. Then have volunteers read the paragraph aloud, using the past tense. Ask: Which reading makes you feel more involved in the lives of this family?

Using Language Have students identify contractions in this chapter—*it's, won't, he's, doesn't*. Make sure students understand what a contraction is and what the apostrophes stand for in these contractions. Have students use contractions in original sentences.

SUPPORTING LEARNING

English Language Learners The chapter gives the Nahuatl words for *mother* and *father*: *nantli* and *tahtli*. Encourage students to share the words for *mother* and *father* in their native languages. Create a display of words for *mother* and *father* using words provided by students and those found on an online translation site such as *http://freetranslation.paralink.com/remote.asp*.

Struggling Readers Distribute the main idea map graphic organizer (see the back of this guide) with *Education* in the center. Students can add details from the chapter about the education of the sons and daughter in the family.

EXTENDING LEARNING

Enrichment A group of students can access thumbnail images of Tenochtitlan art and architecture at *http://instructional1.calstatela.edu/bevans/Art446-12-Aztec*. They can select images to enlarge and then download them to create an illustrated presentation to share with the class.

Extension Have groups write scripts and act out scenes from the lives of the family described in the chapter. Each scene should include a narrator to explain the setting, as well as other characters.

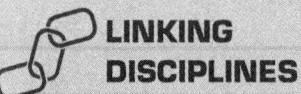

LINKING DISCIPLINES

Science Students can access an online calendar converter that shows the Aztec calendar equivalent of any date entered: solar year, 13-day period, and day. The site can be found at *www.azteccalendar.com/calendar.html*. Combining these details with other Aztec calendar information, students can use the converter to illustrate a report to the class.

THEN and NOW

The Aztecs went to great lengths—and heights—to honor their gods. High on the slopes of Mexico's tallest mountain archaeologists discovered a 15th-century Aztec shrine. They believe the stone shrine located at 14,000 feet was built in honor of the rain god and may have also been part of an Aztec astronomical observatory.

THE LEGEND OF THE FIFTH SUN

Directions
Read the story below, a retelling of an Aztec legend that the family in the chapter might have told. Then answer the questions, using complete sentences.

> When it was time for a Fifth Sun, the creator gods realized there was a problem. The Fifth Sun could only be made from the sacrifice of an existing god.
>
> So the creator gods built a huge fire, but none of *them* was willing to be the sacrifice. Finally they decided that either Nanhuatzin or Tecuciztecatl had to sacrifice himself and become the Fifth Sun. Nanhuatzin was not a popular choice because his body was covered with scabs. So Tecuciztecatl was the first choice to become the Fifth Sun. But each time he ran toward the fire he stopped short. After four tries it was clear: Tecuciztecatl was too afraid to sacrifice himself.
>
> Then Nanhuatzin stepped up and bravely threw himself into the fire. He became the Fifth Sun. Seeing this bravery, Tecuciztecatl got up his courage and jumped into the fire too. He became the moon.
>
> The creator gods then looked in all four directions in the sky but could not see the new sun. Later they discovered that the Fifth Sun would not rise unless he received the hearts and blood of other gods for his food and drink. This angered Lord Morning Star, the fiercest of the 1,600 gods. But Lord Morning Star lost a duel with the Fifth Sun and was sent to the underworld. The other gods then agreed to sacrifice themselves so that the Fifth Sun would rise each day.

1. How does this legend explain the Aztec practice of killing captives and offering their hearts and blood to the Sun God?

   _____

   _____

2. In Aztec legends gods often have human characteristics. What are some of the ways in which the gods in this story act like humans?

   _____

   _____

3. Why would listeners to this story find fire a believable way to make a sun?

   _____

   _____

CHAPTER TEST 11

THE ANCIENT AMERICAN WORLD

NAME _____ DATE _____

A. MULTIPLE CHOICE

Circle the letter of the best answer for each question.

1. Which of the following was **not** one of the rights of Mexica women?
   a. to inherit property
   b. to bring a case before councils of justice
   c. to be a warrior in the emperor's army
   d. to weave with gold thread

2. Many Mexica traveled around Tenochtitlan by
   a. canoe.
   b. horse-drawn wagon.
   c. chariot.
   d. sailboat.

3. In studying for the priesthood, the youngest son studied
   a. sweeping and cleaning.
   b. reading, geography, laws, myths, and astronomy.
   c. farming techniques, singing, and dancing.
   d. fighting and taking captives.

4. Which of the following seemed to be signs that the Triple Alliance was in danger of ending?
   a. the tribute that Texcoco and Tlacopan paid to Tenochtitlan
   b. the eruption of a volcano and the appearance of comets
   c. the inauguration of the new emperor Moctezuma II
   d. an armed attack on Tenochtitlan by its two allies

5. According to the Legend of the Fifth Sun, the only way to make sure the sun will rise is to perform
   a. dances.
   b. plays.
   c. sacrifices.
   d. magic.

B. SHORT ANSWER

Write one or two sentences to answer each question.

6. For what occupations did Aztec children receive training?

7. How did parents in the Aztec Empire treat their children?

8. Why didn't the other members of the Triple Alliance agree with Moctezuma II becoming emperor in 1502 CE?

C. ESSAY

On a separate sheet of paper, write an essay discussing the types of education available to Aztec children. Include details about education presented in the chapter.

UNIT 5: WAR OF THE WORLDS

PAGES 90–105

Chapter 12 War of the Worlds: The Aztec Encounter the Spaniards
Chapter 13 War of the Worlds, Continued: The Inca and the Spaniards in South America

UNIT OBJECTIVES

Unit 5 covers the period from 1493 CE through 1532 CE and examines the impact of the initial contact between Europeans and the Aztec and Inca populations. In this unit your students will learn

- the reaction of Moctezuma and Atahualpa to the invading Spaniards, Hernán Cortés and Francisco Pizarro.
- how Cortés and Pizarro conquered the Aztec and Inca Empires.
- the significance of smallpox to the success of the Spaniards.

PRIMARY SOURCES

Unit 5 includes excerpts from the following primary sources:

- Bernal Díaz, *The True History of the Conquest of New Spain*
- Alva Ixtilxochitl, *XIII relación*
- Illustration from *Florentine Codex*
- Unkown Aztec author, *Unos anales históricos de la nación mexicana*
- Anonymous Aztec scribe, *Poem*
- Guamán Poma, *Letters to a King*
- Pedro de Cieza de León, *The Discovery and Conquest of Peru*
- Juan de Betanzos, *Narrative of the Incas*

Unit 5 also includes pictures of the following artifacts, which can be analyzed as primary sources:

- Map of Tenochtitlan
- Sculpture of double-headed serpent
- Illustration of Inca emperor Huayna Capac
- Portrait of Emperor Atahualpa
- Portrait of Francisco Pizarro
- Illustration of Pizarro ordering assassination of Atahualpa
- Inca-Spanish drinking vessel

BIG IDEAS IN UNIT 5

Conquest and **culture clash** are the two big ideas in Unit 5. There are few more cataclysmic encounters in world history than that between the Spanish conquistadors and the people of the Aztec and Inca Empires. The conquest of the Aztec and Inca Empires was achieved quickly; the culture clashes ignited by the conquistadors are still felt today.

Discuss the phrase *culture clash* with students and ask what images it suggests to them. Ask: Is it possible for cultures to mesh, not clash? What are some examples in their own lives? Point out that they will be reading about a clash of cultures that began in the 16th century and whose repercussions are still felt today.

GEOGRAPHY CONNECTION

Have students study a topographical map of Mexico, either from a world atlas or from a website such as *http://homepage.mac.com/eluna58/PhotoAlbum10.html*. Point out that Cortés had led his army from the shores of the Gulf of Mexico inland to Tenochtitlan. Have students describe the terrain over which the Spaniards and their allies marched, and the difficulties that they would encounter. Then refer students to the map on page 101 so that they can get an idea of the size and topography of the Inca Empire. Have students use the map scale to estimate the length of the empire (about 3,500 miles).

TIMELINE

1493 CE	Huayna Capac becomes Inca emperor
1519 CE	Spaniard Cortés arrives on Mexico's shores
1521 CE	Cortés and Native allies conquer Aztec Triple Alliance
1526 CE	Smallpox invades South America
1532 CE	Francisco Pizarro conquers Inca Empire
1535 CE	Guamán Poma born in Peru
1567 CE	Guamán Poma begins letter to king of Spain

UNIT PROJECTS

On Trial: Cortés, Pizarro, Moctezuma, and Atahualpa

Divide the class into groups of judges, prosecutors, and defenders. The accused: Cortés, Pizarro, Moctezuma, and Atahualpa. Have the prosecutors write statements accusing Cortés and Pizarro of lying and committing war crimes such as the massacre of unarmed civilians, and Moctezuma and Atahualpa of failing to defend their people from the invading Spaniards adequately. The defenders can write statements in defense of each of the accused. Judges will hear the arguments and make a ruling.

Epidemic

Challenge a group of students to become experts in the contagious diseases that ravaged the inhabitants of the Americas with the arrival of Spaniards. For example, scientists blame measles, mumps, influenza, typhus, and smallpox for reducing the population of the Inca Empire from 12 million to 960,000 in the course of a century. On an illustrated timeline, the group can identify landmarks in the history of these diseases.

From the Horses' Mouths

Invite students to present the Spaniards' horses' views of Mesoamerica and South America. "Spokeshorses" can comment on traveling across the ocean, through jungles and mountains, and into battle. Have students answer questions such as: How many and what kind of horses did Cortés and Pizarro bring from Spain? How did people in the Americas react to horses? Did the horses wear armor? How important were horses to the Spaniards' victory over the Aztec and Inca?

The Fates of the Conquistadors

Have small groups research the later life of Pizarro and Cortés. What happened to them after they conquered the Inca and Aztecs? What honors were bestowed on them by Spain? They can also learn more about Hernando de Soto, who is mentioned in Chapter 12 as one of Pizarro's soldiers. What further adventures did he have in the Americas? Have groups give an oral report of their findings to the rest of the class.

ADDITIONAL ASSESSMENT

For Unit 5, divide the class into groups and have them all undertake the On Trial project so you can assess their knowledge of the forces at work in the Aztec and Inca empires at the time of the Spanish conquest. Use the scoring rubric at the back of this guide to assess students' work, and have students rate their own work with the self-assessment rubric.

LITERATURE CONNECTION

There are numerous books that students can enjoy that will broaden their knowledge of the Aztec and Inca civilizations at the time of the Spanish conquest. Suggest some of the following to students:

- Burr, Claudia. *Broken Shields*. Toronto: Groundwood Books, 1997. Nonfiction. AVERAGE. This book relates the Spanish conquest of the Aztecs, using centuries-old words and illustrations. The text is adapted from Friar de Sahagun's 16th-century history of New Spain.
- Duran, Gloria. *Malinche: Princess of Cortez*. Linnet Books, 1993. Fiction. ADVANCED. This story of La Malinche, Cortés's interpreter, sheds a sympathetic light on a young woman generally thought of as a traitor to her people.
- Meltzer, Milton. *Ten Kings and the Worlds They Ruled*. New York: Orchard Books, 2002. Nonfiction. EASY. The life and world of Atahualpa is included in this book about 10 famous rulers from around the world.
- MacDonald, Fiona. *Inca Town*. Philadelphia: Franklin Watts, 1999. Nonfiction. EASY. An aerial view of an Inca town, based on the great city of Cuzco, provides insight into the culture, religion, daily life, and arts and crafts of these ancient people.

UNIVERSAL ACCESS

The following strategies are designed to cover a range of learning styles and reading, language, and skill levels. This section includes suggestions for differentiating instruction to meet the diverse needs of your students.

Reading Strategies

- To facilitate reading these chapters, point out features such as illustrations and information in the side columns that students will encounter as they read.
- Call on students to read sections of the chapters aloud. Encourage students to make their voices expressive and to use hand gestures where appropriate. Fit the reading passage to the abilities of each student.
- Divide the class in half. One half of the class should read the chapters from the point of view of the Spaniards. The other half should read the chapters from the point of view of the Aztecs or Inca. Bring the class together to discuss the conquest from both points of view.

Writing Strategies

- Have students write an essay reacting to this statement: Moctezuma and Atahualpa misjudged the Spaniards because "in the ancient Americas warriors did not claim to come in peace and then attack." Ask students to use details from the chapters in their essay.
- Ask students to create a cause and effect chart to describe the Spaniards' interaction with the Aztec and Inca Empires.
- Have students use the timeline graphic at the back of this guide to organize the events of the conquest of the Aztec and Inca empires. You may want students to make a parallel timeline for the Inca: one for the inner turmoil of the Inca Empire and one for the Inca contact with the Spanish.

Listening and Speaking Strategies

▶ Groups of volunteers can create skits based on information in the text. For example, Moctezuma's indecision about reacting to the Spaniards' arrival; De Soto's approach to Atahualpa at the hot spring; Cortés's recruiting allies among Native people.

▶ Encourage a group of students to prepare and present a "person on the street" reaction to the arrival of the Spaniards in Tenochtitlan.

▶ Divide the class into small groups. When students have completed reading the chapters and taking notes, have them draw parallels between the conquest of the Aztecs and the Inca. Give them categories: purpose of Spaniards, tactics of Spaniards, reaction of Aztecs/Inca, fate of emperor, final outcome. Have groups orally retell the similar details of the two conquests.

UNIT VOCABULARY LIST

The following words that appear in Unit 5 are important for your students' understanding of the social studies content as well as for development of literacy. Use these words for vocabulary study or to reinforce language arts skills (e.g., synonyms, compound words, prefixes and suffixes, and related words). The words are listed below in the order in which they appear in each chapter.

Chapter 12	**Chapter 13**
ravenous	gold-plated
trek	virus
overwhelm	incensed
causeway	scrape
adobe	treacherous
abdomen	ascent
mestizo	reckless
vaccine	petite
	utmost
	consternation
	litter
	blunder
	periodically

THE ANCIENT AMERICAN WORLD

WAR OF THE WORLDS: THE AZTEC ENCOUNTER THE SPANIARDS

PAGES 90–97

FOR HOMEWORK
STUDENT STUDY GUIDE
pages 33–34

conquistador "conqueror" in Spanish

CAST OF CHARACTERS

Cortés, Hernán (err-NAHN cor-TESS) explorer who conquered the Aztec Empire for Spain

Díaz, Bernal del Castillo (bear-NAHL DEE-ahz del cah-STEE-yo) Spanish foot soldier who described conquest of Mexico by Spain

Moctezuma II (Moke-teh-ZOO-mah) the second Aztec emperor; captured by the Spaniards

Malintzin (mahl-EEN-tzeen) Nahua native interpreter for Cortés during the conquest of Mexico by Spain

CHAPTER SUMMARY

The chapter focuses on the events between 1519 CE and 1521 CE, when the Spanish conquistadors arrived in Mesoamerica and through luck, disease, native allies, and deception conquered the Aztec Empire.

PERFORMANCE OBJECTIVES

▶ To interpret the reaction of Moctezuma to the arrival of Cortés
▶ To summarize how the Spaniards defeated Moctezuma and conquered the Aztec Empire
▶ To describe the role of Malintzin in the Spaniards' success
▶ To point out and describe on a map Cortés's route from Spain to Tenochtitlan

BUILDING BACKGROUND

Discuss with students the defining historical events in their lifetimes. Explain that in this chapter, they will read about the arrival of Spaniards in Tenochtitlan in November 1519—a defining event that changed the Mesoamerican world forever.

WORKING WITH PRIMARY SOURCES

The World in Ancient Times Primary Sources and Reference Volume features a poem written by an Aztec soldier, Temiltzin of Tlateloclo. Following that are two accounts written by Bernal Díaz, a Spanish soldier with Cortés. Call on volunteers to give expressive readings of these works. After the readings, have students discuss what they think each writing is about. Have them compare and contrast the accounts (one is a poem, the others are eyewitness descriptions), and talk about how each reflects the writer's point of view.

GEOGRAPHY CONNECTION

Location/Movement   Provide students with a world or historical atlas so they can calculate the distance from Spain to Mesoamerica, and from the Gulf Coast, where Cortés landed, to Tenochtitlan. Students can also refer to a map of the Aztec Empire at its greatest extent to see the prize claimed by Cortés.

READING COMPREHENSION QUESTIONS

1. Why did Cortés and his army and allies march to Tenochtitlan? (*to seize the Aztec Empire and its ruler; to convert native people to Christianity; to acquire gold*)
2. Why did some native people whom Cortés met along the way become his allies? (*They were sick of paying tribute to Moctezuma and were willing to fight against him.*)
3. What made Moctezuma indecisive about welcoming Cortés? (*He wasn't sure if Cortés was an enemy or a priest of TQ, the god who had promised to return in the Aztec year One Reed, the same year Cortés appeared.*)
4. Distribute copies of the blackline master for Chapter 12 and have students summarize the factors that led to the fall of the Aztec Empire.

CRITICAL THINKING QUESTIONS

1. About 64 years elapsed between the events Bernal Díaz experienced and publication of his book. What effect would such a long wait have had on the accuracy of his story? (*Possible answer: Waiting such a long time might have made Díaz's memory of events unreliable.*)
2. Was Cortés's conquest of Moctezuma and Tenochtitlan inevitable? Why? (*Students will probably say yes, given the Spaniards' advantages in weapons, horses, and allies. Cortés also benefited from Moctezuma's indecision and the inadvertent spread of disease among the Aztec population.*)
3. The authors call Malintzin "fearless," and Diaz called her "the great beginning of our conquests." How do you think she would have described herself? (*Students' answers should acknowledge the picture the authors present, that of a slave trying to survive.*)
4. Cortés came to see the desire for gold as a "disease." How did the Spaniards' greed affect the fate of Tenochtitlan and the Aztec Empire? (*With or without gold, the city and empire were doomed; the Spaniards came to Mexico to make a world in their own image, not to preserve what was there.*)

SOCIAL SCIENCES

Science, Technology, and Society Have students investigate and report on the reaction of peopleto Popocatepetl, Mexico's active volcano, today and at the time of the Spanish conquest. Popocatepetl impressed Cortés, and its eruption was seen as a bad omen by his victims. For historical information and responses to recent volcanic activity, students can access *http://news.nationalgeographic.com/news/2000/12/1221_volcano.html*.

READING AND LANGUAGE ARTS

Reading Nonfiction Have students assess the value of firsthand quotes with specific reference to quotes used in this chapter. Ask: How do the quotes help you visualize events? What bias might be present in firsthand accounts? Why should historians search out quotes from more than one source?

Using Language Help students identify the adjectives and verbs that describe Cortés's advance on Tenochtitlan in the description beginning "Hungry for riches" on page 91. Students might identify the adjectives *hungry, steaming, snow-covered, bitter, ravenous,* and *cold* and the verbs *shivered* and *hunched*. Have students continue through the next paragraph and then use some of these words in original descriptive sentences.

SUPPORTING LEARNING

Struggling Readers To help students understand Malintzin's role as Cortés's slave and translator, have students create a main idea map graphic organizer (see the back of this guide) with *Malintzin* in the center and details from the chapter in surrounding circles.

EXTENDED LEARNING

Enrichment Mexico City was built on the ruins of Tenochtitlan. Have students report on archaeological excavations in Mexico City.

Extension Have a group of students write and perform monologues in which Malintzin tells about her life at various stages, including her role in Moctezuma's downfall. A narrator can introduce Malintzin and explain how people view her today.

WRITING

Persuasion Have students write a letter from the point of view of a compassionate Spaniard criticizing Cortés's treatment of Moctezuma and attempting to persuade him to preserve the city of Tenochtitlan.

LINKING DISCIPLINES

Health Have students investigate and report on the risks of smallpox today. They can find information at *www.bt.cdc.gov/agent/smallpox/disease/faq.asp*.

THEN and NOW

The smallpox epidemic that the Spaniards brought spread so fast that one scientist estimates that the population of the Valley of Mexico fell from 1.6 million in 1519 to 900,000 in 1521 due to smallpox alone.

CORTÉS CONQUERS THE AZTECS

Directions
In the circles, write details about how each of the factors contributed to the fall of the Aztec Empire at the hands of Cortés and the conquistadors.

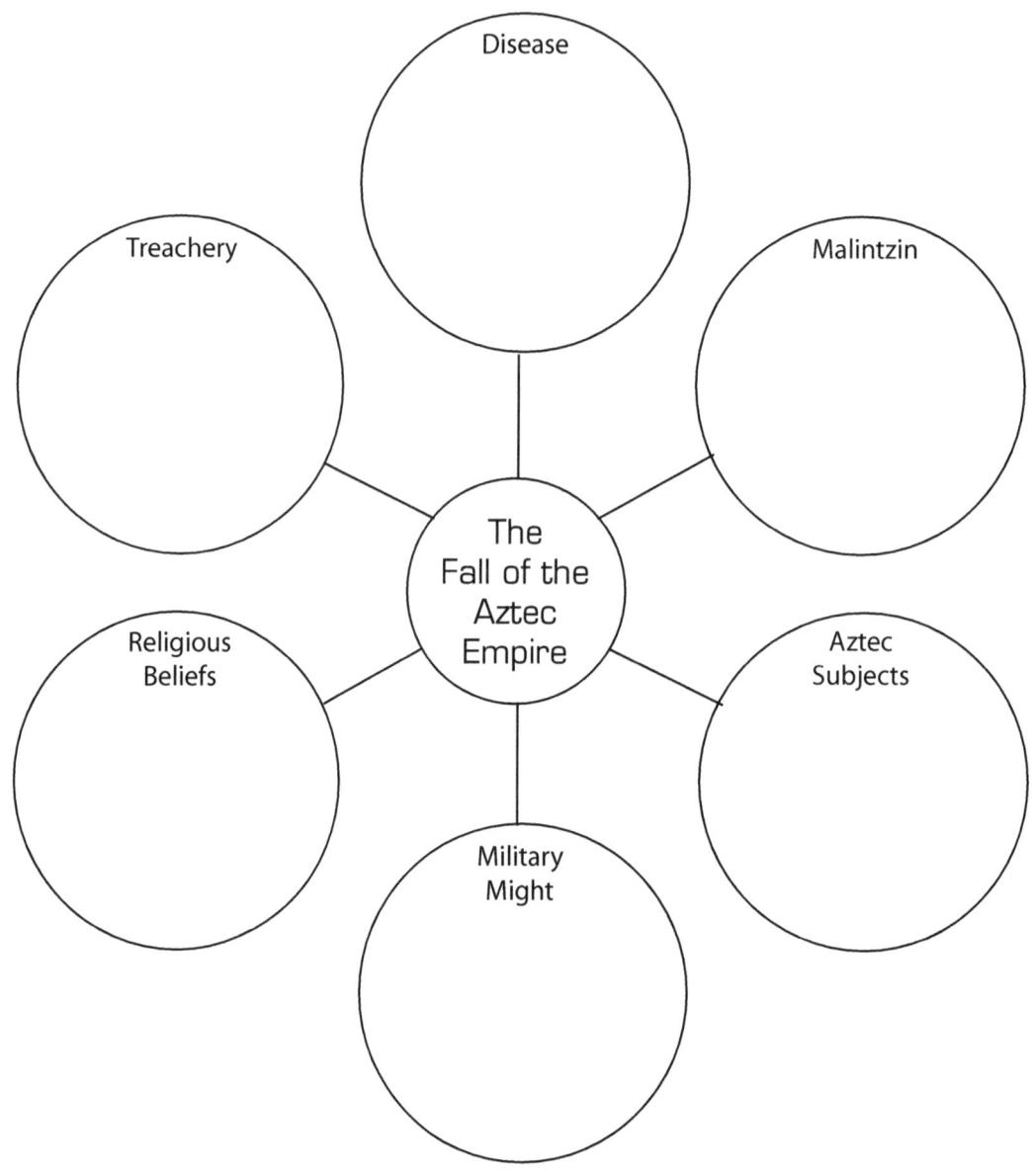

CHAPTER TEST 12

THE ANCIENT AMERICAN WORLD

NAME _____ DATE _____

A. MULTIPLE CHOICE

Circle the letter of the best answer for each question.

1. Which of the following was **not** a hardship that Cortés and his men encountered on their march to Tenochtitlan?
   a. hurricanes
   b. snowy mountains
   c. volcanoes
   d. steaming jungles

2. Why did Moctezuma have trouble making up his mind about Cortés?
   a. He had heard both positive and negative things about Spain.
   b. He thought Cortés might be a returning priest of the Feathered Serpent.
   c. He thought Cortés might have come to pay tribute to him.
   d. He hoped the invaders would go back where they came from.

3. The wonders of Tenochtitlan did not distract the invaders from their true purpose of
   a. relaxing in the marketplace.
   b. stealing the wealth of the Aztecs.
   c. learning to speak the Aztec language.
   d. buying food.

4. Why did Moctezuma agree to give all his gold to the Spaniards?
   a. Cortés asked politely.
   b. Moctezuma planned to steal it back as soon as he was free.
   c. Cortés wanted it for the king of Spain, not himself.
   d. Moctezuma was afraid for his life.

5. After Moctezuma was killed, the Aztecs fought back, chasing the Spaniards into the countryside. The Spaniards finally got control of Tenochtitlan by
   a. negotiating a peace treaty.
   b. burning the city and then starving the residents.
   c. destroying the *chinampas*.
   d. converting all the Aztecs to Christianity.

B. SHORT ANSWER

Write one or two sentences to answer each question.

6. Why were the Spaniards overwhelmed by the city of Tenochtitlan?

   _____

   _____

7. What conflicting stories are told about the death of Moctezuma?

   _____

   _____

8. What were the key elements of the Spanish victory over the Aztecs?

   _____

   _____

C. ESSAY

On a separate sheet of paper, write an essay explaining this statement: "Malintzin was the key to the bloodless capture of Moctezuma."

CHAPTER 13

WAR OF THE WORLDS, CONTINUED: THE INCA AND THE SPANIARDS IN SOUTH AMERICA

PAGES 98–105

FOR HOMEWORK
STUDENT STUDY GUIDE
pages 35–36

CAST OF CHARACTERS

Huayna Capac (WHY-nah KAH-pahk) powerful late Inca emperor; his name means "excellent youth" in Quechua

Atahualpa (ah-tah-WHAL-pa) last Inca emperor; his name means "wild turkey cock" in Quechua

Huascar Inca successor to Emperor Huayna Capac, his father; half-brother of Atahualpa; his name means "gentle hummingbird" in Quechua

Pizarro, Francisco (fran-CEASE-co pee-SAHR-ro) conquistador who took over Inca Empire for Spain

Cieza de Léon, Pedro de (PEH-dro deh see-EH-sah deh leh-OWN) Spanish chronicler of the Inca world

Guamán Poma (gwa-MAHN PO-mah) native South American who wrote about the lost Inca world

CHAPTER SUMMARY

Smallpox and internal disputes in the imperial family threatened the Inca Empire even before Francisco Pizarro arrived. Taking advantage of the chaotic situation, Pizarro managed, through deception, to gain the land and wealth of the Inca Empire.

PERFORMANCE OBJECTIVES

▶ To understand the expanse and wealth of the Inca Empire
▶ To assess how disease and internal Inca disputes led to Pizarro's victory over Atahualpa
▶ To summarize the actions taken by Pizarro, De Soto, and Atahualpa that led to Spain's conquest of the Inca Empire

BUILDING BACKGROUND

Ask students how many of them have had a contagious disease, such as a cold, or the flu, chickenpox, mumps, or measles. Then ask if any of them have been given shots to prevent their getting diseases. Discuss how infectious diseases spread from one person to another. Explain that in this chapter they will find out how smallpox, arriving in the Inca Empire before the Spaniards, contributed to the end of an empire.

WORKING WITH PRIMARY SOURCES

Invite volunteers to read aloud the Inca messengers' descriptions of the Spaniards on pages 100 and 101. Students should read with expression and try to convey the amazement and awe of the residents of Cajamarca observing the Spaniards. Have them imagine and talk about the impact that seeing Europeans for the first time would have had on the Inca witnesses. Discuss how their appearance was deceiving to the Inca, and what happened as a result.

GEOGRAPHY CONNECTION

Movement   Students can find a topographic map of the Inca Empire showing the invasion route of Pizarro at *www.lib.utexas.edu/maps/historical/shepherd/conquest_peru_1531_3.jpg*. Have students hypothesize why Pizarro took almost two years (January 1531–November 1532) to make his final approach to Cajamarca and the capture of Atahualpa. (*They were moving through sometimes hostile territory, had to build a base for their operations, and were hampered by supply problems and the terrain.*)

READING COMPREHENSION QUESTIONS

1. What mountain range dominated the Inca Empire? (*the Andes*)
2. How did the Spaniard Francisco Pizarro approach Peru? (*by boat from Panama*)
3. Why would a Spaniard answer an Inca who asked, "What do you eat?" by saying "Silver and gold"? (*to trick the person into giving him silver and gold*)

CHAPTER 13

4. What advantage over the Inca did horses give the Spaniards? (*Horses could carry riders, move faster than people, and tire less quickly. A soldier on a horse towered over a soldier standing on the ground. The Inca had no animals they could ride.*)

CRITICAL THINKING QUESTIONS

1. Why is "War of the Worlds, Continued" a good title for this chapter? (*The events in this chapter continue to describe the spread of disease and the violent quest for gold and conquest begun in 1519.*)
2. Was Pizarro's victory over Atahualpa at Cajamarca inevitable? Why? (*Students may say no, given the Inca's superior numbers. But Pizarro, like Cortés, benefited from the spread of deadly disease among the native population and from Atahualpa's ignorance of the deceptive ways of the Spaniards. Eventually the Spaniards would have prevailed.*)
3. Explain the statement, "the Inca Empire was a disaster" before the Spaniards attacked. (*Civil war between Atahualpa and his half brother after the death of their father left the empire unstable and open to attack.*)
4. Distribute copies of the blackline master for Chapter 13. Completing the cause and effect chart will help students understand the events that led to the fall of the Inca Empire.

SOCIAL SCIENCES

Economics Have students investigate the value in today's dollars of the 13,400 pounds of gold and 26,000 pounds of silver collected by Pizarro from Atahualpa.

READING AND LANGUAGE ARTS

Reading Nonfiction Have students read aloud the first five paragraphs of the chapter and point out the foreshadowing in paragraph four. Ask students to identify the two forces that would change the Inca world forever (*the light-skinned bearded men and smallpox*). Discuss the effectiveness of beginning a chapter about the end of the Inca Empire with a description of its strengths.

Using Language Direct students to look at the first paragraph on page 102. Ask them to identify the personal pronouns in the paragraph and explain to whom each of them refers. Students can then identify the possessive pronouns in the second paragraph.

SUPPORTING LEARNING

Struggling Readers To better understand events in the chapter, have students create a simple family tree showing the Inca rulers mentioned in the chapter, their relationship to each other, and their fates.

EXTENDING LEARNING

Enrichment Have a group of students prepare a report on the fate of Francisco Pizarro after the conquest. They should answer questions such as, What were his rewards? What enemies did he make among other conquistadors? Students can find information about his assassination online at *www.archaeology.org/online/features/peru/pizarro.html*.

Extension Have students create a skit of Atahualpa bargaining with the Spaniards for his freedom. Students can mark off an area 17 feet by 22 feet (the dimensions of his cell) and act out the Spaniards' response to the offer and ultimate betrayal of the bargain.

THE ANCIENT AMERICAN WORLD

WRITING

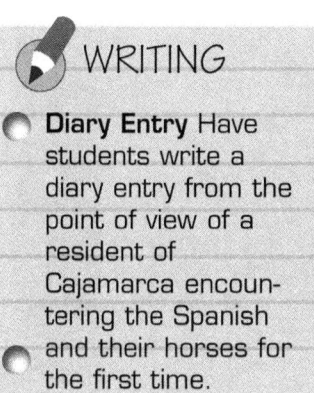

Diary Entry Have students write a diary entry from the point of view of a resident of Cajamarca encountering the Spanish and their horses for the first time.

LINKING DISCIPLINES

Math Students can investigate how to calculate the volume of Atahualpa's cell, assuming his reach extended 7 feet high, the other dimensions being 22 feet by 17 feet. They can present their findings to the class.

THEN and NOW

In 1551 Francisco Pizarro, by then governor of Peru, was assassinated in Lima by rivals. Pizarro's head was buried separately from his body, which was not officially identified until 1977.

CHARTING THE CONQUEST OF THE INCA EMPIRE

Directions
Complete the chart by writing in each missing cause and effect.

Cause	Effect
1. Smallpox, brought by invading Spaniards who are immune to it, spreads through the Americas.	The Inca emperor Huayna Capac dies of smallpox.
2. Huascar Inca succeeds his father, Huayna Capac.	
3.	Atahualpa escapes from and captures Huascar, then murders his family.
4.	Francisco Pizarro and a few soldiers enter the city of Cajamarca, knowing Atahualpa is nearby.
5. DeSoto finds Atahualpa at a hot springs and lies to him.	
6. Atahualpa enters Cajamarca with 5,000 unarmed men.	
7.	Atahualpa learns to speak and read Spanish and to play chess. He sends secret orders to kill Huascar.
8. Atahualpa knows the Spaniards want gold and silver; he wants freedom.	
9.	The Inca Empire's lands and wealth belong to Spain.

CHAPTER TEST 13

THE ANCIENT AMERICAN WORLD

NAME _____ DATE _____

A. MULTIPLE CHOICE

Circle the letter of the best answer for each question.

1. How far did the Inca Empire stretch from north to south?
   a. 350,000 miles
   b. 35,000 miles
   c. 3,500 miles
   d. 350 miles

2. Which of the following events was **not** a cause of the unrest in the Inca Empire in 1532?
   a. the death of Emperor Huayna Capac
   b. the spread of smallpox in the northern part of the empire
   c. the fighting between Huayna Capac's two sons over who would be emperor
   d. a celebration of Inti, the god of the sun

3. Pizarro took his small army and went to Cajamarca to face Atahualpa because he knew that
   a. Atahualpa kept lots of gold and silver there.
   b. the Inca Empire was in chaos.
   c. his men would benefit from a long march in the mountains.
   d. DeSoto would enjoy the hot springs.

4. Atahualpa went with unarmed men to meet Pizarro because
   a. according to the rules of war that he knew, there would not be a battle.
   b. he thought he would be fighting a duel with Pizarro.
   c. the priest did not look threatening.
   d. he thought he would be talking to DeSoto.

5. Atahualpa offered gold and silver to Pizarro in order to
   a. gain his freedom.
   b. send the Spaniards back to Mexico.
   c. destroy his brother.
   d. save himself from death.

B. SHORT ANSWER

Write one or two sentences to answer each question.

6. Why was the Inca Empire a "disaster" by 1532?

   _____

   _____

7. Why couldn't Huascar Inca take over the empire after Atahualpa was killed by the Spaniards?

   _____

   _____

8. What role did Manco Capac play in the end of the Inca Empire?

   _____

   _____

C. ESSAY

Write an essay on a separate sheet of paper agreeing or disagreeing with this statement: Pizarro had what Cortés called the "disease of the heart that can only be cured by gold." Use details from the chapter to support your point of view.

THE ANDEAN WORLD
PAGES 106–126

Chapter 14 Roller-Coaster Roads: Up and Down the Andean World
Chapter 15 A Tale of Two Cities: The Oldest Towns in the Americas
Chapter 16 The Thunderous Temple: Andean People Connect

UNIT OBJECTIVES

Unit 6 covers the period from 5000 BCE through 400 BCE. From agriculture to trade to religion, the Andean world gave rise to fascinating cultures. In this unit your students will learn how ancient Andean people

- ▶ shared agricultural resources.
- ▶ built mounds and trading centers.
- ▶ engineered religious experiences that spread powerful symbols.

PRIMARY SOURCES

Unit 6 includes pictures of the following artifacts and excerpts from the following primary sources:

- ▶ Pedro Cieza de León, *Chronicle of Peru*
- ▶ Inca llama sculpture
- ▶ Mounds of Aspero and Caral
- ▶ Reed bags, Caral, Peru
- ▶ Bone flutes, Caral, Peru
- ▶ Sculptures from temple at Chavín de Huántar, Peru
- ▶ Lanzón sculpture, Chavín de Huántar, Peru
- ▶ Textile, Chavín de Huántar, Peru
- ▶ Gold plaque, Chavín de Huántar, Peru

BIG IDEAS IN UNIT 6

Agriculture, religion, and **connection** are the big ideas in Unit 6. From the vertical organization of agricultural distribution in the Andes to the religious and trading centers of Aspero and Caral, resources were shared by ancient Andean people. Shared religious experiences and symbols characteristic of Chavín soon branched out from Chavín to forge strong connections among people elsewhere.

Ask students to think about where people can share resources today. Besides visiting soup kitchens and food pantries, how do needy people get food? Ask students if they have any experience with food co-ops, places where people contribute their time in exchange for lower food prices. Explain that in this unit they will read about people who, thousands of years ago, developed sophisticated ways to connect people with the food they needed.

GEOGRAPHY CONNECTION

Supplement the maps in the text by providing students with more detailed maps of the Andes and the coastal regions of Peru. An interesting topographic map of Peru that includes the route that Pizarro took in his conquest of the Incas is available online at *www.lib.utexas.edu/maps/historical/shepherd/conquest_peru_1531_3.jpg*. This will help students understand more fully the idea of "up and down" as it relates to the Andean civilizations.

TIMELINE

5000 BCE	Coastal Peruvians grow cotton, weave cloth
3000 BCE	Villages established at Aspero and Caral
2857 BCE	First high mound built at Aspero
2750 BCE	Pirámide Mayor built at Caral
2627 BCE	First sunken plazas built at Caral
2558 BCE	Second high mound built at Aspero
2000 BCE	Pottery making begins in Peru
1900 BCE	Highland Peruvians hammer sheets of gold
1840 BCE	Coastal Peruvians build first U-shaped temple
1800 BCE	Coastal people move inland
600 BCE	Chavín de Huántar first settled
400 BCE	Chavín de Huántar becomes important religious and trade center

UNIT PROJECTS

Potato Panel

Have a group of students find out more about potato cultivation in the Andes. A good source of information about potatoes in Andean life, past and present, is *http://news.nationalgeographic.com/news/2002/06/0610_020610_potato.html*.

Engineering Wonders

A group of students can prepare an illustrated presentation of the engineering feats that archaeologists have uncovered at Aspero, Caral, and Chavín. These include the mounds at Aspero and Caral and the sewer and air-flow systems at Chavín. The presentation should explain the connection between engineering and the religious experience at Chavín.

Textile Wonders

Invite students to create an in-depth report on Andean textiles from early forms of weaving at the Guitarrero Cave (page 125) to the tie-dyed bird designs of the Chavín era (page 124). Students can bring their report into the present by talking about the textiles made in the Andes today.

Animals of the Andes

Have a group of students investigate and prepare an illustrated report on the llama, vicuña, and alpaca. The report should include pictures of the animals and a discussion of their uses, past and present.

ADDITIONAL ASSESSMENT

For Unit 6, divide the class into groups and have them all undertake the Engineering Wonders project so you can assess their knowledge of the technological sophistication of the Andean civilizations. Use the scoring rubric at the back of this guide to assess students' work, and have students rate their own work with the self-assessment rubric.

LITERATURE CONNECTION

There are various translations of *Chronicle of Peru* by Pedro de Cieza de León available, and students can read them with a partner or parent to learn more about the living conditions and lifestyles of ancient Andean peoples. Excerpts from the work are also available online. Many of the books about pre-Inca civilizations are intended for older audiences, but partners can gain important insight from them. Suggest some of the following to students:

- Burger, Richard. *Chavín and the Origins of the Andean Civilization*. New York: Thames & Hudson, 1995. Nonfiction. ADVANCED. This book gives an overview of the Chavín culture and what scholars can explain about its origin, growth, and fall.
- Cobb, Vicki. *This Place Is High: The Andes Mountains of South America*. New York: Walker Books, 1993. Nonfiction. EASY. The book, set in the High Andes of Bolivia and Peru, describes life two and a half miles above sea level, and the ways the native peoples, plants, and animals have adapted to it.
- Davies, Nigel. *The Ancient Kingdoms of Peru*. New York: Penguin, 1998. Nonfiction. ADVANCED. This informative book gives a good overview of pre-Columbian Peru.
- Kirkpatrick, Sidney. *Lords of Sipan: A True Story of Pre-Inca Tombs, Archaeology, and Crime*. New York: William Morrow, 1992. Nonfiction. ADVANCED. The book recounts how Peruvian archaeologist Walter Alva out-maneuvered grave robbers, smugglers, and government interference to excavate one of the richest deposits of pre-Columbian artifacts in South America.
- Martell, Hazel. *Civilizations of Peru: Before 1535*. Austin, TX: Raintree Steck-Vaughn, 1997. Nonfiction. AVERAGE. An examination of several of the more important ancient civilizations of Peru, including the Inca, Chavín, Paracas, Nazca, Moche, Tiahuanaco, Huari, and Chimu.

UNIVERSAL ACCESS

The following strategies are designed to cover a range of learning styles and reading, language, and skill levels. This section includes suggestions for differentiating instruction to meet the diverse needs of your students.

Reading Strategies

- There are unfamiliar words in this unit that are not defined. Suggest that students add them to a class word file. Students can create word cards for each chapter. On each card, students should write the word, define it, and use it in a sentence. They may wish to illustrate the word as well. Have them keep individual word lists in their history journals so they can refer back to the words when doing homework or doing a project in a small group.
- Have partners read sections of the chapters to each other and then ask each other questions about the content: What is the main idea of this passage? What details or examples support the main idea?
- Have groups of three students read this unit, one chapter per student. Each group member should take notes on the reading. Members should come together to tell each other what they learned about the time and place covered by each chapter.
- Before students read Chapter 14, read aloud the excerpts from Pedro de Cieza de León's work. Have students summarize his description of the people and the land. Then have students read the chapter to complete their understanding of the topic.

Writing Strategies

- Have students work in small groups to write proposals for doing archaeological research at one of the places mentioned in the unit. Explain that in this part of the proposal they don't have to be concerned about the budget for the project. Instead they should describe the place they want to study and explain why they want to learn more about it.
- There are strong visual images in each chapter: Cieza de Léon and his overburdened horse moving along a steep mountain road in the Andes; Ruth Shady at the mounds of Caral; pilgrims nervously listening to the temple's

roar at Chavín. Have students choose one image from each chapter and write how it affects them.
- Have students use the main idea map graphic organizer at the back of this guide to organize information in this unit. Have them write *Andean World* in the central circle, and then complete the diagram with details about the geography and the people's response to it, *ayllus,* important cities, and religion.

Listening and Speaking Strategies

- Divide half the class into small groups. Have two groups create monologues—one for a pilgrim at Chavín and one for an engineer who developed the air duct and roaring-water systems there. Each can give a perspective on Chavín. Groups should present their monologues to the other groups, which can prepare questions after the monologues.
- Have the rest of the class form small groups to hold a press conference. The subject is the foods that ancient people ate in the high Andes and the Supe Valley. Students should be prepared to answer questions from the rest of the class and explain the *ayllu* system, which led to an exchange of foods among regions.
- Chapter 15 presents this important question: Can the ancient sites of Aspero and Caral be called cities? Elicit from students the definition of a city, and allow them to express their opinions on the question.

UNIT VOCABULARY LIST

The following words that appear in Unit 6 are important for your students' understanding of the social studies content as well as for development of literacy. Use these words for vocabulary study or to reinforce language arts skills (e.g., synonyms, compound words, prefixes and suffixes, and related words). The words are listed below in the order in which they appear in the chapters.

Chapter 14	**Chapter 15**	**Chapter 16**
ingot	ceremonial	mucus
whittle	colossal	oracle
hammock	breathtaking	subside
desolate	sunken	ordeal
hollow	amphitheater	supernatural
ravine	rainforest	cult
lugging	potluck	batik
quinoa	corrosive	tie-dyed
furrow		solder
		renaissance

CHAPTER 14

ROLLER-COASTER ROADS: UP AND DOWN THE ANDEAN WORLD

PAGES 106–112

FOR HOMEWORK
STUDENT STUDY GUIDE
pages 37–38

condor Andean vulture

CAST OF CHARACTERS

Cieza de Léon, Pedro de (PEH-dro deh see-EH-sah deh leh-OWN) Spanish chronicler of the Inca world

- **Diary Entry** Ask students to write a diary entry describing a journey (a vacation or a trip to the store) using non-judgmental words and conveying a sense of place and weather, as Cieza de Léon does in his writings.

CHAPTER SUMMARY

This chapter presents aspects of the ancient Andean world through the eyes of an intrepid Spaniard of the 16th century CE, Pedro de Cieza de Léon. His travels in the Andes frame the story of a system of agricultural distribution that maximized resources at different altitudes to benefit everyone.

PERFORMANCE OBJECTIVES

▶ To describe the variety of topography and climate in the Andean world
▶ To summarize the system for distributing food among Andean people at different altitudes
▶ To explain how the contributions of the Spanish explorer, Pedro de Cieza de Léon, help our understanding of the Andean world

BUILDING BACKGROUND

Start by asking students how they like their potatoes—as chips, mashed, fried, baked, in soup or salad? How frequently are potatoes eaten by their families? Explain that the potatoes of the Americas—there were almost 4,000 varieties in the Andes—were an export as valuable as gold. In this chapter they will read about the potatoes a Spanish explorer tasted in the Andes five centuries ago and an ancient agricultural system that reached from the seacoast into the highest mountains.

WORKING WITH PRIMARY SOURCES

Have volunteers read aloud the excerpts from Cieza de Léon's book that appear in this chapter. Discuss the difficulty of writing and traveling as he did and assess the usefulness of his work to his contemporaries and to people today. Interested students can read a longer excerpt from the *Chronicle of Peru* online at *www.admin.northpark.edu/dkoeller/Classes/Sources/deLeon.html*.

GEOGRAPHY CONNECTION

Location A topographical map of the west coast of South America would help students see the diversity of terrain that Cieza de Léon crisscrossed on his journey. Small groups can work around a computer to access satellite images of the Andes at *www.geo.cornell.edu/geology/cap/CAP_gen/CAP_TM.html*.

READING COMPREHENSION QUESTIONS

1. What inspired Cieza de Léon to travel to South America? (*his glimpse of the treasures captured there and sent back to Spain*)
2. What was travel in the Andes like for Cieza de Léon? (*He rode on horseback on Inca roads that wound up high mountains and down into lowlands.*)
3. What connection is there between ancient Andean trails and the Inca roads that Cieza de Léon traveled? (*The Inca used the ancient trails up and down the mountains as the basis for their roads.*)
4. How did the *ayllu* system help people during times of drought or flood?

CHAPTER 14

(*Food supplies were kept in warehouses at different elevations and were made available to members of the* ayllu *who needed them.*)

CRITICAL THINKING QUESTIONS

1. Why is a record such as Cieza de Léon's *Chronicle of Peru* so valuable to historians today? (*His nonjudgmental look at a long-vanished world means we can see what he saw without having to filter out his preconceived beliefs.*)
2. What made the *ayllu* system work? (*strong connections among people; willingness to share and to trust that others would share with you*)
3. What important legacy did ancient Andean peoples give to the Inca? (*Their system of trails connected the high mountains with coastal areas and rainforests. These trails became Inca roads that Cieza de Léon and others traveled on during the post-Inca period.*)

SOCIAL SCIENCES

Science, Technology, and Society Distribute copies of the blackline master for Chapter 14. Students can complete the *ayllu* organization chart to better understand the social system that ancient Andean people devised to share resources at different altitudes.

READING AND LANGUAGE ARTS

Reading Nonfiction Have students assess the value of using Cieza de Léon's travels to frame information about agricultural distribution in the Andes. First have students locate the transition between the two sections of the chapter (page 109, *His account left a trail of clues . . .*) and the point at which Cieza de Léon reenters the chapter (page 112, last sentence) to close the frame around the story of the *ayllu* system.)

Using Language Review with students the last paragraph on page 108 describing the coastal desert and the road back into the mountains. Have students analyze the description to discover the words and phrases that create strong visual images.

SUPPORTING LEARNING

English Language Learners To make sure students understand the chapter title and references within the chapter, encourage students to discuss their experiences on roller coasters or mountain roads. Make a word web for *roller coaster* and then have students use the related words in original sentences.

Struggling Readers Have students use the outline graphic organizer (see the back of this guide) to distinguish the two parts of the chapter—the story of Cieza de Léon and the story of ancient Andean agricultural distribution.

EXTENDING LEARNING

Enrichment A group of students can access information from the Library of Congress to prepare a report to the class on the geography of Peru at http://countrystudies.us/peru/25.htm.

Extension Have a group of students develop a skit in which they interview Pedro de Cieza de Léon about his travels in the Andes and his 8,000-page chronicle. Students can use information in their book as well as other sources, such as www.admin.northpark.edu/dkoeller/Classes/Sources/deLeon.html, which has an excerpt from his book.

LINKING DISCIPLINES

Math Challenge a group of students to calculate the estimated weight of the 8,000 handwritten pages that Cieza de Léon's horse was carrying at the end of his travels. The group should offer written documentation of the procedures they used and the assumptions they made.

THEN and NOW

Scientists are working to preserve the genetic diversity of the ancient staple crop of the Andes. The International Potato Center (CIP) has genetic information on 3,800 varieties of potatoes grown in the Andes. CIP manages experimental stations where scientists from 25 countries conduct research in Andean mountain and rainforest agriculture.

NAME DATE

CHARTING ANDEAN AGRICULTURE

Directions
At each level in the chart, fill in information from the chapter about climate and foods. Then, on a separate sheet of paper, write a paragraph explaining how the *ayllu* warehouse system worked.

Puna

Climate

Foods

Rainforests

Climate

Foods

Lake Titicaca

Climate

Foods

Pacific Coast

Climate

Foods

CHAPTER TEST 14
THE ANCIENT AMERICAN WORLD

NAME _____ DATE _____

A. MULTIPLE CHOICE

Circle the letter of the best answer for each question.

1. Which word is **not** a good description of Cieza de Léon?
   a. curious
   b. adventurous
   c. nonjudgmental
   d. lazy

2. The captain of the ship that Cieza de Léon sailed on at age 13 was motivated to
   a. find a passage to India and get gold.
   b. help the people of South America.
   c. travel the roads of the Andes.
   d. bring back piles of potatoes.

3. Which of the following did Cieza de Léon report seeing on his travels?
   a. snakes, crocodiles, mangoes
   b. tigers, coconuts
   c. Inca royalty, cattle
   d. llamas, potatoes, quinoa

4. The *ayllu* system was made up of groups of unrelated
   a. writers.
   b. rulers.
   c. families.
   d. experts.

5. The warehouses of the *ayllu* system were
   a. guarded by soldiers.
   b. closed to anyone who did not pay gold.
   c. open to anyone in the *ayllu* who needed supplies.
   d. places where llamas could rest.

B. SHORT ANSWER

Write one or two sentences to answer each question.

6. What variations in climate did Cieza de León note in his travels through Peru?
   _____
   _____

7. What regions did the *ayllu* system link together?
   _____
   _____

8. What did the Inca emperors do to improve the *ayllu* system?
   _____
   _____

C. ESSAY

On a separate sheet of paper, write an essay that describes the *ayllu* system. Include details about the kinds of food that were grown or gathered at each point in the system.

A TALE OF TWO CITIES: THE OLDEST TOWNS IN THE AMERICAS

PAGES 113–119

FOR HOMEWORK
STUDENT STUDY GUIDE
pages 39–40

Pirámide Mayor "great pyramid" in Spanish

- **Process** Have students read the Warped Idea sidebar on page 114 and write a short process description of their own. Topics might include making a bed, cleaning your teeth, putting on socks, or making microwave popcorn.

CHAPTER SUMMARY

The oldest towns in the Americas are in Peru. The discoveries made by archaeologists at the two sites—Aspero on the coast and Caral in the Supe Valley—and the questions that remain to be answered are the focus of this chapter.

PERFORMANCE OBJECTIVES

▶ To summarize the significance of the mounds found at Aspero and Caral
▶ To describe how the Pirámide Mayor at Caral was constructed
▶ To understand the ongoing questions and concerns of archaeologists working at these sites

BUILDING BACKGROUND

Read the first sentence of the chapter aloud. Ask students to speculate where in the Americas these oldest towns were found. Then explain that they are in Peru in South America. Invite students to use the map of the hemisphere to trace a route from your town to Lima, Peru.

WORKING WITH PRIMARY SOURCES

Have students examine the photographs of artifacts in the chapter, particularly the reed bags filled with rocks on page 116 and the bone flutes on page 119. Discuss what conclusions they can draw about the people of Caral from these artifacts. Have students explain the significance of each item as it relates to the construction of Caral and what the center may have been used for. Students can also listen to an interview with Dr. Ruth Shady at www.archaeologychannel.org/ caralint.html. Advanced readers can read and report on the article in *Science* describing Shady's work at Caral (Shady Solis, Ruth, et al. "Dating Caral, a Preceramic Site in the Supe Valley on the Central Coast of Peru." *Science* 292: 723–26, 2001).

GEOGRAPHY CONNECTION

Location On a map of Peru, have students locate Aspero and Caral (using the map on page 116 as a guide), the Supe Valley, and other features—the Pan-American Highway, the Andes Mountains, the Pacific Ocean.

READING COMPREHENSION QUESTIONS

1. What questions did archaeologists have about Aspero when they first excavated it? (*Was it a city? What did people do there? Was it a ceremonial center?*)
2. What surprised the archaeologists excavating Aspero? (*evidence that people ate only seafood and did not grow maize or beans*)
3. What surprised the archaeologist Ruth Shady at Caral? (*the size of the site and its age*)
4. What discovery at Caral reminded archaeologists of ancient Egypt? (*The homes next to the mounds where the workers could live were like the homes of Egyptian pyramid builders.*)

5. What are some of Shady's concerns about the condition of the Caral ruins? (*Rain, wind, and air pollution are destroying paint; structures are crumbling.*)

CRITICAL THINKING QUESTIONS

1. Why haven't archaeologists answered all their questions about Caral and Aspero? (*Students should recognize the enormity of excavating sites like Caral and Aspero. Elicit that an archaeologist's techniques for digging, recording finds, and drawing conclusions are labor-intensive and time-consuming.*)
2. What evidence at Caral did Ruth Shady find that told her that the city was a ceremonial and trading center? (*sunken pits lined with benches where people could sit to watch a ceremony; musical instruments that could have been part of a procession; remains of trade items such as seafood from the coast*)
3. How did aerial photography and radiocarbon dating help archaeologists at Caral? (*Aerial photographs revealed mounds at the site; radiocarbon dating established that the mounds were probably the oldest in the Supe Valley but not older than Aspero.*)
4. Distribute copies of the blackline master for Chapter 15. Completing the chart will help students compare the Aspero and Caral sites.

SOCIAL SCIENCES

Science, Technology, and Society Have students work in groups to outline the steps in building the Pirámide Mayor (page 115). Then ask them to compose a list of questions they have about the materials or the process. Another group can research answers to the questions by using print or on-line resources, such as *Smithsonian Magazine* (www.smithsonianmag.si.edu/smithsonian/issues02/aug02/pdf/smithsonian_august_2002_first_city_in_the_world.pdf).

READING AND LANGUAGE ARTS

Reading Nonfiction Ask students to identify some of the specific ways that the authors put readers "in the picture" in this chapter (*using the second person and describing details of the journey to each of the sites, such as "17 bumpy miles later" and "You'll notice rain, wind, and air pollution are . . . "*).

Using Language Point out the idiom/pun on page 114 and explain the expression "know beans about" to students unfamiliar with the expression.

SUPPORTING LEARNING

Struggling Readers Have students use the main idea map graphic organizer (see the back of this guide) to organize the chapter details. They can put "oldest settlements" in the center and add details about Aspero and Caral.

EXTENDING LEARNING

Enrichment Invite a group of students to learn more about archaeology in Peru. They can read about and report on recent discoveries in valleys near the Supe Valley at www.stonepages.com/news/archives/001070.html.

Extension Invite a group of students to act out the process of building the Pirámide Mayor—breaking stones and filling bags to carry to the site. Students can explain what they are doing (to a new worker on the mound) and comment on their progress. The aim of their skit is to give an idea of the work involved in building the pyramid.

LINKING DISCIPLINES

Math Have a group of students calculate the size in feet of the Pirámide Mayor at Caral from dimensions given in the text on page 116. Using an encyclopedia or on-line resources, students can compare the size of the Pirámide Mayor to the Great Pyramid of Egypt.

THEN and NOW

Recent radiocarbon dating of samples from pyramid mounds and houses in the Fortaleza and Pativilca valleys of Peru suggest that by 3100 BCE there were complex societies with large populations and monumental architecture in these valleys as well as in the nearby Supe Valley. Have students list questions they would like to ask about the newly discovered sites.

THE ANCIENT AMERICAN WORLD

CHAPTER 15 BLM
THE ANCIENT AMERICAN WORLD

NAME _____ DATE _____

COMPARING ARCHAEOLOGICAL SITES

Directions
Fill in the chart with information from the chapter to compare Aspero and Caral. (Write a question mark if information cannot be found.) Then, on a separate sheet of paper, write a paragraph explaining why archaeologists think Caral was a trading center as well as a ceremonial center.

	Aspero	**Caral**
Food supply		
Occupations of residents		
Population		
Size of site		
Number of mounds		
Size of mounds		
Oldest mound		
Largest mound		
Unanswered questions		
Concerns of archaeologists		

CHAPTER TEST 15

THE ANCIENT AMERICAN WORLD

NAME   **DATE**

A. MULTIPLE CHOICE

Circle the letter of the best answer for each question.

1. What was unusual about the evidence that archaeologists dug up at Aspero?
    a. It was very ancient.
    b. It had special religious meaning.
    c. It showed that the people did not plant crops.
    d. It indicated advanced farming techniques.

2. The age of the buildings at Caral showed that
    a. Caral was the oldest archaeological site in Peru.
    b. people had moved inland much earlier than had been thought.
    c. the builders of Caral used outdated methods.
    d. Caral was the capital of a great empire.

3. The finding of clam shells at Caral and cotton-wrapped corpses at Aspero seems to prove that the people at both sites
    a. were self-sufficient.
    b. were educated.
    c. lived a comfortable life.
    d. traded with each other.

4. Caral differed from Aspero because the people who lived at Caral
    a. grew crops.
    b. ate seafood.
    c. built mounds.
    d. lived in a rainforest.

5. Archaeologists agree that Caral was a
    a. city.
    b. ceremonial center.
    c. government center.
    d. university center.

B. SHORT ANSWER

Write one or two sentences to answer each question.

6. How did the people of Caral build the Pirámide Mayor?

_____

_____

7. What do scholars think was the purpose of the small houses of wood and mud at Caral?

_____

_____

8. What evidence do most archaeologists need to call an ancient site a city?

_____

_____

C. ESSAY

Write an essay on a separate sheet of paper summarizing the evidence found at Aspero and Caral. Include what needs to be done to prove that the two sites were or were not cities.

CHAPTER 16: THE THUNDEROUS TEMPLE: ANDEAN PEOPLE CONNECT

PAGES 120–126

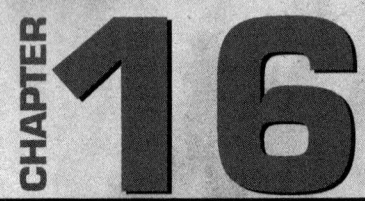

FOR HOMEWORK
STUDENT STUDY GUIDE
pages 41–42

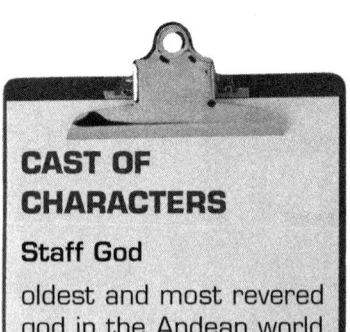

CAST OF CHARACTERS

Staff God
oldest and most revered god in the Andean world

WRITING

- **Poetry** Have students write a poem using either the words for popular Andean symbols that united people—*jaguar, eagle, cat, snake*—or current words that unite people around the world—*peace, music, family, love*. The poem can rhyme, or not, but should convey a sense of connectedness among people.

CHAPTER SUMMARY

Excavation of the major ceremonial site at Chavín de Huántar reveals sophisticated engineering and religious symbols that created strong connections between widely different Andean cultures.

PERFORMANCE OBJECTIVES

▶ To describe the experience of pilgrims at the temple at Chavín de Huántar
▶ To explain the water and air systems used at the Chavín temple
▶ To summarize some of the symbols used in the Chavín religion and the ways that the people of the Andes translated the symbols into art

BUILDING BACKGROUND

Discuss how symbols show a shared interest among people who are otherwise very different. Some symbols that connect people today might be political party pins, team caps, product logos, or T-shirt slogans. Explain that in this chapter students will read about religious symbols that influenced the art of people from varied Andean cultures.

WORKING WITH PRIMARY SOURCES

Have students choose one of the illustrations of artwork in the chapter—the Lanzón, the textile, the hammered gold plaque—and write a brief description of what they see in the illustration and why they think it was a chosen for this chapter. Assign three students the task of digging deeper into the carving, metalwork, and textiles of the Chavín period and reporting back to the class. Spanish speakers can access the website of Luis Lumbreras, the archaeologist cited in the chapter, at *http://chavin.peruculturual.org.pe*.

GEOGRAPHY CONNECTION

Place Have students get more information about Chavín at *http://studentweb.tulane.edu/~tluka/*. Have students draw conclusions about the site, its climate, and its topography.

READING COMPREHENSION QUESTIONS

1. Why did pilgrims come to Chavín? (*to visit the oracle and get information about the future*)
2. What were some of the symbols that connected people in the Andes to the religion at Chavín? Where were they used? (*Jaguars, cats, snakes, and eagles appear in tapestries, as gold figures, and on pottery.*)
3. What were some new techniques in art that developed along with an interest in Chavín's powerful symbols? (*weaving with wool that held dye better than cotton; using alloys of gold, copper, and silver that could be soldered to give dimension to gold objects; batiking and tie-dyeing fabrics*)
4. What god, called "son of Lanzón" by the authors, was found in the enlarged temple at Chavín? (*the Staff God*)

CRITICAL THINKING QUESTIONS

1. How did engineering heighten the pilgrims' experience at Chavín temple? (*Some of the sounds and sights that scared pilgrims and convinced them of supernatural powers were made possible by engineering—loud rushing sounds were made by a sewer system inside the temple; air ducts made it possible to have air to breathe while walking a long way in windowless passages.*)
2. How did the priests benefit from the Chavín religion? (*Pilgrims brought food and gifts to the temple. Interpreting the oracle's answers gave priests control over people's actions.*)
3. Explain why people all over the Andes responded to the symbols from Chavín. (*Students should mention the idea of rebirth, in which old symbols take on new life. The symbols of jaguar, cat, eagle, and snake were not new and everybody recognized them, but suddenly people had new ideas about portraying them.*)

SOCIAL SCIENCES

Science, Technology, and Society Have a group of students prepare an illustrated report on the technique of making an alloy of silver, gold, and copper. Students can explain the advantages of the alloy (its strength meant it could be soldered, unlike pure gold) and how this led to the creation of "three-dimensional" figures.

READING AND LANGUAGE ARTS

Reading Nonfiction Have students look at paragraph two of the chapter and analyze the words and phrases used to create an uneasy feeling like that felt by pilgrims who traveled to the temple at Chavín de Huántar. Ask students to explain briefly the purpose of making the visit scary for pilgrims.

Using Language Discuss correct capitalization of the cardinal directions—*north, south, east,* and *west*—and their adjective forms.

SUPPORTING LEARNING

English Language Learners Point out the pun on page 123 ("see if this theory holds water") and discuss puns in general. Encourage students to keep a page in their history journals to collect puns they make up or hear from others.

Struggling Readers Have students use the sequence of events graphic organizer (see the back of this guide) to better understand the experiences of pilgrims at the Chavín temple.

EXTENDING LEARNING

Enrichment Spanish-speaking students can access Luis Lumbreras's website and report back to the class about the construction of the old temple at Chavín (*http://chavin.perucultural.org.pe/csubterran.shtml*). A Chavín site in English that references the archaeologist Richard Burger is at *http://huaraz.com/culturachavin*. All students can enjoy Luis Lumbreras's photographs of Chavín at his website.

Extension Have a group of students role-play engineers and priests from Chavín in a panel discussion about the temple, its special effects, and the Lanzón. Students can find information at *http://huaraz.com/culturachavin*.

VOCABULARY

Lanzón "lance," from Spanish; name for a Peruvian sculpture shaped like a lance or spear

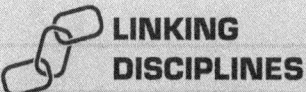

LINKING DISCIPLINES

Art Assign a group of students to define *renaissance* by using a dictionary or thesaurus and apply the word to the explosion of Andean art described in the chapter. To see examples of Andean art from this period, students can use print resources such as Rebecca Stone-Miller, *Art of the Andes: From Chavín to Inca*, recommended on the Further Reading page of their book, or images from the Peabody Museum site listed on their book's Websites page.

THE ANCIENT AMERICAN WORLD | 105

CHAPTER BLM 16
THE ANCIENT AMERICAN WORLD

NAME _____ **DATE** _____

CHAVÍN'S INFLUENCE

Directions
In the circles, write details about Chavín's influence on different arts, based on information in the chapter. Then answer the question below.

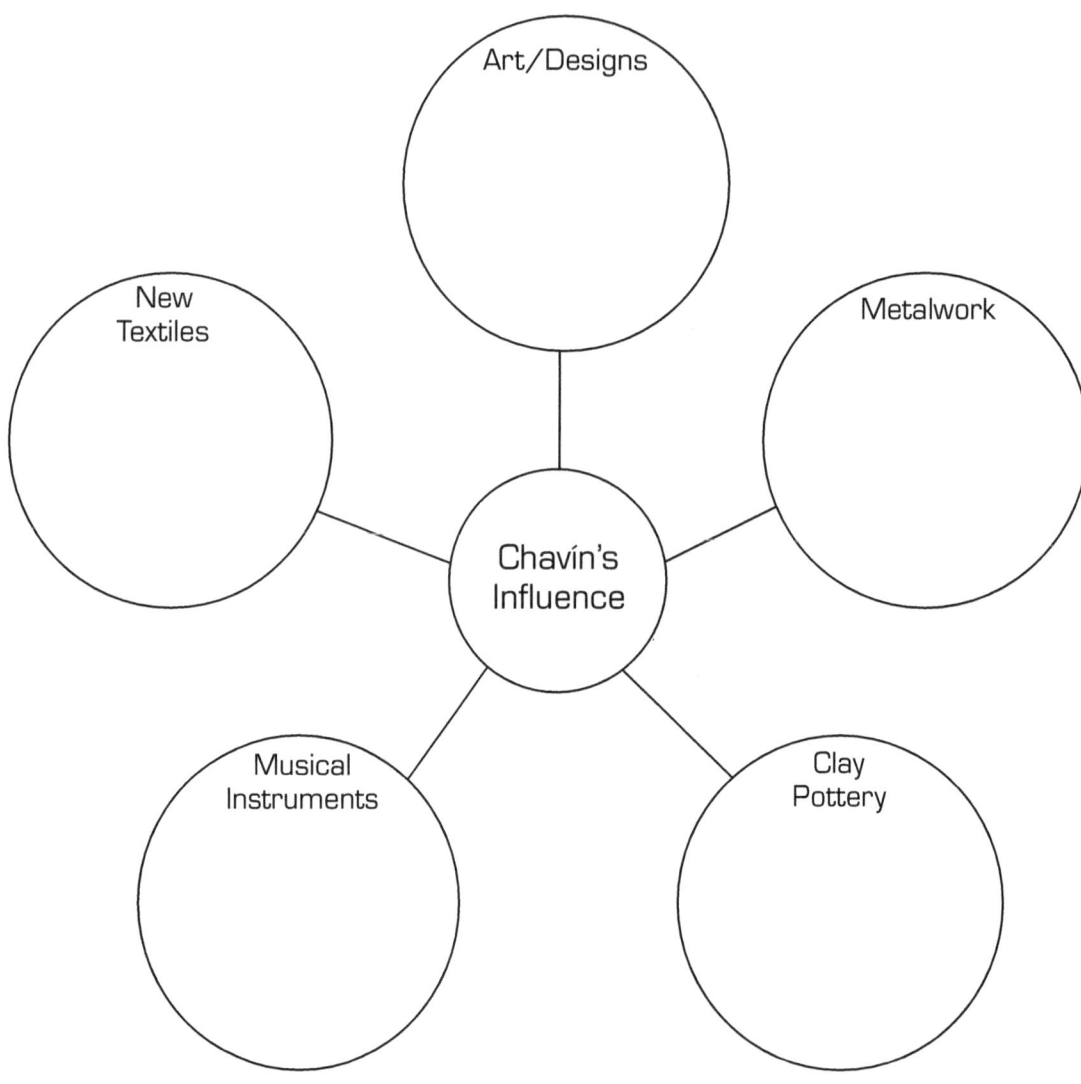

According to the chapter, an alloy is a mixture of metals that is stronger than the original metals. Explain why *alloy* would be a good word to use to describe the Andean world under the Chavín cult's influence.

CHAPTER TEST 16

THE ANCIENT AMERICAN WORLD

NAME _____ DATE _____

A. MULTIPLE CHOICE

Circle the letter of the best answer to each question.

1. Which of the following was **not** used to impress pilgrims at Chavín Huántar?
   a. thunderous roaring sounds
   b. monstrous carved heads
   c. a long walk through a maze of dark, windowless hallways
   d. cold hands that grabbed their arms in the dark

2. The first step for a pilgrim at Chavín was
   a. hearing the oracle speak.
   b. meeting the Staff God.
   c. waiting in a walled pit under monstrous carved heads.
   d. walking through a windowless, dark maze.

3. Engineers developed a sophisticated system of air ducts to
   a. bring water into the temple to frighten pilgrims.
   b. make it possible to breathe in the winding, windowless tunnels.
   c. permit pilgrims to listen to the oracle.
   d. heat the temple's passageways.

4. The Lanzón was placed so that it symbolically connected
   a. east and west.   c. art and engineering.
   b. pilgrims and priests.   d. men and women.

5. The symbols of the Chavín religion gave new life to
   a. old designs.   b. old pilgrims.
   c. the Lanzón.   d. the high Andes.

B. SHORT ANSWER

Write one or two sentences to answer each question.

6. Why did pilgrims come to Chavín?

_____

_____

7. What influences, besides religious, did the Chavín cult have on ancient Peruvians?

_____

_____

8. If Chavín wasn't the biggest, oldest, or most original religious site in the Andean world, why was it so important?

_____

_____

C. ESSAY

On a separate sheet of paper, write an essay explaining this statement: "When modern Peruvians wonder how they can unit themselves as a single nation with shared beliefs, they look back 2,500 years to Chavín."

UNIT 7: HIGHLAND AND COASTAL EMPIRES BEFORE THE INCA

PAGES 127–146

Chapter 17 On Top of the World: Highland Empires in the Andes
Chapter 18 The Man with the Gold Earrings: Moche Artists in Coastal Peru
Chapter 19 Chan Chan: Capital City of the Andean Kingdom of Chimor

UNIT OBJECTIVES

Unit 7 covers the period from 300 BCE through 1470 CE, a period that saw the rise and fall of great cities, amazing art and engineering, and monumental architecture. In this unit your students will learn
- the impact of Tiwanaku on other highland cultures.
- how vertical irrigation helped Wari.
- the incredible art and engineering of the Moche.
- the significance of the royal compounds of Chimor.

PRIMARY SOURCES

Unit 7 includes pictures of the following artifacts and excerpts from the following primary sources:
- Pedro Cieza de León, *The Incas*
- Kalasasaya Gateway, Tiwanaku, Bolivia
- Ponce Stela, Tiwanaku, Bolivia
- Wari figurine
- Tomb of Moche warrior-priest, Huaca Sipán, Peru
- Moche brick-maker marks
- Moche warrior earring
- Vase painting of Moche sacrificial ceremony
- Moche portrait jar
- Moche monkey-head bead
- Chimú myth
- Bricks, Chan Chan
- Decorated adobe wall, Chan Chan

BIG IDEAS IN UNIT 7

City and **art** are the big ideas in Unit 7. *What does it take to make a city?* is the question that Unit 7 answers—food, water, government, help for people in hard times, places for people to live, work for people to do, and places for the dead. The unit discusses art and architecture in four different cultures, Tiwanaku, Wari, Moche, and Chimor. Art in Tiwanaku and Moche included centralized monumental displays, whereas in Chimor kings were isolated behind high thick walls, with their own artists and craftsmen living nearby.

Ask students to describe cities they know well. List the ways those cities are the same and how they differ. Explain that in these chapters students will visit cities of the past that had very different fates.

GEOGRAPHY CONNECTION

As students read the unit, have them note differences in the geography of the various empires. Help them recognize that, although these chapters are about Andean empires, there are great variations across the region.

TIMELINE

300 BCE	Tiwanaku first settled
100 CE	Moche people begin building Huacas of the Sun and Moon
200 CE	Tiwanaku residents begin massive building effort
560 CE	Government established at Wari
635 CE	Flood destroys capital of Moche kingdom
700 CE	Tiwanaku largest Andean city
900 CE	Chimú begin building city of Chan Chan
1000 CE	Tiwanaku abandoned
1100 CE	Wari government collapses; city abandoned
1450 CE	Chan Chan second-largest Andean city
1465 CE	Inca cut off water supply to Chan Chan
1470 CE	Inca Empire conquers Chimú Empire

UNIT PROJECTS

Lake Titicaca

Invite a group of students to investigate and report on Lake Titicaca—its size, elevation, climate (*http://countrystudies.us/bolivia/26.htm*), importance to Tiwanaku and Wari, and the recent discovery of a temple under its waters (*http://news.bbc.co.uk/1/hi/world/americas/892616.stm*).

Press Conference: Ancient Cities

Students role-play a panel of experts, each of whom comes from the heyday of these ancient cities—Tiwanaku, Wari, Cerro Blanco, Sipán, and Chan Chan. Panelists should be prepared to describe the outstanding monuments, statues, or other features of his or her city; explain the climate, agriculture, and water sources of the city; and tell why the city will be remembered. Other students can play the role of the press, asking questions (based on information in the unit chapters).

Taking It with You: Death in the Andean World

Have a group of students investigate and report on Andean peoples' beliefs about the afterlife. Students can report on tomb excavations in Sipán and Chan Chan that reveal what Andean pre-Inca cultures considered necessary for the afterlife.

Water Technology

From the mound at Tiwanaku with its imitation mountain spring, to the vertical irrigation of Wari, to the deep wells of Chan Chan, this unit is brimming with information about Andean cultures and water. Divide the class into small groups of students; have each group take a specific technology and report on it in detail. Topics include developing irrigation techniques (particularly in high mountain settings), finding water supplies in arid regions, and incorporating water in ceremonial architecture. When the groups have presented their findings, the class can draw conclusions about connections among Andean cultures.

ADDITIONAL ASSESSMENT

For Unit 7, divide the class into groups and have them all undertake the Press Conference project so you can assess their knowledge of the Andean empires. Use the scoring rubric at the back of this guide to assess students' work, and have students rate their own work with the self-assessment rubric.

LITERATURE CONNECTION

There are various translations of *Chronicle of Peru* by Pedro de Cieza de León available, and students can read them with a partner or parent to learn more about the living conditions and lifestyles of ancient Andean peoples. Excerpts from the work are also available online. Many of the books about pre-Inca civilizations are intended for older audiences, but partners can gain important insight from them. Suggest some of the following to students:

- Donnan, Christopher. *Moche Portraits from Ancient Peru*. Austin, TX: University of Texas Press, 2004. Nonfiction. ADVANCED. The book documents how the Moche portrait tradition evolved, how the portraits were produced and distributed, who they portrayed, why they were made, and how they were used in Moche society.
- Moseley, Michael. *Incas and Their Ancestors: The Archaeology of Peru*. New York: Thames & Hudson, 2001. Nonfiction. ADVANCED. The book presents the extraordinary saga of the Incas and the prehistoric Andean cultures upon which they built.
- Von Hagen, Adriana. *The Cities of the Ancient Andes*. New York: Thames & Hudson, 1998. Nonfiction. AVERAGE. This book offers a stimulating introduction to cities in the pre-Columbian Andes. At the start of each chapter on a civilization, there is a short description of what life would have been like in that city.

UNIVERSAL ACCESS

The following strategies are designed to cover a range of learning styles and reading, language, and skill levels. This section includes suggestions for differentiating instruction to meet the diverse needs of your students.

Reading Strategies

- To facilitate students' reading, point out features such as illustrations, information, and definitions in the side columns that students will encounter as they read.
- Add definitions of unfamiliar words to the class's word file. Encourage students to review all the words in the file and announce that you will be holding a reverse spelling bee. Deal out the word-file cards to small groups of students. Call on each group in turn to be the "Challenger" and to spell a word out loud, reading off the card. Students in other groups volunteer to be "Responders," defining each word and using it in a sentence. Award points for correct definitions and appropriate word use. (Students can prepare for this contest by keeping word lists in their history journals and studying them before the event.)
- Call on students to take the role of tour guide by reading the descriptions of places in these chapters aloud. Fit the reading passages to the abilities of each student.

Writing Strategies

- Have students retell the Inca creation myth and compare it to the Aztec myth about the sun and moon (Chapter 17). Have students write their own story explaining why the moon's light is dimmer than the sun's.
- Descriptions of the work of archaeologists appear in each of the chapters in Unit 7. Have students create a two-column chart with the headings *Agriculture* and *Art* and ask students to use the chart to record archaeological discoveries from different cultures in each category.
- There are strong visual images of objects and places in Unit 7. Have pairs of students choose an image, such as the Bearded Statue of Tiwanaku, the split-level apartments of Wari, the gold earrings of the Lord of Sipán, or the compound of the king at Gran Chimú. Then ask students to write a script for the narrator of a TV show called *Images of the Past*.

Listening and Speaking Strategies

- As you read portions of the chapters, call on volunteers to describe the various experiences and scenes presented in the unit chapters. For example, opening the Lord of Sipán's tomb; living in one of the split-level apartment complexes of Wari; discovering that ancient raised-field agriculture around Lake Titicaca still works today. Encourage a group of students to prepare and present an interview in which a reporter for the *Chan Chan Times* interviews servants about what it's like inside the king's walled compound.

UNIT VOCABULARY LIST

The following words that appear in Unit 7 are important for your students' understanding of the social studies content as well as for development of literacy. Use these words for vocabulary study or to reinforce language arts skills (e.g., synonyms, compound words, prefixes and suffixes, and related words). The words are listed below in the order in which they appear in the chapters.

Chapter 17	**Chapter 18**	**Chapter 19**
grimacing	honeycomb	famine
splendor	runt	overpower
preside	goldsmith	handiwork
metropolis	crumpled	labyrinth
eave	confetti	purveyor
niche	miniature	millstone
	eyewitness	inheritance
	reenact	eternity

CHAPTER 17

ON TOP OF THE WORLD: HIGHLAND EMPIRES IN THE ANDES

PAGES 127–132

FOR HOMEWORK
STUDENT STUDY GUIDE
pages 43–44

VOCABULARY

Tiwanaku can be spelled at least six different ways, including *Tiahuanaco* and *Tihuanacu*. Present-day Bolivians who live near the ruins of the city spell it *Tiwanaku*.

CAST OF CHARACTERS

Staff God oldest and most revered god in the Andean world

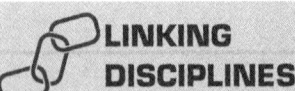
LINKING DISCIPLINES

Science Have students investigate why water in ditches around the raised fields near Lake Titicaca keeps the crops from freezing. Invite a group to create a demonstration to illustrate the phenomenon.

CHAPTER SUMMARY

Tiwanaku and Wari, highland empires near Lake Titicaca, captured the imaginations of the Inca (who made Tiwanaku the site of their creation story), European explorers of the time (Cieza de Léon was impressed), and today's archaeologists, who note Tiwanaku's widespread influence on Andean cultures.

PERFORMANCE OBJECTIVES

▶ To identify connections between Tiwanaku and Wari
▶ To summarize the creative water technologies used in Tiwanaku and Wari
▶ To explain how the Inca showed their regard for Tiwanaku

BUILDING BACKGROUND

Ask students about mountains they have seen or climbed. Talk about the high Andes and give students an idea of their elevations compared to the Rocky Mountains in North America or the Himalayas in Asia. Ask the class to describe challenges of farming high in the mountains. Explain that in this chapter they will be reading about two highland cultures of the Andes whose people solved the problem of getting water to their terraced fields on steep mountainsides.

WORKING WITH PRIMARY SOURCES

Ask students to look carefully at the image of the Staff God on page 129 and describe it briefly in a journal entry to share with the class. Then ask a group of students to investigate and report to the class about the Staff God images of Tiwanaku and their resemblance to the Staff God at Chavín.

GEOGRAPHY CONNECTION

Interaction This chapter offers an exceptional opportunity to show not only how humans interact and change the environment to suit their needs (the raised fields of Tiwanaku) but how they develop systems because of the environment (the *ayllu* of Wari). Have students pose questions about these two concepts and use them to guide their study of the two cities.

READING COMPREHENSION QUESTIONS

1. How did Cieza de Léon describe the statues at Tiwanaku? (*"stone idols," "of human size and shape," "features beautifully carved," "seem the work of great artists," "giants"*)
2. Where does the Staff God of Chavín make an appearance at Tiwanaku? (*in the center of the plaza and standing guard at what archaeologists call "the Gateway of the Sun"*)
3. What was unusual about Wari's mountainside irrigation system? (*It consisted of vertical canals that diverted mountain streams to water the terraced fields.*)
4. How did Wari's government make sure everyone took part? (*It fed people at feasts if they worked and grew crops for the government.*)

CRITICAL THINKING QUESTIONS

1. What evidence is there of shared ideas between Chavín, Tiwanaku, and Wari? (*Staff God images and statues; canals to move water*)
2. Compare Cieza de Léon's responses to Tiwanaku and Wari. What can you conclude about him? (*He was impressed by the artistry he saw in statues at Tiwanaku, remarking that they "seem the work of great artists," but was not impressed with the "old" buildings that had fallen into "ruin and decay" at Wari. Conclusion: He was not interested in long-ago history, but he did feel responsible to record everything he saw, even if he wasn't that impressed with it.*)
3. Which of the features of Tiwanaku or Wari impresses you most? Why? (*Responses will vary.*)

SOCIAL SCIENCES

Civics In Wari the government adapted the food-sharing *ayllu* into a system that benefited both the government and the people. Have students draw a diagram showing how the system worked. Then ask them to state a conclusion about who benefited most.

READING AND LANGUAGE ARTS

Reading Nonfiction Chapter 17 tells a tale of two cities—Tiwanaku and Wari. Ask students to identify the transition between the two parts of the chapter (paragraph three, page 130) and to identify the rhetorical device the authors use to switch topics from one city to the other.

Using Language First ask students to locate the hyphenated words in the chapter (*man-made, split-levels, give-and-take, almost-free*). Then have them identify each word as a noun or adjective and speculate about why they are hyphenated.

SUPPORTING LEARNING

Struggling Readers Distribute copies of the blackline master for Chapter 17 to help students organize information about Tiwanaku and Wari.

EXTENDING LEARNING

Enrichment Radiocarbon dating has been used to show that farmers near Lake Titicaca planted crops in raised fields for 2,000 years before the Spaniards came. Have a group of students explain the process of radiocarbon dating to the class and describe some of its applications.

Extension Clark Erickson reintroduced raised-field farming to people near Lake Titicaca in the 1980s. Have students create a skit about his work. They can find information in the chapter and in an online interview with him at *http://archaeology.about.com/cs/agriculture/a/erickson2_p.htm*. Students can play the roles of Erickson and his assistants and of local farmers who at first resist the idea. A narrator can set the scene.

WRITING

Description The people in Wari perfected a system of vertical irrigation to get water to their mountainside terraced fields. The system is described briefly in the chapter. Ask students to write a succinct paragraph describing how water gets to their home and where it comes from.

THEN and NOW

International archaeologists diving in Lake Titicaca located the ruins of a Tiwanaku temple and other structures 1,000 to 1,500 years old. Archaeologists made over 200 dives to depths of as much as 100 feet to photograph the ruins. Despite the find, scientists say that legends about a lost city under the lake have no foundation. Invite students to write a fanciful legend about the lost city of the lake.

THE ANCIENT AMERICAN WORLD

CHAPTER 17 BLM
THE ANCIENT AMERICAN WORLD

NAME _____ DATE _____

COMPARING TIWANAKU AND WARI

Directions
Use information from the chapter to complete the chart comparing and contrasting Tiwanaku and Wari. If no information is given in the chapter, leave the space blank. Use complete sentences.

Points of Comparison	Tiwanaku	Wari
1. Where is the city? When was it founded?		
2. What was the tallest structure, and how tall was it?		
3. What is the most impressive work of art?		
4. What is the city's claim to fame in farming?		
5. What was the population and the area of the city at its peak?		
6. When and why did the city finally fall?		
7. What is one more fact, myth, or question about the city you can add?		
8. How did the city influence other cities and how was it influenced?		

NAME _____ DATE _____

CHAPTER TEST 17
THE ANCIENT AMERICAN WORLD

A. MULTIPLE CHOICE

Circle the letter of the best answer for each question.

1. The largest city in the ancient Andean world from 100–1000 CE was
   - a. Wari.
   - b. Titicaca.
   - c. Tiwanaku.
   - d. Chavín.

2. What makes it difficult to grow crops near Lake Titicaca?
   - a. killer frosts several times a year
   - b. very hot temperatures
   - c. flooding from the lake
   - d. animals eating the crops

3. The water in ditches around the raised fields
   - a. keeps crops cool.
   - b. keeps crops warm so they don't freeze.
   - c. prevents animals from eating the crops.
   - d. provides a place for farmers to cool off.

4. Which of the following ideas did Wari people come up with on their own?
   - a. Staff God images
   - b. raised fields for farming
   - c. patios outside apartments
   - d. vertical irrigation canals

5. When Wari organized itself into a capital city, the government
   - a. offered people feasts in exchange for work.
   - b. built housing in exchange for work.
   - c. gave people food without requiring them to work.
   - d. required everyone to raise their own food.

B. SHORT ANSWER

Write one or two sentences to answer each question.

6. Why do archaeologists think that the Staff Gods of Tiwanaku were influenced by Chavín?
   _____
   _____

7. What made early settlement around Lake Titicaca possible?
   _____
   _____

8. What did the people of Wari do during times of food shortages?
   _____
   _____

C. ESSAY

On a separate sheet of paper, write a list of questions you would like to ask Cieza de León about his visit to Tiwanaku. Then pose his responses.

CHAPTER 18
THE MAN WITH THE GOLD EARRINGS: MOCHE ARTISTS IN COASTAL PERU
PAGES 133–139

FOR HOMEWORK
STUDENT STUDY GUIDE
pages 45–46

VOCABULARY

Moche comes from the word *Mochica*, the language spoken in the Moche Valley when Pedro de Cieza de León visited in the 16th century

huaca Quechua for "sacred"; any object with sacred powers; it could be a mountain, spring, temple, rock, or pyramid.

CAST OF CHARACTERS

Warrior-Priest the most important figure in Moche civilization; often portrayed in Moche art

CHAPTER SUMMARY

In this chapter students follow archaeologists in the step-by-step excavation of a treasure-filled Moche tomb. They gain an appreciation of Moche artists, whether working on the Huaca of the Sun at Cerro Blanco or adding tiny turquoise details to a golden earring.

PERFORMANCE OBJECTIVES

▶ To describe the superb artistry of the Moche
▶ To understand the monumental structures the Moche built at Cerro Blanco
▶ To summarize how archaeologists solved the mystery of who else was buried in the tomb of the Lord of Sipán

BUILDING BACKGROUND

Ask students what they think of when they hear the word *pyramid*. They may mention Egypt or Mesoamerican cultures. Explain that Andean cultures also built pyramids, not of rocks but of mud bricks. In this chapter they will read about some of the world's finest artists and craftspeople.

WORKING WITH PRIMARY SOURCES

Students can read Walter Alva's firsthand account of excavating the tomb of the Lord of Sipán in the October 1988 issue of *National Geographic* or online at http://muweb.millersville.edu/~columbus/data/ark/ALVA-01.ARK.

GEOGRAPHY CONNECTION

Regions Have students locate the Moche River cultures on the map on page 144. Then ask a group of students to use an encyclopedia to find out more about the climate and resources of the coastal region of Peru and report their findings to the class.

READING COMPREHENSION QUESTIONS

1. Who brought the pyramid/tomb in Sipán to Walter Alva's attention? (*The police showed him stolen artifacts that had been recovered from looters.*)
2. Why hadn't the pyramid of Sipán been excavated before? (*The larger pyramids in Cerro Blanco seemed more interesting.*)
3. What gave Walter Alva and his team the idea that the man buried in the Sipán tomb was important? (*the expensive things he was buried with—golden headdress and earrings; the people who were buried with him*)
4. What inventions are Moche artists known for? (*molds for pottery and a technique for coating copper with gold*)
5. Distribute copies of the blackline master for Chapter 18 and have students organize details about the Moche craftspeople.

CRITICAL THINKING QUESTIONS

1. What did you find most interesting about the discovery of Lord Sipán? (*Responses will vary but will probably include the gold jewelry and the other bodies buried in his tomb.*)
2. How did Christopher Donnan solve the mystery of who was buried with the Lord of Sipán? (*His experience in looking at photographs of Moche paintings led him to recognize that a story had been reenacted in the tomb.*)
3. What conclusions did Walter Alva draw from the artifacts found in the Lord of Sipán's tomb? (*that there were master craftsmen in all the Moche settlements, not just in large towns or cities; the person in the tomb was probably a great warrior of some kind because of the quantity and quality of items buried with him*)

SOCIAL SCIENCES

Science, Technology, and Society On page 139 the authors mention two "inventions" of Moche artists—using molds to make pottery and coating copper with gold. Divide the class into groups to investigate these techniques and report to the class. Duplicate topics as necessary. The website *www.allperu.com/PERU2A1a.htm* is a source of information. Students can see examples of Moche pottery and jewelry at the Peabody Museum website recommended on the Websites page of their book.

READING AND LANGUAGE ARTS

Reading Nonfiction Have students read aloud the subtitle of this chapter and remind them that *Highland* was part of the subtitle for Chapter 17. In light of this information, have them predict what they will find in Chapter 18.

Using Language Have students use a dictionary to discover the etymology of *archaeology* (from the Greek *archaio-* + *-logia*, or "ancient science"). Elicit that archaeology is the scientific study of ancient humans. Have students list and define related words (*archaeologist, archaeological, archaeologically*) and use them in sentences.

SUPPORTING LEARNING

Struggling Readers Distribute copies of the sequence of events graphic organizer (see the back of this guide) and have students fill in the first box with the arrest of the looters. Have them list all the events that led to the discovery of the gold earrings.

EXTENDING LEARNING

Enrichment Invite a group of interested students to find out what is being done to prevent the looting of Moche artifacts today. The group can present the information to the class.

Extension Have a group of students investigate the Huaca of the Sun and Huaca of the Moon in the Moche city of Cerro Blanco. (An online source of information is *www.inkanatura.com/coastchiclayotrujillosunandmoontemples.asp*.) Then have students write information about the two Huacas on colored-paper "bricks" labeled with the students' own "maker's marks." (See page 134.) Use the bricks for a bulletin board display.

WRITING

Dialogue Divide the class into pairs and have each pair write a short conversation between two members of Walter Alva's team. The two are exchanging ideas and information about the mystery of the people buried in the Lord of Sipán's tomb. Suggest that students write sentences, read them aloud, and make changes to make the conversation sound more realistic.

LINKING DISCIPLINES

Art Have students find out more about Moche art and artists online at *www.tribalarts.com/feature/moche*. Students can make copies of the artwork and report on the interpretations of the subjects.

THE ANCIENT AMERICAN WORLD

EXPERT MOCHE CRAFTSPEOPLE

Directions
Excavations of Moche Empire sites have revealed that the Moche were expert artists. Complete the web with details from the chapter about the objects that the Moche produced. Then answer the question below.

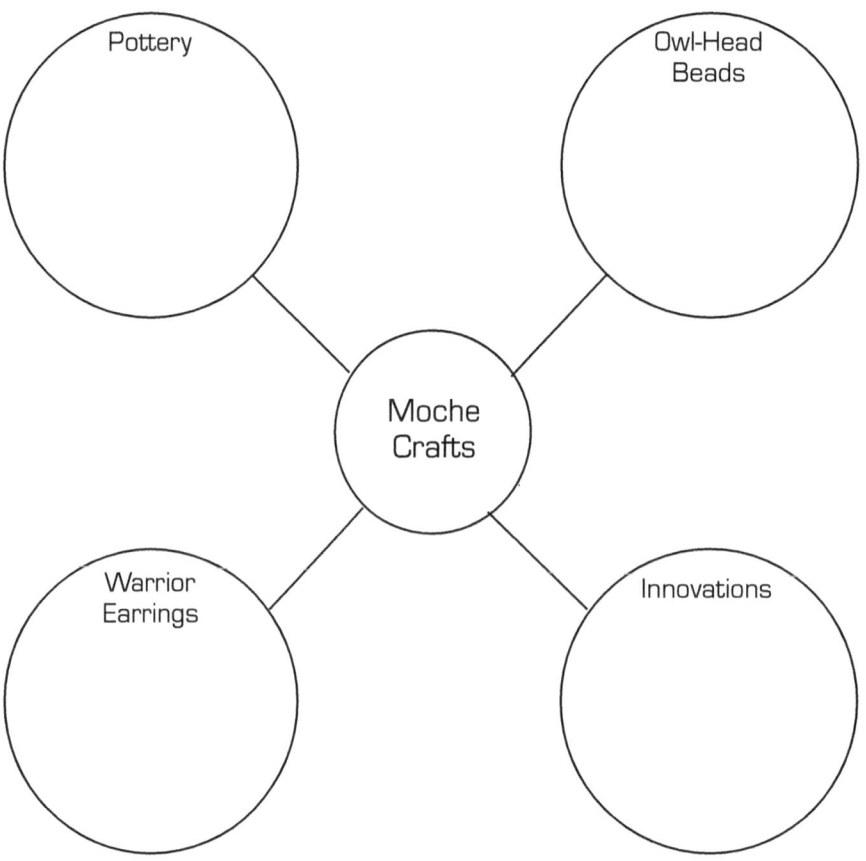

From the details about Moche art and other information in the chapter, write conclusions about the artists using these categories:

- ▶ artistic skill
- ▶ reasons for creating the objects
- ▶ ability to come up with new techniques

_____
_____
_____
_____

NAME _____ DATE _____

A. MULTIPLE CHOICE

Circle the letter of the best answer for each question.

1. Which of the following is **not** one of the things found in the tomb with the Lord of Sipán?
   - a. skeleton of a sacrificed man
   - b. skeleton of a dog
   - c. beautiful golden earrings
   - d. a mummy

2. The team excavating the tomb in Sipán referred to the important man buried there as a
   - a. warrior-priest.
   - b. sacrifice.
   - c. murder victim.
   - d. master goldsmith.

3. The Moche kingdom was located
   - a. along the coast of Peru.
   - b. in the highlands of Peru.
   - c. on the shores of Lake Titicaca.
   - d. in the Andes rainforest.

4. Moche pottery often features
   - a. llamas and other animals.
   - b. important people.
   - c. the mark of the person who made it.
   - d. images of gods.

5. The discovery of the Lord of Sipán's tomb can be compared to the discovery of King Tut's tomb because
   - a. the Lord of Sipán's body was inside a mummy case.
   - b. golden masterpieces were buried with him.
   - c. a footless man was buried with him.
   - d. the Lord of Sipán was as powerful as King Tut.

B. SHORT ANSWER

Write one or two sentences to answer each question.

6. Why did the people of Moche build pyramids?

   _____
   _____

7. What makes Moche painted pottery so beautiful?

   _____
   _____

8. Why were the Moche artists the finest in the Andean world?

   _____
   _____

C. ESSAY

On a separate sheet of paper, write an essay explaining how Christopher Donnan figured out the reason that six people and a dog were buried in the tomb with the Lord of Sipán.

CHAPTER 19
CHAN CHAN: CAPITAL CITY OF THE ANDEAN KINGDOM OF CHIMOR
PAGES 140–146

FOR HOMEWORK

STUDENT STUDY GUIDE
pages 47–48

CAST OF CHARACTERS

Taycanamu (tay-cah-NAH-mu) founder of the Andean kingdom of Chimor

VOCABULARY

anonymous *an + onyma* = "without" + "name" in ancient Greek; an anonymous person's name is unknown

Chan Chan "Sun Sun" in Quechua

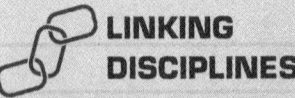

LINKING DISCIPLINES

Math Have students calculate the area in square feet of the largest royal compound at Chan Chan, which measured 0.5 mile x 0.25 mile (page 143).

CHAPTER SUMMARY

From the time of their mythical origins to their conquest by the Inca, the Chimú dominated hundreds of miles of coastal territory in what is now Peru. The chapter focuses on the fortified compounds where the kings of Chimor lived a lifestyle they expected would follow them to the afterlife.

PERFORMANCE OBJECTIVES

▶ To summarize the myth about the founding of Chimor
▶ To describe a king's walled compound at Chan Chan and the surrounding homes and workshops of his craftsmen and nobles
▶ To explain the burial practices of the Chimú

BUILDING BACKGROUND

Write the saying "You can't take it with you" on the board and elicit comments about its meaning. Explain that the people they will read about in this chapter, like the pharaohs of ancient Egypt, not only believed they could but that they should be buried with their most valuable possessions.

WORKING WITH PRIMARY SOURCES

Have students examine the image of the decorated adobe wall on page 142. Students can trace the design and identify the images listed in the caption. Then they can copy the elements of the design onto paper to create their own decoration for the classroom wall.

GEOGRAPHY CONNECTION

Regions Have students locate Chan Chan on the map on page 144. Have small groups investigate the Chimor region's climate and physical features. One useful source is www.tulane.edu/~latinlib/chanchan.html.

READING COMPREHENSION QUESTIONS

1. What former culture did the Chimú take over and absorb into their kingdom? (*the Moche*)
2. How did one archaeologist react to a stately palace compound that had a single entrance door in the high thick walls? (*He felt like a prisoner.*)
3. How did the kings of Chimor support themselves? (*They collected tribute from people they had conquered.*)
4. What was the point of tight security for the palace compounds? (*to keep intruders out; to protect the valuable wells and the royal inhabitants*)
5. Distribute copies of the blackline master for Chapter 19 so students can retell the story of Chimor's "rocky start."

CRITICAL THINKING QUESTIONS

1. What is the reasoning of those who think a total of ten kings ruled Chimor? (*At Chan Chan they have discovered ten palace compounds built with varying styles of adobe bricks. The bricks indicate to one archaeologist that each compound was built by a different king.*)
2. How did the king of Chimor control his subjects? (*by forcing them to pay tribute, by forcing craftsmen and other workers to live outside his palace compound and giving them only limited privileges*)

SOCIAL SCIENCES

Civics Guide students in drawing a diagram to illustrate the custom of split inheritance, to show why there were multiple palace compounds at Chan Chan. Explain how this system differs from the traditional inheritance arrangement, in which a ruler's heir inherits everything.

READING AND LANGUAGE ARTS

Reading Nonfiction Discuss the effectiveness of starting this chapter with a retelling of the legend of Taycanamu. Have students point out the sentence that tells readers they are moving from legend to history: "Here legend becomes real history."

Using Language Have student volunteers read aloud the sidebar The Care and Feeding of a King (page 143). Define unfamiliar words and then discuss the meaning of the names in capital letters and quotation marks. Also explain the meaning and purpose of this primary source, to describe how a Chimú king was treated.

SUPPORTING LEARNING

English Language Learners On page 141 the authors give examples of the compounds of famous modern people: Bill Gates, the Kennedys, and Saddam Hussein. Make sure students understand what the purpose of a compound is, and the point of these examples of compounds. Clarify who the people are, if their names are unfamiliar.

Struggling Readers Distribute the main idea map graphic organizer (see the back of this guide) to help students organize the information in the chapter.

EXTENDING LEARNING

Enrichment Chan Chan has been listed as an endangered World Heritage Site since 1986. A group of students can find out why at *www.globalheritagefund.org/where/nomination_chanchan.html* and report to the class about what is being done to protect Chan Chan. Another source is *http://whc.unesco.org/sites/366.htm*.

Extension Have a group of students create a skit based on the sidebar The Care and Feeding of a King, page 142. Roles can include the king and each of the servants listed in the sidebar.

WRITING

- **Personal Letter** Students can write a letter from the point of view of a person visiting one of the craftspeople at Gran Chimú. The letter writer can remark on the size of Gran Chimú, describe a worker's home, and comment on privileges the craftspeople enjoy.

THEN and NOW

The archaeological site at Chan Chan has been on the World Heritage in Danger list since 1986. The adobe structures at Chan Chan require continuous conservation efforts because adobe is subject to natural erosion when exposed to air and rain. Steps to prevent erosion and theft have been taken.

THE ANCIENT AMERICAN WORLD

NAME _____   DATE _____

TELLING THE TALE OF CHIMOR'S ROCKY START

Directions
Read the legend of Chimor's founding on page 140. Then divide the story into six scenes. In each box, draw one of the scenes and write a caption on the line below the box.

CHAPTER TEST 19

THE ANCIENT AMERICAN WORLD

NAME _____ DATE _____

A. MULTIPLE CHOICE

Circle the letter of the best answer for each question.

1. Taycanamu was important to Chimor because he
   a. came out of the sea.
   b. got rid of the former king.
   c. led the Chimú to the Moche Valley.
   d. taught the Chimú to make gold jewelry.

2. In the dry coastal desert of Chimor, it rained
   a. once a year.
   b. once every 10 years.
   c. once every 30 years.
   d. once every 100 years.

3. When a Chimú king died, his body was mummified and he was buried
   a. in the desert outside Chan Chan.
   b. in his palace compound.
   c. in a pyramid.
   d. in a deep well.

4. In Chimor, "split inheritance" meant that a son who became king
   a. could not inherit his father's property; he had to get his own.
   b. inherited his father's compound.
   c. had to share his father's compound until he got his own.
   d. had to give half his inherited wealth to the poor.

5. The Inca conquered Chimor by
   a. setting fire to Chan Chan.
   b. defeating the king in a duel.
   c. cutting off Chan Chan's water supply.
   d. offering Chimor's people gold to surrender.

B. SHORT ANSWER

Write one or two sentences to answer each question.

6. How does the real history of the Chimú people match the legend of their origins?
   _____
   _____

7. What special privileges did the craftspeople of Chan Chan have?
   _____
   _____

8. Why was conquering new territory of such importance for each new Chimú king?
   _____
   _____

C. WRITING

On a separate sheet of paper, write an essay explaining this statement: "The palace compound was the king's home in both life and death."

THE INCA EMPIRE

PAGES 147–160

Chapter 20 Cuzco Rules: The Inca in the Land of the Four Quarters
Chapter 21 Chosen Girls and Breechcloth Boys: Life in the Inca Empire
Epilogue   The Legacy of the Ancient Americas

UNIT OBJECTIVES

Unit 8 covers the period from 1438 CE through 1532 CE, the short time that the Inca Empire shone so brightly. In this unit your students will learn

- ▶ how the first Inca emperor came to power.
- ▶ how the Inca emperor rewrote history to maintain and expand power.
- ▶ the techniques by which 40,000 Inca were able to rule a kingdom of 10 million non-Inca subjects.
- ▶ what life was like for an Inca boy or girl.

PRIMARY SOURCES

Unit 8 includes excerpts from the following primary sources:

- ▶ Bernabé Cobo, *History of the Inca Empire*
- ▶ *Khipu*

Unit 8 also includes pictures of the following artifacts, which can be analyzed as primary sources:

- ▶ Inca clay watering vessel
- ▶ Guamán Poma
- ▶ Chosen Woman figurine

BIG IDEAS IN UNIT 8

Power and **control** are the big ideas in Unit 8. As the Inca exerted their power, toppling kingdoms and expanding their empire, they used that power to control the population and to expropriate technologies of older cultures, claiming them as Inca originals. Discuss with students how they would feel if someone took credit for an idea of theirs. Explain that in these chapters they will be reading about the Inca who "borrowed" ideas from the peoples they conquered, claiming they were Inca ideas.

GEOGRAPHY CONNECTION

Have students study the map on page 10, showing the Inca Empire in 1525, at its greatest extent. Compare this map to the map on pate 144, showing the pre-Incan cultures to 1100. Use the maps to point out the kingdoms that the Inca conquered on their sweep to power.

TIMELINE

1438 CE	Pachacuti defeats Chanca; Inca expansion begins
1470 CE	Incas conquer Chimú Empire
1471 CE	Pachacuti's son, Topa Inca, becomes emperor
1493 CE	Topa Inca's son, Huayna Capac, becomes emperor
1527 CE	Huayna Capac dies; sons struggle for power
1526 CE	Smallpox spreads through South America
1532 CE	Francisco Pizarro executes Atahualpa; conquers Inca Empire
1535 CE	Pedro de Cieza de León arrives in Peru

UNIT PROJECTS

Unknotting Khipu

A group of interested students can investigate *khipu* by visiting the Peabody Museum's *khipu* database (*http://khipukamayuq.fas.harvard.edu*). The site is primarily for researchers, but there are clear explanations of *khipu* construction and use. The examples and analysis of *khipu*, while complicated, give a sense of its amazing complexity as a communication device.

Saving the Inca High Road

Inca roads were—and still are—engineering marvels. A group of students can investigate a project to conserve and revitalize the ancient Gran Ruta Inca, the High Road. This route through the mountains was a network of ancient footpaths totaling more than 15,000 miles. According to the World Conservation Union, sections of the Gran Ruta Inca in the high Andes are walkable today. Students can present information about the roads of the Inca Empire, their condition today, and plans for their preservation.

Inca Emperors

Have small groups use resources in the library/media center to learn more about the Inca emperors. Have groups research the five emperors included in the book (Chapters 13 and 20): Pachacuti, Topa Inca, Huayna Capac, Huascar Inca, Atahualpa, and Manco Capac. Students should find and report on the length of their reigns, their most important characteristics and accomplishments, and their deaths.

Inca Society

Have small groups use online or print encyclopedias to find out more about the administration of the Inca Empire and the classes of its society. Groups should create and display diagrams showing the organization of Inca administration and society.

ADDITIONAL ASSESSMENT

For Unit 8, divide the class into groups and have them all undertake the Inca Emperors and Inca Society projects so you can assess their knowledge of the Inca Empire. Use the scoring rubric at the back of this guide to assess students' work, and have students rate their own work with the self-assessment rubric. Distribute the library/media center log so students can evaluate their sources as they conduct their research.

LITERATURE CONNECTION

There are some translations of Bernabé Cobo's works available online and in print. Students can benefit by reading excerpts with a partner or parent, or you can read sections out loud. Suggest some of the following books to students:

- Cobo, Bernabé. *History of the Inca Empire*. Translated by Roland Hamilton. Austin, TX: University of Texas Press, 1983. Nonfiction. ADVANCED The book is an account of the character, appearance, and dress of the Inca people as well as a superb resource of Inca legends, history, and social institutions.
- Daniel, A. B. *Incas: The Puma's Shadow*. New York: Simon & Schuster, 2002. Fiction. AVERAGE. A tale of splendor and savagery unfolds as the Incan civilization is haunted by omens, shaken by civil war, and shattered by European conquest.
- Martell, Hazel. *Civilizations of Peru: Before 1535*. Austin, TX: Raintree Steck-Vaughn, 1997. Nonfiction. AVERAGE. The book is an examination of several of the more important ancient civilizations of Peru, including the Inca, Chavin, Paracas, Nazca, Moche, Tiahuanaco, Huari, and Chimu.

UNIVERSAL ACCESS

The following strategies are designed to cover a range of learning styles and reading, language, and skill levels. This section includes suggestions for differentiating instruction to meet the diverse needs of your students.

Reading Strategies

- Have students use a K-W-L chart to assist them in their reading about the Inca. Preview Chapters 20 and 21 and have students fill in the first column of the chart with what they *know* about the subject. Have them write what they *want to know* about the subject in the second column. When they are finished with the chapters, have them complete the third column by writing what they *learned*.
- Instead of having a chronological organization, Chapter 21 deals with several subtopics under the general topic of controlling the population. Have students create main idea statements for each subtopic. Then have them point out details or examples that support the main ideas.
- Many more of the illustrations in Guamán Poma's *Letters to a King* are viewable online at the Royal Library of Denmark website: *www.kb.dk/elib/mss/poma/index-en.htm*. Students can look at these pictures to get a better idea of what Poma's letters were about.

Writing Strategies

- After reading Chapter 20, have students write a paragraph explaining "expropriation" of other cultures' ideas as a tactic of the Inca.
- Ask students to write a short essay explaining how the Four Quarters division of the Inca Empire helped the emperor control it.
- Encourage students to write an essay comparing and contrasting the education of boys and girls in the Inca Empire.
- Have students use the Main Idea and Details graphic organizer at the back of this guide to organize information in this unit. For example, students can write *Inca Government* in the central circle, and fill the surrounding circles with details about the emperor, the division of the empire into four quarters, the administration of the empire, and so on. Other topics include Inca religion, Inca borrowings, and Inca life.

Listening and Speaking Strategies

- Have pairs of students read this unit, one chapter per student. Each group member should take notes on the reading. Pairs can compare notes about what they learned about Pachacuti and daily life in the Inca Empire.
- Have students present first-person reports of the following events: attending a human sacrifice selection event; hearing about Huayna Capac's fateful

dream; and listening to Pachacuti define himself as a god. In their reports students should convey a sense of the audience's mood.
- ▶ Have student volunteers read passages from the material written by Garcilaso de la Vega and Bartholomé de las Casas in *The World in Ancient Times Primary Sources and Reference Volume* aloud to the class to reinforce details in the unit.

UNIT VOCABULARY LIST

The following words that appear in Unit 8 are important for your students' understanding of the social studies content as well as for development of literacy. Use these words for vocabulary study or to reinforce language arts skills (e.g., synonyms, compound words, prefixes and suffixes, and related words). The words are listed below in the order in which they appear in the chapters.

Chapter 20
insignificant
successor
slingshot
showcase
addictive
coincidence
subjugate
divine
hostage
currency
decimal

Chapter 21
sheltered
spindle
dormitory
famished
breechcloth
rebellious
mutiny
exile
pestilence
epidemic
quest

CUZCO RULES: THE INCA IN THE LAND OF THE FOUR QUARTERS

PAGES 147–152

FOR HOMEWORK

STUDENT STUDY GUIDE
pages 49–50

CAST OF CHARACTERS

Pachacuti (pah-chah-KOO-tee) first Inca emperor; name means "cataclysm," or "He Who Remakes the World" in Quechua

Guamán Poma (gwa-MAHN PO-mah) native South American who wrote about and drew pictures of the Inca world

 WRITING

- **Persuasion** Have students write a letter from the point of view of a Chimú, now a subject of the Inca Empire. The letter should try to persuade a Chimú friend to either accept or reject the emperor Pachacuti's view that Inca are the best and other cultures are inferior.

CHAPTER SUMMARY

Winning wasn't *just* an option for the Inca; it was the *only* option. Pachacuti, their first emperor, burst on the scene in 1438 with a victory over the Chanca. He never looked back, and he went on to rewrite history, launching an empire and a dynasty and expanding his power until the Inca had swallowed far older cultures, like Chimor.

PERFORMANCE OBJECTIVES

- To explain Pachacuti's goals and the nature of the Inca Empire he created
- To define some of the ways the Inca controlled conquered people in their empire
- To summarize the ways the Inca "borrowed" ideas and technology from other cultures and claimed them as their own

BUILDING BACKGROUND

Remind students that they read about the Inca in Chapter 13, which described the end of the Inca Empire and the victory of Francisco Pizarro. Explain that now they have an opportunity to learn how the Inca Empire started, how it expanded, and how it ruled its subjects in its brief history (less than 100 years).

WORKING WITH PRIMARY SOURCES

Have students read the excerpts from the work of Garcilaso de la Vega in *World in Ancient Times Primary Sources and Reference Volume* to learn more about the first Inca king and the splendor of the Inca palaces.

GEOGRAPHY CONNECTION

Region   Refer students to the map of the Inca Empire on page 101. Have them use the map scale to calculate the size of the empire at its greatest extent.

READING COMPREHENSION QUESTIONS

1. How did Pachacuti react when the powerful Chanca army attacked Cuzco in 1438 CE? (*He defended the kingdom although his father and brother ran away.*)
2. How did Pachacuti convince people he was the son of the sun god, Inti? (*He made up a story, one that was remembered hundreds of years later.*)
3. What was the old Wari system of "give to me, I'll give to you"? (*The government provided food and supplies in time of need in return for people's working for the government.*)
4. Pachacuti tried to erase all pre-Inca history. How do we know he didn't succeed? (*Today's archaeologists and historians have uncovered evidence of older cultures; storytellers in the past kept the ideas and accomplishments of older cultures alive.*)

CRITICAL THINKING QUESTIONS

1. How do the authors describe Pachacuti's methods of gaining and keeping personal control of the Inca Empire? (*"proceeded to crown himself king"; "erased his brother from memory"; "reshaped kingdoms as if they were fresh clay"; "oldest royal trick"; "borrowed from older cultures but made sure Inca got all the credit"; "fooled everyone with his official Inca history"*)
2. What were some of the ways that 40,000 Inca controlled 10 million non-Inca? (*Everyone had to learn Quechua so that there was a single [single? or common?] language; local leaders became emperor's commanders and tax collectors; improved roads meant better communications; and the warehouse system meant no one went hungry.*)
3. What kind of power did the interpreters of *khipu* have? (*They were among the very few people in the empire who understood what was being communicated by* khipu, *so theoretically it was possible for them to influence decisions by manipulating the making and interpretation of* khipu.)
4. Distribute copies of the blackline master for Chapter 20. In completing the activity, students will appreciate the extent to which the Inca appropriated the ideas of other cultures.

SOCIAL SCIENCES

Economics   The Inca Empire had no currency. Define *currency* and discuss with students the benefits or drawbacks of an economy without currency. Ask them to imagine their lives without it. Then ask: Are credit cards and on-line shopping making currency unnecessary?

READING AND LANGUAGE ARTS

Reading Nonfiction   Point out the reference to the Internal Revenue Service on page 151. Ask students whether this reference and the joking remark, *Inca Revenue Service*, help or distract readers trying to understand taxation in the Inca Empire.

Using Language   Invite students to read the first paragraph of the chapter aloud. Discuss the figurative language: "a tiny mole" and "a fleck of dust on the face of." Define any unfamiliar words. Have students write original sentences using figurative language of their own.

SUPPORTING LEARNING

Struggling Readers   Have students complete a timeline graphic organizer (see the back of this guide) order to understand how the Inca Empire got its start.

EXTENDING LEARNING

Enrichment   Invite a group of students to investigate and report on the Khipu Data Base website, part of the Peabody Library at Harvard University *http://khipukamayuq.fas.harvard.edu/index.html*. The group can give the class a sense of the complexity of *khipu* and an idea of the purpose of the database.

Extension   Have students role-play a scene in which Pachacuti, having taken command of the Inca at Cuzco and won the battle, declares himself emperor and commands that his brother be erased from memory. Other characters can play the role of his generals and other advisors. Students can decide what the Inca people felt about Pachacuti's meteoric rise to power.

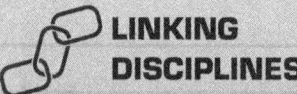

LINKING DISCIPLINES

Art   Have a group of students prepare a display of Inca art with images from the Peabody Museum's website (listed on the Websites page of the student book) or from other print or online resources.

THEN and NOW

Every year, tens of thousands of tourists visit the 500-year-old Inca city of Machu Picchu, high in the Andes Mountains. It has been suggested that a cable car be built to make it possible for more people to get there. But some people worry that the ancient ruins are already suffering from too much tourism and are at risk of landslides. They suggest limiting the number of tourists. Have students write a list of questions they would like answered to help them form an opinion about limiting or encouraging tourism to the site.

THE ANCIENT AMERICAN WORLD

CHAPTER 20

THE ANCIENT AMERICAN WORLD

BORROWING FROM OLDER CULTURES

Directions

Use the chart below to identify ideas and ways of doing things that the Inca borrowed from older cultures such as the Chimú or Wari. In the left column are ideas that Pachacuti claimed were Inca ideas. In the right column, record the names of the people who had each idea first. Then answer the question below, using complete sentences.

"It's an Inca idea!"	"It was our idea first!"
1. Terraced fields on high mountains	
2. *Khipu*	
3. Warehouses of supplies for emergencies	
4. Free feasts in exchange for working for the government	
5. Staff God	
6. Vertical irrigation canals in mountains	
7. Split inheritance	
8. Mummifying the royal family	

Pachacuti claimed that the Andean people who came before the Inca were "uncivilized savages." Write a paragraph stating your opinion of Pachacuti's statement. Support your opinion with details from the chart. Include what you think Pachacuti was trying to do by making this statement.

_____
_____
_____
_____

NAME   DATE

A. MULTIPLE CHOICE

Circle the letter of the best answer for each question.

1. Before Pachacuti became emperor, he was
   - a. next in line to rule Cuzco.
   - b. a soldier in the Cuzco army.
   - c. a farmer in Cuzco.
   - d. second in line to be ruler of Cuzco.

2. Pachacuti convinced people in his empire that he was royal by telling them
   - a. the sun god was his father.
   - b. his own father was a king.
   - c. he was the sun god.
   - d. he worshipped the sun god.

3. The royal dynasty Pachacuti founded ruled for
   - a. hundreds of years.
   - b. 100 years.
   - c. almost 100 years.
   - d. less than 50 years.

4. Inca messengers traveled quickly over the empire's network of roads and trails
   - a. on foot.
   - b. on horseback.
   - c. in carriages pulled by llamas.
   - d. in vehicles pulled by people.

5. The Inca system of split inheritance and mummifying members of the royal family after death
   - a. was an original idea of Pachacuti's.
   - b. came from the Chimú culture.
   - c. was originally used in Chavín.
   - d. did not continue under Pachacuti.

B. SHORT ANSWER

Write one or two sentences to answer each question.

6. Why was the Inca Empire known as the Land of Four Quarters?

7. How did Inca army commanders get people to provide the labor for projects like building roads?

8. How did the Inca Empire improve on the *ayllu* system?

C. ESSAY

On a separate sheet of paper, write an essay explaining this statement: "Pachacuti tried to erase thousands of years of pre-Inca history."

CHAPTER 21
CHOSEN GIRLS AND BREECHCLOTH BOYS: LIFE IN THE INCA EMPIRE
PAGES 153–158

FOR HOMEWORK
STUDENT STUDY GUIDE
pages 51–52

CAST OF CHARACTERS

Pachacuti (pah-chah-KOO-tee) first Inca emperor; name means "cataclysm" or "He Who Remakes the World" in Quechua

Huayna Capac (WHY-nah KAH-pahk) powerful late Inca emperor; his name means "excellent youth" in Quechua

Pizarro, Francisco (fran-CEES-co pee-SAHR-ro) conquistador who took over Inca Empire for Spain

 **VOCABULARY**

Mama Kona "Mother" + "Chosen Woman" in Quechua

mitmaq (MEET-mahk) Incan colonizers; Quechua for "displaced people"

CHAPTER SUMMARY

The chapter takes us into the lives of boys and girls in the Inca Empire. The empire's control extended to the lives of its youngest inhabitants, and their choices in life were strictly limited. But the control of the Inca came at a price—revolts on the part of conquered peoples were common. By the time of the last emperor, the Inca Empire was deeply divided.

PERFORMANCE OBJECTIVES

▶ To explain the expectations and demands on boys and girls in the Inca Empire
▶ To define some of the ways the Inca controlled people, even children
▶ To describe the internal disarray of the Inca Empire at the time the Spaniards invaded

BUILDING BACKGROUND

Begin a discussion of the high expectations the Inca had for their children and of the limited roles that they could play by talking about choices your students have made and will make in their lives. Point out that their freedoms are far beyond the wildest imaginings of the Inca youth they will be reading about.

WORKING WITH PRIMARY SOURCES

Have students read the excerpt from Bartholomé de las Casas's book on the destruction of the Indies in *The World in Ancient Times Primary Sources and Reference Volume*. Use this excerpt as a springboard to discuss how people of different cultures interact.

GEOGRAPHY CONNECTION

Movement Have students review the map on page 101 showing the extent of the Inca Empire at the time of Huayna Capac's death. Have students identify northern Ecuador, the area Huayna Capac was planning to conquer next.

READING COMPREHENSION QUESTIONS

1. Explain the significance of these ceremonies focused on children: hair-cutting; selection at age 10 (girls); selection at age 14 (girls); naming at age 14 (boys); naming at age 14 (girls). (*hair-cutting—temporary name given to child learning to walk; selection at age 10 (girls)—sacrificed or sent to House of Chosen Women for education; selection at age 14 (girls)—sacrificed or became Mama Konas; naming at age 14 (boys)—celebrated a boy's maturity; naming at age 14 (girls)—celebrated a girl's maturity*)
2. How did the government get involved in marriages? (*If two men wanted to marry the same woman, the commander of their district would decide which man could marry her.*)
3. What part of Huayna Capac's dream came true? (*He dreamed about pestilence and died of smallpox along with many others.*)

4. Why do the authors say "the empire was too divided" to stop the Spaniards' conquest? (*There were rebellions among subjects, disagreements among nobles over Huayna Capac's actions, and attempted overexpansion of the empire.*)
5. Distribute copies of the blackline master for Chapter 21 so students can assess the legacies of Ancient America and Europe as described in the Epilogue.

CRITICAL THINKING QUESTIONS

1. How do you think people felt when their child was selected for sacrifice? (*Possible answer: As Incas, they were honored; as parents, they felt regret.*)
2. The *mitmaq* system was supposed to control rebellions. Do you think it worked? (*Responses will vary. Some students may think that the relocated Incas who were supposed to be good examples might have become rebellious because they were relocated and that the rebels who were removed would have become even more restless.*)

SOCIAL SCIENCES

Science, Technology, and Society   Have students expand on the information about the classification of human toolmaking in the sidebar Hard Rock, Heavy Metal (page 153). They can define the three ages and give examples of specific tools and cultures that used them. We are living in what has been the Information Age. Have students assess the usefulness of that description of human toolmaking today.

READING AND LANGUAGE ARTS

Reading Nonfiction   Have students read the first paragraph of the chapter and identify the phrase that is the main point of the chapter, linking the treatment of children and how the empire became so powerful ("*they had almost total control of Inca subjects, including children*"). Ask students to identify the topics covered in the chapter that are related to this main idea of control.

Using Language   Direct students to look at the sidebar From Head to Toe on page 157 and to identify the adjectives and nouns. Invite students to write descriptions of what they are wearing using adjectives and nouns and to share the results with the class.

SUPPORTING LEARNING

Struggling Readers   To better understand the chapter, have students create a main idea and details graphic organizer (see the back of this guide).

EXTENDING LEARNING

Enrichment   Have a group of students prepare a report on an Inca girl sacrificed high in the Andes whose mummy was discovered in 1996. Students can read about her in Johan Reinhard's *Discovering the Inca Ice Maiden* (National Geographic Society, 1998) and find information online at *www.archaeology.org/ 9601/newsbriefs/icewoman.html*. They can view a virtual autopsy of the mummy at *www.nationalgeographic.com/andes/autopsy/intro.html*. Assign a group of students to read the book, view the autopsy, and then report to the class.

Extension   Have students present the pros and cons of life as a member of "Team Inca" in a panel discussion. Students can take the roles of rebels, team-player *mitmaqs*, and Inca authorities. A moderator can call on the panel speakers to answer questions based on information in the chapter.

WRITING

- **Poetry** Have students write a poem about the children in this chapter, the "Chosen Girls" and "Breechcloth Boys." Students can write the poem as an acrostic so that the first letters of each line in a stanza spells *Inca*, or can write a poem in the shape of a mountain, such as the one where the Ice Maiden was found.

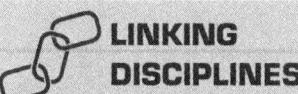

LINKING DISCIPLINES

Science Have a group of students investigate volcanoes in the Andes. The activity of one volcano, Sambancaya, disrupted the resting place of the Inca Ice Maiden. Students can report to the class about other volcanoes, their elevation, and the potential impact on the people who live there.

THE ANCIENT AMERICAN WORLD

CHARTING LEGACIES

Directions
Some of the items in the chart are legacies of ancient Americans, some are legacies of the Europeans who conquered the Americas, and some are common to both cultures. For each item, indicate with a check mark which culture it came from. Where an item is a legacy of both, check both columns.

Americas	Legacy	Europe
	1. chocolate	
	2. horse	
	3. potatoes	
	4. art	
	5. cattle	
	6. architecture	
	7. wheel	
	8. maize (corn)	
	9. mathematics	
	10. goats	
	11. books	
	12. chicken	
	13. vertical irrigation	
	14. metal plow	
	15. peanuts	
	16. sheep	
	17. rubber	
	18. calendar	
	19. ball games	
	20. roads	

Choose one legacy of the ancient Americans. On a separate sheet of paper, write a paragraph explaining its importance to us today.

CHAPTER TEST 21

THE ANCIENT AMERICAN WORLD

A. MULTIPLE CHOICE

Circle the letter of the best answer for each question.

1. The Inca emperors created the largest Bronze Age empire by
   a. maintaining total control over their subjects.
   b. allowing their subjects to live as they chose.
   c. controlling only adult subjects.
   d. controlling only children.

2. Life turned serious for 10-year-old girls because they could be
   a. married at that age.
   b. picked to be human sacrifices.
   c. sent as hostages to other emperors.
   d. stricken with a disease.

3. In the Inca Empire, the larger the family
   a. the less land it had for its own use.
   b. the more land it had for its own use.
   c. the fewer duties the children had.
   d. the greater the time for playing.

4. If people in an area rebelled, the Inca authorities might
   a. put them in prison.
   b. exile them to other areas.
   c. execute them.
   d. take their children to be sacrificed.

5. The growing pains of the empire during the rule of Huayna Capac included all of the following **except**
   a. revolts by conquered peoples.
   b. a plague of moths.
   c. less land to bring in tribute.
   d. unhappiness of Inca nobles.

B. SHORT ANSWER

Write one or two sentences to answer each question.

6. How did the Inca government control the lives of young girls?

7. What were some reasons that people would rebel against the empire?

8. Who were the *mitmaq*, and why were there so many of them in the Inca Empire?

C. ESSAY

On a separate sheet of paper, write an essay explaining this statement: "In the Inca world it was a high honor to be chosen for sacrifice."

WRAP-UP TEST

THE ANCIENT AMERICAN WORLD

NAME _____ **DATE** _____

Directions

Answer each of the following questions on a separate sheet of paper.

1. Agriculture was central to life in Mesoamerica and South America. The following is a list of some of the crops and techniques that originated in the Americas:

   ▶ potatoes
   ▶ chocolate (cacao)
   ▶ maize, squash, and beans (the Three Sisters)
   ▶ vertical irrigation
   ▶ mounded-earth fields surrounded by water-filled ditches

   For each crop on the list, tell with which part of the Americas it was first associated. Then write a sentence for each technique explaining what it is and why it was used.

2. For each city, explain its location and then write a paragraph describing a sight you might have seen there in its heyday.

   ▶ Teotihuacan
   ▶ Palenque (Bone)
   ▶ Chichén Itzá
   ▶ Tenochtitlan
   ▶ Chavín
   ▶ Machu Picchu

3. Mesoamericans were the only ancient people in the Americas to invent a system of writing. Write a paragraph explaining which Mesoamerican culture produced the most writing, describe their writing, and give an example of where their writing can be seen today.

4. Volcanoes, rainforests, high mountains, rivers, coastal deserts—the landforms and climate of the Americas affected agriculture, trade, communication, and conquest. Write two paragraphs. In one, explain how the location of Chichén Itzá helped the Putún Maya. In the other, explain where the system of *ayllu* began and why it was a good solution to a problem based on geography.

5. Copy this idea web on a separate sheet of paper to describe the civilization of the Maya. Tell why their hieroglyphs are important; why their calendar was created; and what happened to their cities.

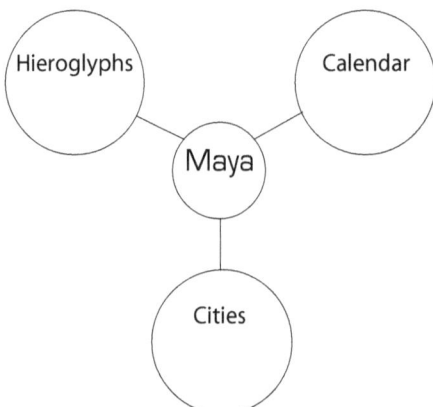

136 WRAP-UP TEST

6. Make an idea web like the one in question 5 to tell about the Aztec Empire. Write *Aztec Empire* in the central circle. In the surrounding circles, describe the location of the empire, what the Triple Alliance was, and the rights of women in the empire.
7. Make an idea web like the one in question 6 to tell about the Inca Empire. Write *Inca Empire* in the central circle. In the surrounding circles, describe the location of the empire, how it was organized, and how the Inca kept records without a written language.
8. Match each of these quotations from the book with the correct civilization (either Maya, Aztec, Inca, or Toltec). Then write a sentence explaining what the quote tells about the civilization.
    a. "The gods agreed to sacrifice themselves so the Fifth Sun would rise each day."
    b. "'Come here, my child. Have no fear for I am your father, the Sun; I know that you will subjugate [conquer] many nations and take care to . . . remember me in your sacrifices.'"
    c. "Then he fixes his eyes on Tula and in that moment begins to weep. . . . His tears drop by drop perforate [pierce] the stones."
    d. "This is the stone of K'inich Yax K'uk' Mo'."
9. Both Itzcoatl and Pachacuti rewrote history to make themselves more powerful. Write a paragraph about each man explaining who he was and giving an example of how he rewrote history.
10. Match each person with his or her description. Then choose one of the people and on a separate sheet of paper write a paragraph explaining why he or she is remembered.

    _____ Malintzin
    _____ Lady S'ak K'uk'
    _____ Moctezuma
    _____ Hernán Cortés
    _____ Francisco Pizarro
    _____ Atahualpa
    _____ Topiltzin Quetzalcoatl (TQ)
    _____ Lord of Sipán

    a. Spaniard who took advantage of unrest in Inca Empire and conquered it
    b. Last Aztec emperor
    c. Queen who put her 12-year-old son on the throne and restored a Maya dynasty
    d. Slave and translator who aided Spanish conquistador in conquest of Aztecs
    e. Moche warrior-priest buried with beautifully crafted gold jewelry
    f. Spaniard who tricked and killed Aztec leader and then conquered Aztec Empire
    g. Inca leader who was tricked and killed by Pizarro
    h. Legendary Mesoamerican figure linked to feathered serpent god and city of Tula

GRAPHIC ORGANIZERS

GUIDELINES

Reproducibles of seven different graphic organizers are provided on the following pages. These give your students a variety of ways to sort and order all the information they are receiving in this course. Use the organizers for homework assignments, classroom activities, tests, small group projects, and as ways to help the students take notes as they read.

1. Determine which graphic organizers work best for the content you are teaching. Some are useful for identifying main ideas and details; others work better for making comparisons, and so on.

2. Graphic organizers help students focus on the central points of the lesson while leaving out irrelevant details.

3. Use graphic organizers to give a visual picture of the key ideas you are teaching.

4. Graphic organizers can help students recall important information. Suggest students use them to study for tests.

5. Graphic organizers provide a visual way to show the connections between different content areas.

6. Graphic organizers can enliven traditional lesson plans and encourage greater interactivity within the classroom.

7. Apply graphic organizers to give students a concise, visual way to break down complex ideas.

8. Encourage students to use graphic organizers to identify patterns and clarify their ideas.

9. Graphic organizers stimulate creative thinking in the classroom, in small groups, and for the individual student.

10. Help students determine which graphic organizers work best for their purposes, and encourage them to use graphic organizers collaboratively whenever they can.

11. Help students customize graphic organizers when necessary; e.g., make more or fewer boxes, lines, or blanks, if dictated by the exercise..

OUTLINE

MAIN IDEA: _____
_____
_____

DETAIL: _____
_____

DETAIL: _____
_____

DETAIL: _____
_____

MAIN IDEA: _____
_____
_____

DETAIL: _____
_____

DETAIL: _____
_____

DETAIL: _____
_____

Name _____   Date _____

MAIN IDEA MAP

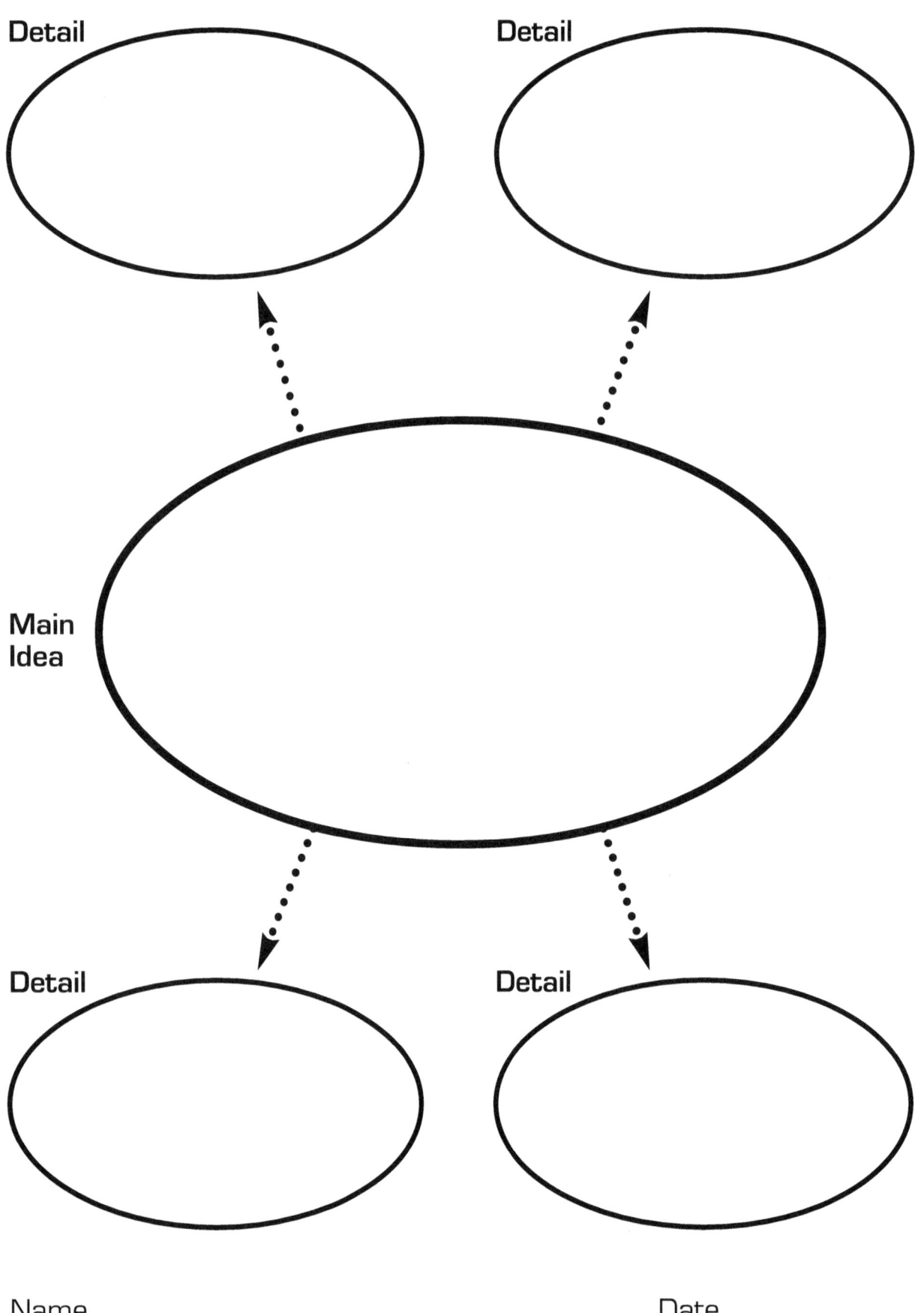

Name _____ Date _____

K-W-L CHART

K	W	L
What I Know	What I Want to Know	What I Learned

Name _____ Date _____

VENN DIAGRAM

Write differences in the circles. Write similarities where the circles overlap.

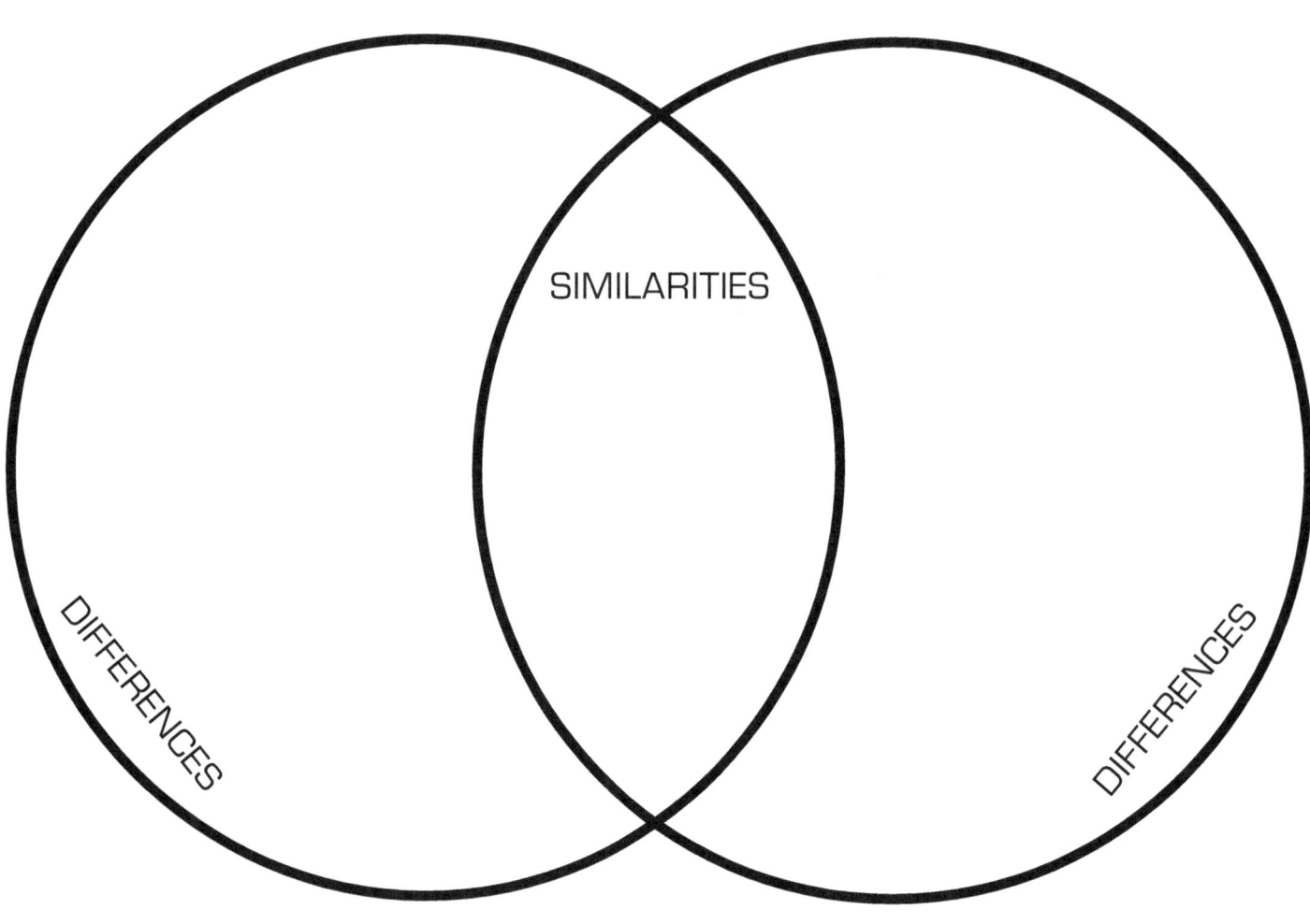

Name _____ Date _____

TIMELINE

DATE

EVENT Draw lines to connect the event to the correct year on the timeline.

Name _____ Date _____

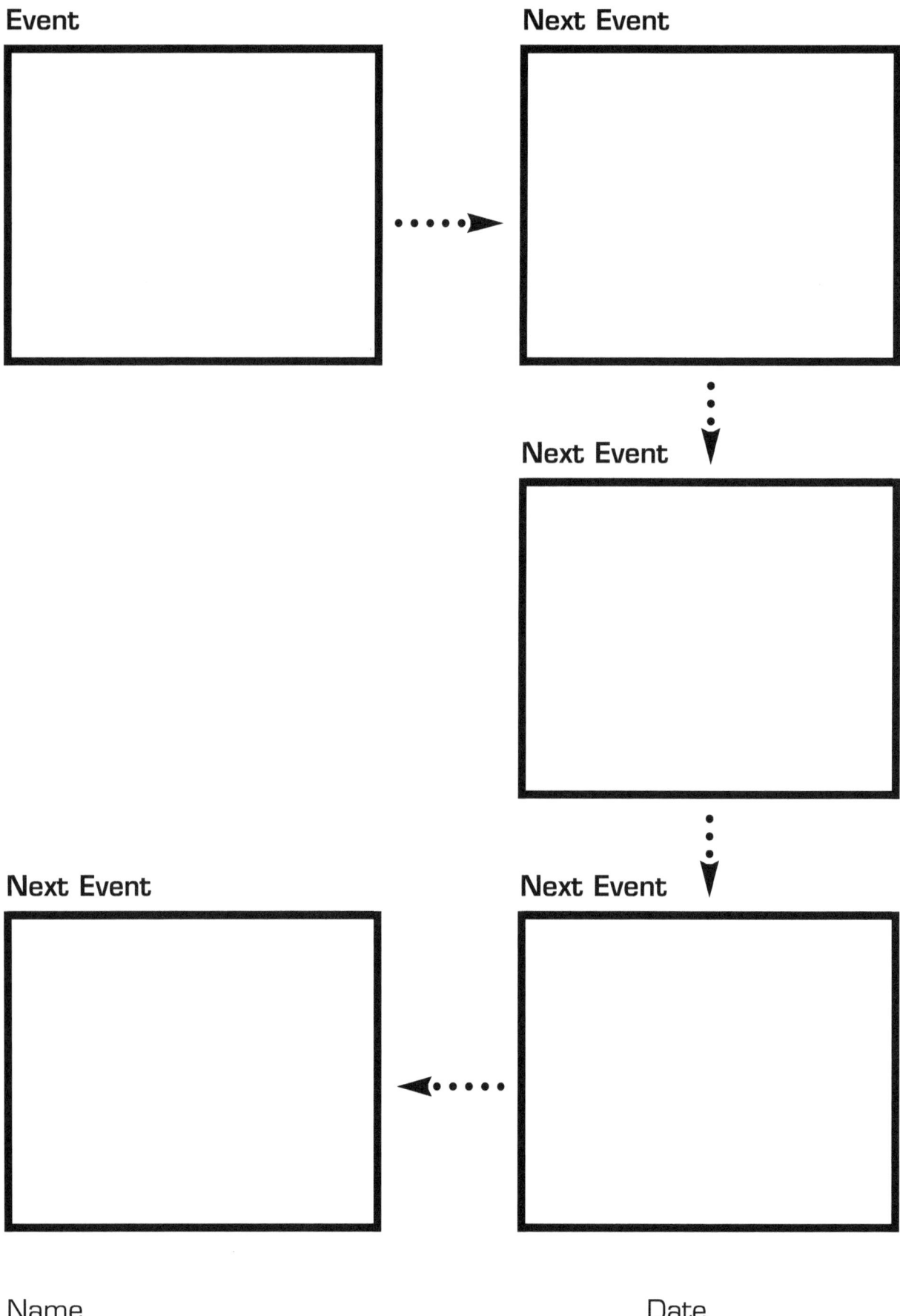

T-CHART

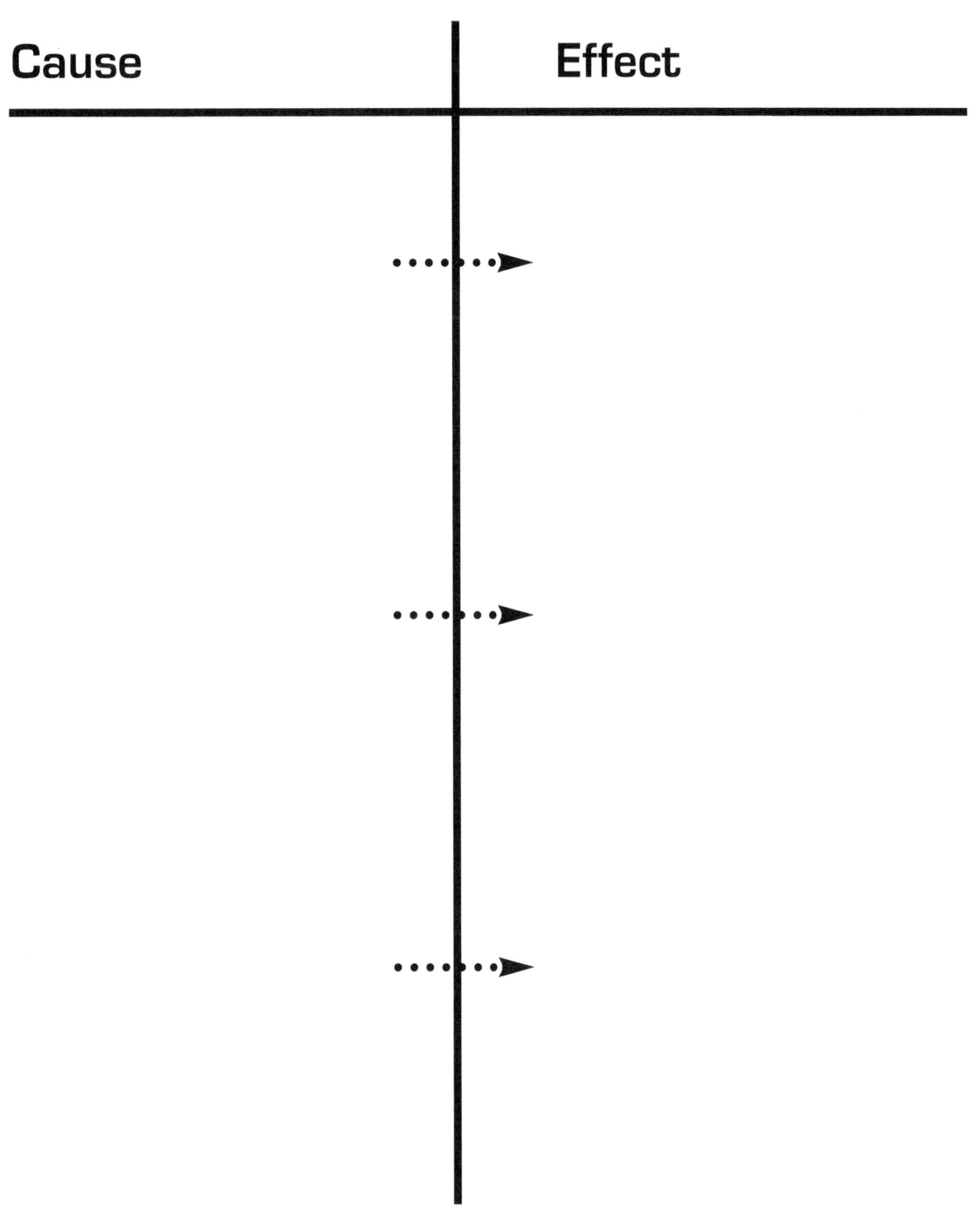

Cause | Effect

Name _____ Date _____

SCORING RUBRIC

The reproducibles on the following pages have been adapted from this rubric for use as handouts and a student self-scoring activity, with added focus on planning, cooperation, revision and presentation. You may wish to tailor the self-scoring activity—for example, asking students to comment on how low scores could be improved, or focusing only on specific rubric points. Use the Library/Media Center Research Log to help students focus and evaluate their research for projects and assignments.

As with any rubric, you should introduce and explain the rubric before students begin their assignments. The more thoroughly your students understand how they will be evaluated, the better prepared they will be to produce projects that fulfill your expectations.

	ORGANIZATION	CONTENT	ORAL/WRITTEN CONVENTIONS	GROUP PARTICIPATION
4	• Clearly addresses all parts of the writing task. • Demonstrates a clear understanding of purpose and audience. • Maintains a consistent point of view, focus, and organizational structure, including the effective use of transitions. • Includes a clearly presented central idea with relevant facts, details, and/or explanations.	• Demonstrates that the topic was well researched. • Uses only information that was essential and relevant to the topic. • Presents the topic thoroughly and accurately. • Reaches reasonable conclusions clearly based on evidence.	• Contains few, if any, errors in grammar, punctuation, capitalization, or spelling. • Uses a variety of sentence types. • Speaks clearly, using effective volume and intonation.	• Demonstrated high levels of participation and effective decision making. • Planned well and used time efficiently. • Demonstrated ability to negotiate opinions fairly and reach compromise when needed. • Utilized effective visual aids.
3	• Addresses all parts of the writing task. • Demonstrates a general understanding of purpose and audience. • Maintains a mostly consistent point of view, focus, and organizational structure, including the effective use of some transitions. • Presents a central idea with mostly relevant facts, details, and/or explanations.	• Demonstrates that the topic was sufficiently researched. • Uses mainly information that was essential and relevant to the topic. • Presents the topic accurately but leaves some aspects unexplored. • Reaches reasonable conclusions loosely related to evidence.	• Contains some errors in grammar, punctuation, capitalization, or spelling. • Uses a variety of sentence types. • Speaks somewhat clearly, using effective volume and intonation.	• Demonstrated good participation and decision making with few distractions. • Planning and used its time acceptably. • Demonstrated ability to negotiate opinions and compromise with little aggression or unfairness.
2	• Addresses only parts of the writing task. • Demonstrates little understanding of purpose and audience. • Maintains an inconsistent point of view, focus, and/or organizational structure, which may include ineffective or awkward transitions that do not unify important ideas. • Suggests a central idea with limited facts, details, and/or explanations.	• Demonstrates that the topic was minimally researched. • Uses a mix of relevant and irrelevant information. • Presents the topic with some factual errors and leaves some aspects unexplored. • Reaches conclusions that do not stem from evidence presented in the project.	• Contains several errors in grammar, punctuation, capitalization, or spelling. These errors may interfere with the reader's understanding of the writing. • Uses little variety in sentence types. • Speaks unclearly or too quickly. May interfere with the audience's understanding of the project.	• Demonstrated uneven participation or was often off-topic. Task distribution was lopsided. • Did not show a clear plan for the project, and did not use time well. • Allowed one or two opinions to dominate the activity, or had trouble reaching a fair consensus.
1	• Addresses only one part of the writing task. • Demonstrates no understanding of purpose and audience. • Lacks a point of view, focus, organizational structure, and transitions that unify important ideas. • Lacks a central idea but may contain marginally related facts, details, and/or explanations.	• Demonstrates that the topic was poorly researched. • Does not discriminate relevant from irrelevant information. • Presents the topic incompletely, with many factual errors. • Did not reach conclusions.	• Contains serious errors in grammar, punctuation, capitalization, or spelling. These errors interfere with the reader's understanding of the writing. • Uses no sentence variety. • Speaks unclearly. The audience must struggle to understand the project.	• Demonstrated poor participation by the majority of the group. Tasks were completed by a small minority. • Failed to show planning or effective use of time. • Was dominated by a single voice, or allowed hostility to derail the project.

NAME _____ **PROJECT** _____

DATE _____

ORGANIZATION & FOCUS	CONTENT	ORAL/WRITTEN CONVENTIONS	GROUP PARTICIPATION

COMMENTS AND SUGGESTIONS

UNDERSTANDING YOUR SCORE

Organization: Your project should be clear, focused on a main idea, and organized. You should use details and facts to support your main idea.

Content: You should use strong research skills. Your project should be thorough and accurate.

Oral/Written Conventions: For writing projects, you should use good composition, grammar, punctuation, and spelling, with a good variety of sentence types. For oral projects, you should engage the class using good public speaking skills.

Group Participation: Your group should cooperate fairly and use its time well to plan, assign and revise the tasks involved in the project.

NAME _____ GROUP MEMBERS _____

_____
_____
_____

Use this worksheet to describe your project by finishing the sentences below.
For individual projects and writing assignments, use the "How I did" section.
For group projects, use both "How I did" and "How we did" sections.

The purpose of this project is to :

[   ]

Scoring Key =   **4** – extremely well
                3 – well
                2 – could have been better
                1 – not well at all

HOW I DID

I understood the purpose and requirements for this project…

I planned and organized my time and work…

This project showed clear organization that emphasized the central idea…

I supported my point with details and description…

I polished and revised this project…

I utilized correct grammar and good writing/speaking style…

Overall, this project met its purpose…

HOW WE DID

We divided up tasks…

We cooperated and listened to each other…

We talked through what we didn't understand…

We used all our time to make this project the best it could be…

Overall, as a group we worked together…

I contributed and cooperated with the team…

NAME _____

LIBRARY/ MEDIA CENTER RESEARCH LOG

DUE DATE _____

What I Need to Find

Brainstorm: Other Sources and Places to Look

Places I **Know** to Look

I need to use:
- ☐ primary
- ☐ secondary

____ sources.

WHAT I FOUND

Title/Author/Location (call # or URL)

	Book/Periodical	Website	Other	Primary Source	Secondary Source	Suggestion	Library Catalog	Browsing	Internet Search	Web link	**How I Found it**	helpful	relevant
_____	☐	☐	☐	☐	☐	☐	☐	☐	☐	☐		_____	_____
_____	☐	☐	☐	☐	☐	☐	☐	☐	☐	☐		_____	_____
_____	☐	☐	☐	☐	☐	☐	☐	☐	☐	☐		_____	_____
_____	☐	☐	☐	☐	☐	☐	☐	☐	☐	☐		_____	_____
_____	☐	☐	☐	☐	☐	☐	☐	☐	☐	☐		_____	_____
_____	☐	☐	☐	☐	☐	☐	☐	☐	☐	☐		_____	_____

Rate each source from 1 (low) to 4 (high) in the categories below

ANSWER KEY

CHAPTER 1

Blackline Master

2. The climate would be tropical: hot and humid near the coasts, all year round.
3. a) 19° N and 99° W; b) 26° N and 98° W; c) 23° N and 90° W.
4. Sierra Madre Occidental; Sierra Madre Oriental

Chapter Test   **A. 1.** d   **2.** b   **3.** a   **4.** b   **5.** d

B. 6. Women prepared and cooked food, spun and wove cloth, and made storage jars. Men built houses, planted and harvested maize, shucked kernels, made tools, and hunted deer.
7. A midden contains all of the things that ancient people have thrown away. An archaeologist could find many artifacts there.
8. It tells what work people did and specific details about how to do those jobs well.
C. Students' essays will vary but should support the idea that ancient Mesoamericans needed goods from different places in the region to survive.

CHAPTER 2

Blackline Master

Use Radiocarbon Dating: animal bone, charcoal, human bone, fossilized seeds. *Use Another Method:* clay bowl, stone tool, gold, basalt chips, stone beads. Students' paragraphs will vary, but should indicate that knowing the dates of formerly living things is important in placing an archaeological site in time.

Chapter Test   **A. 1.** d   **2.** b   **3.** d   **4.** b   **5.** a

B. 6. They became rich by trading the extra maize they were able to grow.
7. Good harvests meant you had extra food to trade and could become rich. This allowed you to hold a feast and gain influence over other people.
8. One theory is that San Lorenzo was invaded by another Olmec group. Another theory is that volcanic eruptions changed the routes of the rivers, interrupting trade and robbing the people of their wealth.
C. Students' essays will vary but should include details about the finds that archaeologists have made and the dates assigned to those finds.

CHAPTER 3

Blackline Master

Monte Albán: 500 BCE–900 CE; city was built because Zapotec abandoned their other towns and moved to a place where they could please the rain god with sacrificial blood; notable architecture includes market, reservoir, palaces, sunken patio, ball court, and temples; building materials include stone, stucco; farming techniques include terraces, irrigation; more than 20,000 residents; city might have been abandoned because of competition from other cities or city became too large to govern; sports included ball games; water source was rivers in the surrounding valleys; advantages of location were central location linking three valleys; disadvantages of location were dry mountain. *El Mirador:* 350–200 BCE; city was built to take advantage of new farming lands and jungle wildlife; notable architecture includes Tigre Pyramid, raised roads, and the Danta Complex; building materials include stone, stucco, limestone powder; farming techniques include raised fields fertilized with organic matter from swamps; number of residents is unknown; city might have been abandoned after too many trees were cleared and erosion spoiled the farm fields; sports are unknown; water source was surrounding swamps; advantages of location were easy hunting of jungle animals and availability of land for farming; disadvantages of location were difficulty of creating farm fields and roads to get from one place to another.

Chapter Test   **A. 1.** a   **2.** c   **3.** c   **4.** a   **5.** a

B. 6. One Earthquake was leader of a village that was defeated by San José Mogote. The portrait was placed in the victorious village's temple to show their victory and to warn others against making war against them.
7. They had safety in numbers, they could shop easily, and finding a mate was easier.
8. The Maya of Mirador built their roads by hand, raising them above the level of the swamps.
C. Students' essays will vary, but should include details about the challenges the people faced and their solutions to the problems.

CHAPTER 4

Blackline Master

Apartment compounds: group dwellings size of a city block, separated into three or four aparments, built of adobe and concrete, windowless rooms, sunny courtyards; *Moon Pyramid:* statue of Goddess of Standing Water at base, beginning of Avenue of the Dead; *Avenue of the Dead:* stretched for more than two miles, lined by temples and palaces; *Sun Pyramid:* terraced pyramid that matches the shape of a mountain behind it; *Citadel:* vast temple dedicated to Feathered Serpent god, 200 warriors buried inside as sacrifices; *Great Compound:* marketplace with traders from the Gulf Coast to the Pacific Coast; *Pottery workshop:* hundreds of women molding clay vessels.

Chapter Test   **A. 1.** d   **2.** b   **3.** a   **4.** b   **5.** c

B. 6. The comfortable lodgings were a great improvement over the one-room thatched huts that most Mesoamericans lived in.
7. The pilgrim would have been used to such stories. He would believe that people had to feed the gods on occasion.
8. The traders exhibited their wares in the Great Compound for people to buy.
C. Students' essays will vary but should include details of how the Maya wrote about the city, traded with it, and copied its architecture, as well as the tourists who still come to climb the Sun Pyramid.

CHAPTER 5

Blackline Master

11: one dot and two bars; 12: two dots and two bars; 13: three dots and two bars; 14: four dots and two bars. The number in the place value chart is 423: one 400, one 20, and three ones.

Chapter Test   **A. 1.** c   **2.** a   **3.** d   **4.** a   **5.** a

B. 6. K'uk' Mo' went to Teotihuacan to undergo some sort of ritual. It was possible that the priests crowned him king of Copán
7. Astronomy was important so they could keep a calendar, which told them important dates for agriculture, battle, and other things.
8. The *Popol Vuh* describes how the Maya gods created the world and people and traces the line of one royal family.
C. Students' essays will vary but should include details about how K'inich Yax K'uk' Mo'gained power in the city and other details from Altar Q.

CHAPTER 6

Blackline Master

Have students play the game of *bul* using the gameboard and the suggested game pieces.

Chapter Test   A. 1. a   2. c   3. a   4. b   5. d
B. 6. Only kings could pass on leadership, so Lady Sak K'uk' wouldn't be able to keep the dynasty going.
7. Her major concern was making sure that her son could pass on his kingship to his sons.
8. They were painted red, had multiple doors to let in sunshine, and had porches with high ceilings that gave a feeling of lightness.
C. Students' essays should give the details of how Lady Sak K'uk' was connected with the First Mother in the myths of the people of the city.

CHAPTER 7

Blackline Master

Reasons for fall of Maya kingdoms: drought ruined harvests; disease, possibly anemia, made life miserable; erosion of farmland would ruin harvests and cause starvation; greedy outsiders interrupted trade and blocked goods from getting to jungle cities; vandals attacked and destroyed the cities; people moved to a simpler life in unspoiled forests.

Chapter Test   A. 1. b   2. b   3. d   4. b   5. b
B. 6. They would have wanted to destroy the palace to destroy the city's power as a sacred place.
7. Their homes wouldn't have been burnt, so they could take away their belongings in several trips.
8. Her study of bones shows that the people suffered from anemia, but that the disease did not come from starvation, so she believes it came from a widespread infectious disease.
C. Students' essays should include details of what made life uncertain for the Maya in the lowland cities.

CHAPTER 8

Blackline Master

Embroidered cloaks, Chichén Itzá/Isla Cerritos, Slaves inland, Blocks of salt
Blocks of salt, Isla Cerritos/Cozumel, Slaves inland, Spiny oyster shells
Spiny oyster shells, Cozumel/Tabasco, Slaves inland, orange bowls
Have students show their work on the map.
Students' paragraphs should explain that Chichén Itzá was a good place for the traders to set up a marketplace because it was centrally located between their coastal ports.

Chapter Test   A. 1. a   2. a   3. d   4. b   5. c
B. 6. The warfare of the southern Maya cities interrupted trade, allowing the Putún Maya to step in and take over the trading cities.
7. They had to fight the residents to take over Chichén Itzá.
8. The Feathered Serpent god reveals himself on two days a year at sunrise, when the nine stepped levels of a pyramid cast a serpent-like shadow.
C. Students' essays should include details and examples from the chapter of how the trade web worked.

CHAPTER 9

Blackline Master

Craftsmen were highly skilled and famous: fact, yes. *Maize grew so big...*: myth. *A carving of a warrior...*: fact, yes. *Two pyramids were built...*: fact, yes. *Houses had porches and patios*: fact, yes. *Red, yellow, and brown...*: myth. *All the residents were rich*: myth. *Quetzalcoatl invented Toltec crafts*: myth. *Cacao plants were so plentiful...*: myth.
Students' paragraphs should tell about the differences in the size of Tula Chico and Tula Grande, as well as the peaceful nature of Tula Chico as opposed to the aggressive nature of Tula Grande.

Chapter Test   A. 1. c   2. c   3. a   4. d   5. b
B. 6. Wisdom and kindness to other humans were valued by TQ.
7. The society who lived in Tula Chico valued beauty, art, and craftsmanship. The society of Tula Grande was more interested in war and aggressive behavior.
8. They didn't forget Tula. They proudly claimed to be descendants of the Toltecs. Only men from the royal line could rule in the Valley of Mexico.
C. Students' essays should use the details of the myth of TQ to explain how facts turn into fantasy.

CHAPTER 10

Blackline Master

Order of events on the timeline: The god Mexi tells people of Aztlan to leave their homeland. Mexica found Tenochtitlan. Tenochtitlan becomes vassal of Tepanec kingdom. Tenochtitlan, Texcoco, and Tlacopan form Triple Alliance. Triple Alliance defeats Tepanec tyrants. Aztec Empire begins. Aztec Empire spreads throughout most of Mesoamerica. Itzcoatl rewrites history, makes laws favoring king and nobles, and starts a new religion. Spanish conquerors arrive.

Chapter Test   A. 1. c   2. a   3. a   4. b   5. c
B. 6. The Mexica came from Aztlan, a mythical place in northeastern Mexico. They supposedly told to migrate southward by the god Mexi.
7. The Mexica were the most active warriors, and so won most of the spoils from battle, making them more powerful than the other cities.
8. This myth told that, as god of the sun, Hummingbird on the Left needed a magic substance in human blood to be able to fight his way across the sky every day.
C. Students' essays should include details of how Itzcoatl rewrote history and destroyed the old history and those who taught it, started a new religion that called for massive human sacrifice, and burned all the existing histories of the Mexica.

CHAPTER 11

Blackline Master

1. This legend explains that Fifth Sun would not rise unless it had the hearts and blood of the other gods for his food and drink.
2. None of the creator gods was willing to be the sacrifice. Tecuciztecatl was supposed to be the sacrifice, but was afraid. Nanhuatzin was brave and threw himself into the fire. Seeing this, Tecuciztecatl got up his courage and threw himself into the fire, too.
3. A fire gives off heat and light like the sun does.

Chapter Test   A. 1. c   2. a   3. b   4. b   5. c
B. 6. Aztec children received training to be priests and priestesses, warriors, government workers, and farmers.
7. Aztec parents loved their children dearly, giving them attention and discipline.
8. Tenochtitlan's nobles chose Moctezuma II as emperor by themselves and didn't consult the nobles from the other cities.
C. Students' essays should include details of the education given to Aztec children.

CHAPTER 12

Blackline Master

Disease: Spaniards brought smallpox, to which the Aztecs had no immunity. The disease killed thousands of Aztecs. *Malintzin:* As Cortés's translator, she helped him gain allies and trick Moctezuma. *Aztec Subjects:* The subjects of the Aztecs did not like Aztec rule, and wanted to overthrow them. The Spaniards gave them that chance. *Military Might:* The Spaniards were able to defeat (or at least hold off) the Aztecs in battle. *Religious Beliefs:* When Cortés first arrived at Tenochtitlan, Moctezuma may have thought that he was a priest of the god TQ, who was supposed to come back in that year. *Treachery:* Cortés was able to capture Moctezuma by telling him lies.

Chapter Test   **A. 1.** a   **2.** b   **3.** b   **4.** d   **5.** b

B. 6. Tenochtitlan was larger, cleaner, and taller than any city in Europe. It seemed to float on the lake.
7. One tale says he was stoned to death by his own people. Another says that the Spaniards killed him by stabbing him with swords.
8. The key elements were native allies, luck, disease, and Malintzin.
C. Students' essays will vary but should emphasize that without Malintzin as interpreter and assistant in treachery, Cortés would never have been able to capture Moctezuma bloodlessly.

CHAPTER 13

Blackline Master

2. Atahualpa is angered, and challenges Huascar Inca for control.
3. Huascar Inca has Atahualpa captured.
4. Pizarro knew that the empire was in chaos and that Atahualpa was in Cajamarca.
5. DeSoto brags that the Spaniards can help Atahualpa become emperor.
6. Pizarro captures Atahualpa and massacres the Aztec warriors.
7. Pizarro imprisons Atahualpa for 20 days.
8. Atahualpa has his cell filled with gold and silver to try to win his freedom.
9. Pizarro kills Atahualpa.

Chapter Test   **A. 1.** c   **2.** d   **3.** b   **4.** a   **5.** d

B. 6. The emperor Huayna Capac had died, smallpox was infecting the people, and Atahualpa and Huascar Inca were fighting each other to become emperor.
7. Atahualpa had had him killed.
8. Manco Capac established a city deep in the Peruvian rainforests and periodically raided Spanish settlements.
C. Students' essays will vary but should note that Pizarro was driven to overcome great challenges for gold, and that even the gold that Atahualpa gave up was not enough to satisfy Pizarro.

CHAPTER 14

Blackline Master

Pacific Coast: Climate—dry, hot; Foods—seafood, maize, beans, squash. *Lake Titicaca:* Climate—cold, windy, dry; Foods—various crops. *Rainforests:* Climate—wet, warm; Foods: manioc root. *Puna:* Climate: cold, dry; Foods—potatoes, quinoa. Students' paragraphs should explain the interconnectedness of the people in the *ayllu*, no matter at which level they lived, and the way they shared their food supplies.

Chapter Test   **A. 1.** d   **2.** a   **3.** d   **4.** c   **5.** c

B. 6. He went from cool, wet highlands to hot, dry lowlands.
7. The *ayllu* system linked the seacoast, the highlands, Lake Titicaca, and the rainforests on the eastern side of the Andes.
8. The Inca emperors improved the ancient trails, making them roads.

C. Students' essays should include details about how an *ayllu* was formed, the people who made it up, the locations involved, and the foods that were shared.

CHAPTER 15

Blackline Master

Aspero: Food Supply—mussels, clams, sardines, anchovies. *Occupations of Residents:* fishing, building mounds. *Population:* unknown. *Size of Site:* 37 acres. *Number of Mounds:* 17. *Size of Mounds:* 13–32 feet high. *Oldest Mound:* 2857 BCE. *Largest Mound:* 32 feet high. *Unanswered Questions:* Was it a city? What was it used for? *Concerns of Archaeologists:* Not enough time to excavate the site. *Caral: Food Supply*—squash, beans, seafood. *Occupations of Residents:* farming, building mounds. *Population:* unknown. *Size of Site:* 160 acres. *Number of Mounds:* 6. *Size of Mounds:* one large, five smaller. *Oldest Mound:* 2750 BCE. *Largest Mound:* 5 stories high and the size of four football fields. *Unanswered Questions:* Was it a city? What was it used for? *Concerns of Archaeologists:* Exposed structures are crumbling.

Chapter Test   **A. 1.** c   **2.** b   **3.** d   **4.** a   **5.** b

B. 6. They built it by cutting rocks with stone tools and piling them up to make walls. Then they carried loose rubble in woven reed bags to fill in the mound. Then they plastered and painted the walls.
7. Scholars think they were used to house the people who worked on the mounds.
8. Evidence that a site is a city includes a population of 10,000 living and working at the site and doing different kinds of jobs.
C. Students' essays summarize the evidence found at Aspero and Caral and should state that more research and much more excavation needs to be done at these sites.

CHAPTER 16

Blackline Master

Art/Designs: Jaguar, snake, eagle, and feline designs found on Andean crafts. *Metalwork:* Craftspeople began to use alloys in their work. *Clay Pottery:* Pottery turned into artwork, with hand-shaped snakeheads and painted cats. *Musical Instruments:* In the highlands, conch-shell trumpets have been found. *New Textiles:* Weavers began to use wool, which held colors better. Also learned how to batik and tie-dye.
Alloy is a good word for the Andean world under the Chavín cult's influence because different beliefs, attitudes, and skills were combined to make a stronger, more unified civilization.

Chapter Test   **A. 1.** d   **2.** c   **3.** b   **4.** a   **5.** a

B. 6. Pilgrims came to Chavín to ask the oracle questions about the future.
7. The Chavín cult influenced Peruvian art, metalwork, music, pottery, and textiles.
8. The priests, artists, and builders of Chavín started a renaissance by giving new life to old designs, influencing Peruvians for centuries to come.
C. Students' essays should explain that the example of Chavín gives Peruvians the knowledge that there are things that unite them.

CHAPTER 17

Blackline Master

1. Tiwanaku was below three mountains on the southeastern side of Lake Titicaca. Wari was in a mountain valley 400 miles northeast of Tiwanaku.
2. The tallest structure in Tiwanaku was a 500-foot-tall mound. The tallest structures in Wari were two- or three-story apartment buildings.

3. At Tiwanaku, the most impressive works of art were the giant statues of Staff Gods. At Wari, the most impressive works of art were pots with images of Staff Gods on them.
4. Tiwanaku's claim to fame in farming was raised fields next to Lake Titicaca that were kept from freezing by water-filled ditches. Wari's claim to fame was stone vertical irrigation canals.
5. Tiwanaku grew to be 30 square miles with a population of 34,000. Wari's largest size and population are unknown.
6. Tiwanaku was abandoned in 1100 CE when the level of Lake Titicaca dropped and the crops withered. Wari was abandoned in 1100 CE for unknown reasons.
7. Answers will vary.
8. Tiwanaku's buildings and sculptures show the influence of the Chavín cult. Echoes of Tiwanaku can be seen in Wari's underground drains and images of the Staff Gods. Wari's technique of getting almost-free labor from its people in return for feasts was used throughout the Andes long after Wari fell.

Chapter Test   **A. 1.** c **2.** a **3.** b **4.** d **5.** a
B. 6. The Staff Gods of both places have similarities in their appearance.
7. Early settlement around Lake Titicaca was made possible by farming raised fields next to the lake. Ditches in the fields held water from the lake, which kept the crops from being damaged by frosts.
8. The people of Wari used an expanded *ayllu* system, with colonists being sent to other areas to grow food and then sharing it with the other communities.
C. Students' essays should include details from the chapter.

CHAPTER 18

Blackline Master

Owl-Head Beads: made by master goldsmiths; extremely small and detailed. *Innovations*: potters used molds to make copies of works; learned how to coat copper with gold; turned plain Chavín-style spouted bottles into sculptures. *Warrior Earrings*: three-dimensional warriors of turquoise and gold; set in a gold ear spool; delicate craftsmanship; miniature portraits of buried person. *Pottery*: painted figures seem almost alive; spouted bottles became lifelike sculptures of animals or people's heads. Students' conclusions about the Moche artists will vary, but should support the idea that they were wonderfully skilled and creative people.

Chapter Test   **A. 1.** d **2.** a **3.** b **4.** b **5.** b
B. 6. They built pyramids to ask the gods to keep drought, disease, and other bad luck away.
7. The painted figures almost seem alive, and the pots themselves are lifelike sculptures of animals and peoples' heads.
8. The Moche artists were so skilled because many nobles were asking for their work, so they had a lot of practice.
C. Students' essays will vary but should summarize Donnan's scholarly search through the themes of Moche artwork.

CHAPTER 19

Blackline Master

Possible scenes:
1. Chimú ruler moves capital and is punished and thrown into the Pacific Ocean.
2. Taycanamu comes from across the ocean.
3. Taycanamu leads the Chimú to the Moche Valley.
4. Taycanamu's son and grandson overpower people in valleys to the north and south.
5. The Chimú take over the old Moche irrigation canals and build new ones, turning the scorched desert into lush fields.
6. The Chimú build the city of Chan Chan.

Chapter Test   **A. 1.** c **2.** c **3.** b **4.** a **5.** c
B. 6. The myth tells about Chimú origins and their takeover of the Moche Valley. Real history tells about their takeover of the Moche Valley and what happened afterward.
7. The craftspeople could wear large earrings (a sign of nobility), marry among themselves, and bury their dead in private cemeteries.
8. Each new king had to conquer new territory to get enough tribute to build a new palace.
C. Students' essays will vary but should include an explanation that the king was buried in his palace.

CHAPTER 20

Blackline Master

1. Wari
2. people of the dry coastal valleys, ca. 750 CE
3. *ayllus*; Wari and earlier peoples
4. Wari
5. Tiwanaku
6. Wari
7. Chimú
8. Chimú

Chapter Test   **A. 1.** d **2.** a **3.** c **4.** a **5.** b
B. 6. The Inca Empire was known as the Land of Four Quarters because Pachacuti divided it into four quarters to make it easier to rule.
7. They had the people exchange their labor for free feasts.
8. The Inca improved on the *ayllu* system by improving the old warehouses and adding two sets of new warehouses: one set for crops from the emperor's fields, and one set for surpluses from the people's fields.
C. Students' essays should include details about how Pachacuti proclaimed that people before the Inca were savages and wrote an official history that gave all the credit for innovations to the Inca.

CHAPTER 21

Blackline Master

1. Americas   2. Europe   3. Americas   4. Both
5. Europe   6. Both   7. Europe   8. Americas   9. Both
10. Europe   11. Europe   12. Europe   13. Americas
14. Europe   15. Americas   16. Europe   17. Americas
18. Both   19. Both   20. Both

Chapter Test   **A. 1.** a **2.** b **3.** b **4.** b **5.** b
B. 6. Some girls were picked as "Chosen Women" and separated from their families to be trained to serve the emperor or to become human sacrifices.
7. People would rebel against the emperor's strict rules, such as royal approval for engagements and having to speak Quechua.
8. The *mitmaq* were displaced people, either rebellious people who were moved to other areas or the more willing people who replace the rebellious ones. There were so many because conquered people continued to defy the emperor.
C. Students' essays should include ideas from the Circle of Life sidebar on page 154 and explain that one child was sacrificed so that all the others could live.

WRAP-UP TEST

1. *Potatoes*: Andes mountains. *Chocolate*: Mexico. *Maize, squash, and beans*: Mexico. *Vertical irrigation*: Wari (Andes); used to bring water from high mountain springs to terraced fields. *Mounded-earth fields*: Lake Titicaca (Tiwanaku); used to irrigate fields and keep crops from freezing.

THE ANCIENT AMERICAN WORLD

2. *Teotihuacan:* central Mexico; Street of the Dead, pyramids, temples, palaces. *Palenque:* southern Highlands of Mexico; Temple of the Inscriptions. *Chichén Itzá:* Yucatan Peninsula; pyramids, Great Ballcourt, temples. *Tenochtitlan:* Valley of Mexico; pyramids, floating gardens, causeway, palace. *Chavín:* Andes mountain valley in northern Peru; temple, Lanzon. *Machu Picchu:* Andes Mountains south of Cuzco; mountaintop religious retreat, ceremonial stone column.
3. The Maya produced the most writing. Their writing was hieroglyphic. It can be seen on temples and other buildings. The longest example is on the Hieroglyphic Stairway at Copán.
4. The location of Chichén Itzá was a benefit to the Putún Maya because it was situated inland, an equal distance from important trade cities. The Putún used Chichén Itzá to connect trade with the seaports and highland cities in the Yucatán Peninsula.

The *ayulla* system began in the Andes, where crops varied widely because of the rugged terrain and dramatic changes in altitude. Different groups grew specific crops in their areas and traded them with other groups in other areas, so that all groups could get the food they needed to survive.
5. Their hieroglyphs are important because they tell of a long, detailed history. They created a calendar to keep track of important dates, such as when to plant crops and when to go into battle. Most of their cities were abandoned for various reasons: invasion, disease, lack of food, changes in trade patterns.
6. The Aztec Empire controlled most of Mesoamerica from its capital at Tenochtitlan. The Triple Alliance was an alliance amongst three cities—Tenochtitlan, Texcoco, and Tlacopan—to defeat the city that was oppressing them and rule the Valley of Mexico. Aztec women kept their mother's surname, could inherit land and property, and bring cases against other people in court. The souls of women who died in childbirth went to the highest heaven.
7. The Inca Empire was located in the Andes, with its capital at Cuzco. It stretched 3,500 miles along the coast of South America. It was divided into four quarters, with each quarter subdivided into 20 districts run by a local ruler who sent taxes to the emperor. The Inca kept records using *khipu*, knotted, multicolored ropes.
8. a. Aztec: The quote shows the basis for human sacrifice. **b.** Inca: The quote was part of Pachacuti's efforts to rewrite history and show he was the son of a god. **c.** Toltec: The quote tells of the sadness of the god TQ when his people sided with the god of war. **d.** Maya: The quote tells of the king who founded a long dynasty in Copán.
9. Students' paragraphs will vary but should explain how each ruler rewrote history to make himself seem godlike and destined to rule.
10. Malintzin, d; Lady S'ak K'uk', c; Moctezuma, b; Hernán Cortés, f; Francisco Pizarro, a; Atahualpa, g; Topiltzin Quetzalcoatl (TQ), h; Lord of Sipan, e. Students' explanations will vary.

ANSWERS FOR THE STUDENT STUDY GUIDE

CHAPTER 1

Cast of Characters
1. rain god
2. pottery jars

What Happened When?
around 5000 BCE: Mesoamericans started growing maize
16th century CE: Mesoamericans wrote codices describing tasks of men and women
17th century CE: group of Mesoamericans wrote the *Popol Vuh*
1970s: archaeologists started digging in the Valley of Oaxaca

Do the Math
6,970 years passed between 5000 BCE and 1970 CE.

Word Bank   1. archaeologist   2. hieroglyphics   3. Maya
4. hypothetical

Word Play   1. *Codex* comes from Latin.   2. *Codex* means "a manuscript book."

Critical Thinking   *Men's Tasks:* planted maize, hunted deer, shucked maize kernels from the cob, built houses, harvested maize, made tools from animal bones and obsidian

Women's Tasks: ground maize into cornmeal, cooked tortillas, spun plant fibers into thread, wove cloth, wove baskets, made clay storage jars

Comprehension   1. The Mesoamericans called maize, squash, and beans the "Three Sisters" because they grew so well together.
2. Women probably spent three to eight hours a day grinding corn.   3. Pot irrigation was drawing water from a well with a pot to water crops during droughts.

All Over the Map   Check students' work against map on page 15.

CHAPTER 2

Cast of Characters
Ann Cyphers: archaeologist who studies the Olmec
Matthew and Marion Stirling: archaeologists who have uncovered Olmec stone heads

What Happened When?
1200-600 BCE: dates when Olmec chiseled huge stone heads from basalt
as early as 1300 BCE: Mesoamericans were playing a rubber ball game
around 900 BCE: Olmec abandon San Lorenzo plateau
1990–1994: Ann Cyphers searched for Olmec artifacts
In 1862, 1925, 1940, and 1994, giant Olmec stone heads were found.
According to radiocarbon dating, the Olmec civilization is older. The year 900 BCE came first.

Word Bank   1. La Venta   2. achiote   3. Olmec   4. radiocarbon dating   5. Maya

Critical Thinking   Students' outlines should include details from the chapter.   1. Archaeologists think the Olmec got basalt from a volcanic mountain range 35 miles northwest of San Lorenzo.   2. The Olmec could have floated the rocks down the rivers, or they could have built sledges and hauled the stones to San Lorenzo.

Comprehension   A *realm* is a kingdom.   *Warrior Maiden:* Coyolxauhqui; moon   *God of Fire:* Xiuhtecuhtli; fire   *Smoking Mirror:* Tezcatlipoca; night, war   *Wind:* Ehecatl; wind   *God of Hell:* Mictlantecuhtli; death   *Storm God:* Tlaloc; rain   *Sun Disk:* Tonatiuh; sun   *Two God:* Ometeotl; creation   *Flower Lord:* Xochipilli; games, music   *Young Maize:* Xilonen; maize   *Hummingbird on the Left:* Huitzilopochtli; war, the sun

CHAPTER 3

Cast of Characters
Possible answers: fashionable, ambitious, foolish

What Happened When?
around 500 BCE: Zapotec abandon all their villages and move to Monte Albán
by 400 BCE: Monte Albán has more than 5,000 residents
about 200 CE: Monte Albán is a small kingdom with one ruler
1519 CE: Spaniards name Zapotec carvings *danzantes*
around 900 CE: Monte Albán's population drops to a few thousand
between 350 and 200 BCE: Maya build city of El Mirador
1926 CE: local workers discover El Mirador

Word Bank 1. El Mirador 2. macaws 3. stucco 4. *danzantes*

Word Play As an adjective, remote means "far away" or "in an isolated place." As a noun, it means "mechanism to activate machinery from a distance." Students' sentences will vary.

Critical Thinking The three chiefs lived in three arms of land that formed the Oaxaca valley, SO they could unite without giving up their power over their individual lands. Archaeologists have found mirrors, shell jewelry, and pottery buried in tombs, SO we know that skilled artists and craftspeople lived in Monte Albán. Together the three chiefs tripled their power, SO they controlled enough laborers to build the city. Outside invaders could not attack 20,000 people at once, SO city life was safer than country life. Monte Albán had no water supply, SO a large reservoir was built for storing water. People wanted to please the rain god with sacrificial blood, SO they moved to a sacred mountain where they would make their sacrifices.

Primary Source 1. One Earthquake had a misshapen head because his parents shaped it that way when he was born. 2. One Earthquake might have wanted to farm fertile fields around San José Mogote, or he decided to fight back against the larger city. 3. He probably set the slab in the doorsill so people would remember the victory and would know not to challenge him.

All Over the Map Have students show their work.

CHAPTER 4

Cast of Characters
1. The Storm God had goggles in place of eyes.
2. Warriors in the Storm God's service are also shown wearing goggles.
3. The statue of the Goddess of Standing Water was placed at the base of the Moon Pyramid.
4. the Feathered Serpent god

What Happened When?
50 BCE: first volcanic eruption in Valley of Mexico
400 CE: Teotihuacan has 125,000 residents
550 CE: vandals destroy temples in Teotihuacan
100 CE: construction starts on Teotihuacan
600 CE: much of Teotihuacan burns
1960s: archaeologists begin mapping site of Teotihuacan
1970s: archaeologists prepare a drawing of Teotihuacan

Word Bank 1. Moon Pyramid 2. Teotihuacan

Word Play Obsidian is hard, black, volcanic glass. It comes from a volcano.

Critical Thinking Students' outlines will vary but should include details from the chapter.

All Over the Map Check students' work against map on page 39.

CHAPTER 5

Cast of Characters
K'uk Mo' Ajaw: Maya noble who became king of Copán
Alfred Maudslay: archaeologist who worked in Copán and named Altar Q
David Stuart: epigrapher who deciphered glyphs on Altar Q

What Happened When?
426 CE: K'uk' Mo' Ajaw travels to Teotihuacan to be named king of Copán
1995: K'uk' Mo's bones found
end of 600s CE: height of Copán's power
1884–1886: Alfred Maudslay worked on Copán
1912: sculptures were astronomers discussing the stars.
1970s: sculptures were portraits of kings sitting in order of their rule.
1980s: each king was sitting on his name glyph
1985: first glyph is the one for K'uk' Mo'

Word Bank 1. epigraphers 2. Popol Vuh 3. Altar Q

Word Play 1. Middle English, Old English, Latin 2. Altars are used to make sacrifices or for worship.

Sequence of Events K'uk' Mo' went to a special location, probably in Teotihuacan, to undergo a ritual to become a king. Three days went by, and the name of K'uk' Mo' Ajaw was changed to K'inich Yax K'uk' Mo', to represent his promotion from lord to great sun. K'uk' Mo' was given special goggles to wear, made out of cut shell, and a shield decorated with the image of the War Serpent god. K'uk' Mo' left the city of the gods for the trip home—a difficult journey over rough and dangerous terrain. It took five months for K'uk' Mo' to walk from Teotihuacan to "three mountain place" (Copán). K'uk' Mo' found a wife, and they had a son. 1. Quetzal Macaw Lord; Great Sun Blue-Green Quetzal Macaw 2. Learned One 3. Storm God of Teotihuacan, War Serpent, snake-footed god

CHAPTER 6

Cast of Characters
Scroll Serpent: king of Bone, father of Lady Sak K'uk'
Lady Sak K'uk': daughter of King of Bone; became queen when he died
K'inich Janaab' Pakal I: son of Lady Sak K'uk'
Diego de Landa, Bernardino de Sahagún

What Happened When?
599 CE: Bone loses battle to Calakmul
611 CE: Calakmul attacks Bone again
612 CE: king of Bone dies; Lady Sak K'uk' makes herself queen
647 CE: Hieroglyphic stairway built in Bone
673 CE: Temple of Inscriptions built in Bone
July 29, 615 CE: Lady Sak K'uk' crowns her son king
1956: Pakal's tomb discovered
1990: Linda Schele discovers that glyph for Bone is similar to glyph for Lady Sak K'uk'

Word Bank 1. self-appointed 2. sarcophagus 3. mosaic

Word Play deity: god deify: to make someone into a god
deus, meaning "god"; deicide

Critical Thinking Students' outlines should included details from the chapter.

Comprehension 1. a 2. c 3. b 4. a 5. c

CHAPTER 7

Cast of Characters
Bol: scribe of the king of Aquateca
Takeshi Inomata: archaeologist who excavated the home of Bol
Rebecca Storey: anthropologist who theorized that an infectious disease caused anemia in the people of Aquateca

What Happened When?
early 800s CE: Aquatera invaded
800–900 CE: Maya cities of lowland abandoned
1993 CE: Takeshi Inomata excavates Bol's residence

Word Bank 1. anemia 2. alliance 3. clamber

THE ANCIENT AMERICAN WORLD

Word Play Anthropology means "the study of humans."

Critical Thinking   F; O; O; F; O; F; O; F   Invaders hoped to destroy Aquateca's power as a sacred place.

Summarizing   Drought: would have ruined harvests and caused hunger   Erosion: If Maya cut down too many trees to farm, soil would have been washed away.   Disease/Illness: Anemia or some other disease may have made life unbearable.   Interrupted Trade: Cities would have lost things they needed   War: Invaders may have destroyed cities   Alliances with Other Cities: If one city lost, its allies lost, too.   1. There are 6 million Maya-speaking people today.   2. There are 39 Maya languages today.   3. Many Maya still offer food and drink to the gods and make pottery painted with red designs.

CHAPTER 8

Cast of Characters

Christopher Columbus: Italian explorer who sailed to the Americas
Bartholomew Columbus: Christopher Columbus's brother
Ferdinand Columbus: Christopher Columbus's son

What Happened When?

1502: Columbus meets Maya traders
918 CE: Putún Maya arrive at Chichén Itzá
500 BCE: worship of Feathered Serpent god begins with Olmec

Word Bank   1. awnings   2. mantles   3. inricate

Critical Thinking   Putún Maya: Wore shoulder capes, had long hair with short bangs, in battle, carried round shields painted with dots, worshipped the Feathered Serpent god, hauled trade goods by canoe, Captain Serpent, were expert watermen and traders, won the battle for control of Chichén Itzá   Yucatan Maya: Captain Sun Disk, were farmers, hauled trade goods slowly overland on people's backs, resisted the takeover of Chichén Itzá, in battle, carried rectangular shields, worshipped the rain god, Chac   Both: Spoke Mayan

Sequence of Events   A Putún trader in Tabasco exchanges cacao pods for a shipment of bowls. The trader sails up the west coast of the Yucatán peninsula with the bowls. Hired porters and slaves haul the bowls inland to Chichén Itzá. The bowls are traded for a pile of embroidered cloaks. The trader and his crew head to Isla Cerritos, where the merchant trades the cloaks for blocks of salt. In Cozumel, the trader barters his salt for spiny oyster shells from the Pacific Ocean. The trader heads back home to Tabasco with the oyster shells to begin the circle of trade again.

All Over the Map   Check students' work against map on page 66.

CHAPTER 9

Cast of Characters

Fray Bernardino de Sahagún collected the information in the *Florentine Codex*. Topiltzin Quetzalcoatl was nicknamed TQ.

What Happened When?

16th century CE: native American dictated the legend of TQ to Bernardino de Sahagún
between 700–900 CE: Tula was built in central Mexico
1519 CE: Spaniards arrive in Mexico
around 1588: Florentine Codex arrives at a museum in Florence, Italy
by 950 CE: Tula Grande covered 5 square miles
shortly before 900 CE: original city of Tula burned
By 1150 CE, the city of Tula had grown to 60,000–80,000 people and had become more warlike.

Word Bank   1. penance   2. paradise   3. monumental

Word Play   To *summon* means "to call" or "to ask to appear."

Critical Thinking   Students' outlines will vary but should include details from the chapter.   Tula: Enemies burned it around 900 CE, Warriors in art wear the goggles of the Storm God, Ended around 1150 CE   Teotihuacan: Enemies partly burned it around 600 CE, Has apartment compounds, Ended in 900 CE   Both: Has two pyramids, Beautiful art and architecture   1. Archaeologists call the old Tula Tula Chico and the rebuilt part of Tula Tula Grande.   2. The descendants of the Toltecs were proud of themselves and their ancestors. They believed they were royalty, and that only they could rule the Valley of Mexico.

CHAPTER 10

Cast of Characters

Fray Diego Durán: recorded myths of the Mexica; came to Mexico at age 7; was fascinated by people of Tenochtitlan
Mexi: god of Mexica people; told them to leave Aztlán; told them to move to place where eagle makes a nest in a cactus
Itzcoatl: first emperor of Aztecs; rewrote history; started new religion
Serpent Woman: Itzcoatl's nephew; helped Itzcoatl rewrite history; rewrote story of Hummingbird on the Left

What Happened When?

about 1000 CE: Mexi tells Mexica to leave their homeland
by 1367 CE: Mexica build small kingdom at Tenochtitlan
1428 CE: Triple Alliance overthrows Tepanec
1521 CE: Aztecs conquered by Spaniards
1581 CE: Fray Diego Durán writes The History of the Indies of New Spain

Word Bank   1. vassals   2. tribute   3. multiple

Word Play   Lackey means "a person who is someone's servant or follower."

Cause and Effect   Children of commoners were not taught the new history in school, SO if any of them grew up and became priests and told the old history, the king labeled them evil carriers of false wisdom.   Only nobles could wear shoes and cotton clothing, SO any commoner who dared to dress well or even wear jewelry was put to death.   Serpent Woman created a new national religion that required massive human sacrifice, SO thousands of commoners were sacrificed to the god of the sun.   Itzcoatl worried that he and the nobility would have to share their wealth with the non-royal Mexica, SO he and Serpent Woman wrote a history that explained why only the king and royal families should be wealthy.

Making Inferences   1. Possible answer: Written lies may seem true to people who are told they are the truth and who don't know any different.   2. Propaganda means "ideas spread deliberately to further one's cause or damage another cause."

All Over the Map   Check students' work against map on page 81.

CHAPTER 11

Cast of Characters

Students' sentences about Fray Bernardino de Sahagún and Moctezuma II will vary but should include details from the chapter.

What Happened When?

1502 CE: inauguration of Moctezuma II as Aztec emperor; nobles of other Aztec cities become rebellious
1521 CE: Aztec Empire is conquered by Spaniards and Indian allies led by Hernán Cortés.

156   ANSWER KEY

Word Bank   1. gala   2. humiliation   3. forbidden

Word Play   A *seminary* is a school that trains students to be religious leaders.

Critical Thinking   Women: kept their mother's last name, cooked, gardened, wove cloth for trading, was considered a brave warrior for giving birth, was taught weaving and spinning, could inherit land and property   Men: warrior in the emperor's army, worked in the chinampas, was a stone worker, was a blacksmith, in battles, had to capture someone of their own rank or higher   Both: dedicated at the temple as an infant, had pierced ears   Students' outlines will vary but should include details from the chapter.

CHAPTER 12

Cast of Characters
Hernán Cortés: leader of Spaniards who conquered Aztec Empire
Bernal Díaz: Spanish soldier who wrote about the Aztec conquest
Malintzin: native woman who was Cortés's translator
Moctezuma II: last emperor of the Aztecs

What Happened When?
November 6, 1519 CE: Cortés leads Spaniards into mountains near Tenochtitlan
November 8, 1519 CE: Cortés leads Spaniards into Valley of Mexico
June 30, 1520 CE: "Night of Sorrow," when Spaniards tried to leave Tenochtitlan with their gold
August 1521 CE: Spaniards lay siege to Tenochtitlan
1584 CE: Bernal Díaz publishes *The True History of the Conquest of New Spain*

Word Bank   1. vaccine   2. mestizo   3. adobe

Word Play   Immunity means "having a resistance to a disease."

Sequence of Events   Just in case Cortés was the god Topiltzin Quetzalcoatl, Moctezuma gave the Spaniards a warm welcome. Cortés tricked Moctezuma with words and took him prisoner. As a prisoner, Moctezuma was treated politely and allowed to have his usual comforts. Cortés insisted that Moctezuma turn over his entire fortune as tribute to the Spanish king. Moctezuma was killed, either by Spaniards stabbing him, or by angry warriors throwing stones at him. The Spaniards fled the city with all the gold they could carry. Native people attacked the fleeing Spaniards at night, killing one third of the Spanish army.   1. They burned the city and starved the residents.   2. smallpox and influenza

Think About It   1. Malintzin was sold into slavery by her mother.   2. A tribe gave her to Cortés as a gift. She already knew two languages, and quickly learned Spanish and became Cortés's translator.   3. She hoped to escape slavery.   4. She walked in front of him when they went to meet Moctezuma.

CHAPTER 13

Cast of Characters
Huayna Capac: powerful emperor of Inca
Atahualpa: son of Huayna Capac; fought with Huascar Inca for control of empire
Guamán Poma: Inca writer who wrote *Letters to a King*, intended to tell the Spanish king about the treatment of the Inca people
Huascar Inca: son of Huayna Capac; fought with Atahualpa for control of empire
Francisco Pizarro: leader of Spaniards who conquered Aztec Empire
Hernando De Soto: one of Pizarro's soldiers who tricked Atahualpa into meeting Pizarro
Pedro de Cieza de León: Spanish writer who wrote *The Discovery and Conquest of Peru*
Manco Capac: last son of Huayna Capac who resisted Spanish rule

What Happened When?
1493: Huayna Capac becomes ruler of Inca Empire
1567-1615: Guamán Poma writes *Letters to a King*
November 15, 1532: Pizarro arrives in Cajamarca
1552: Pedro de Cieza de León writes *The Discovery and Conquest of Peru*

Word Bank   1. ascent   2. petite   3. blunder

Critical Thinking   The Spaniards in Cajamarca could see light from thousands of Inca campfires on the hillsides, SO they knew they were hugely outnumbered.   Spanish law required conquistadors to give native people a chance to accept Christianity before blood was shed, SO a friar with a cross and prayer book met Atahualpa and his procession.   He had no immunity against disease brought by the Europeans, SO Huayna Capac died of smallpox.   Atahualpa refused to accept Christianity, SO Pizarro felt justified in slaughtering the unarmed Inca.   Atahualpa believed the Spaniards' claim that they came in peace, SO his Inca warriors brought no weapons, and the armed Spaniards massacred 5,000 of them.

Comprehension   1. Pizarro learned to lie to the native people before attacking.   2. According to Inca rules, warriors wouldn't say they had come in peace and then attack.   3. Atahualpa hoped the Spaniards would let his people mummify his body so his soul wouldn't die, too.

All Over the Map   Compare students' work against map on page 101.

CHAPTER 14

Cast of Characters
Pedro de Cieza de León was adventurous, curious, and determined.

What Happened When?
January 9, 1534: Pedro de Cieza de León sees riches from the Inca Empire
March 1535: Cieza de León sets sail for South America
1541: Cieza de León begins writing Chronicle of Peru
1548: Cieza de León enters Peru
1549: Cieza de León reaches Lake Titicaca
1550: Cieza de León ends his travels in South America

Word Bank   1. manioc   2. condor

Sequence of Events   Cieza de León watched with astonishment as Spanish soldiers unloaded silver and gold from a ship that had been to South America. Cieza de León wanted to see South America for himself. Cieza de León's parents arranged the trip to South America for him. Cieza de León left Seville when he was 13 years old. Six years after Cieza de León landed in South America, he started writing his book about Peru.
1. They wanted to find a route to India and get piles of gold.
2. He did it without judging the South American people.
3. Lake Titicaca is the highest lake in the world.

Outline
Students' outlines should include details from the chapter.   1. llamas   2. They protest and refuse to move.

All Over the Map   Check students' work against map on page 106.

CHAPTER 15

Cast of Characters
Francisco Pizarro: conqueror of Aztec Empire who founded Lima, Peru
Ruth Shady: archaeologist who excavated Pirámide Mayor at Caral

What Happened When?
1. 2750 BCE
2. 2857 BCE
3. 1970s CE

Word Bank 1. colossal 2. corrosive 3. sunken

Word Play Vertical means "in an up-and-down direction." *Horizontal* means "going across." Have students show their drawings of vertical and horizontal lines.

Sequence of Events People cut rocks with stone tools. They piled up rocks to make walls around the base of the pyramid. They made small mesh bags from reeds and filled them with loose rubble. The builders eventually packed the inside walls with more than 7 million cubic feet of rock. They plastered the walls and painted them red.

Multiple Choice 1. c 2. b 3. a 4. a 5. b 6. b 7. The ruins, now exposed to wind and rain and pollution, are crumbling. 8. She hopes they will help the people of Peru remember that their history started long before the Spaniards arrived.

All Over the Map Check students' work against map on page 114.

CHAPTER 16

Cast of Characters
They suspect that it was used to convince people the Lanzón held supernatural powers.

What Happened When?
5000 BCE: coastal people weave first cotton cloth
2000 BCE: coastal and highland potters make first jars
1900 BCE: highland metalworkers hammer sheets of gold
400 BCE: Chavín cult begins to influence other areas
1976 CE: archaeologists test sound effects of sewer system in Chavín

Word Bank 1. alloy 2. batik

Word Play 1. Batik comes from Malay. 2. Possible pronunciations are buh-TEEK or BAT-ik.

Primary Source Students' outlines will vary but should include details from the chapter.

Comprehension 1. The religion at Chavín served to connect different Peruvian cultures because its art style and religious ideas influenced others. 2. The benefits of being a temple priest included being able to tell people what to do and receiving food from the pilgrims. 3. Peruvian craftspeople used jaguars, cats, and snakes in their designs.

CHAPTER 17

Cast of Characters
Pedro de Cieza de León's journal *The Incas* was published in 1553.

What Happened When?
1. 300 BCE
2. 1000 BCE
3. 1000 CE

Go Figure 2,000 years

Word Bank 1. metropolis 2. whither 3. grimacing

Word Play Tiahuanaco, Tihuanacu

Critical Thinking Tiwanaku: Sunken square plaza, the Bearded Statue, raised fields for crops Wari: multistory apartment buildings, terraced mountainside fields for crops, new walls built with ancient stones, evidence of feasts and parties, mountainside irrigation canals Both: Pottery with images of the Staff God, underground drains and channels

Sequence of Events The creator made the world but left it in darkness. The creator caused the sun and moon to emerge from an island in Lake Titicaca. The jealous sun threw ashes in the moon's brighter face and dimmed her light. The creator went to Tiwanaku and modeled animals and people out of clay. The creator painted clothes on the tribes of people and gave them food, language, and songs. The creator ordered the tribes of people to go into caves, lakes, and hills. The creator told the tribes to emerge and settle in their assigned places.

CHAPTER 18

Cast of Characters
Walter Alva: archaeologist who excavated Sipán
Christopher Donnan: interpreted findings at Sipán according to themes in Moche art

What Happened When?
100 CE: first stage of smallest period at Sipán completed
16th century CE: Pedro de Cieza de León visits Moche Valley; names people after their language, Mochica
1986 CE: looters are stopped from digging in pyramids, Walter Alva begins excavations

Word Bank 1. runt 2. goldsmith 3. confetti

Critical Thinking Students' outlines will vary but should include details from the chapter.

Cause and Effect Walter Alva had seen many owl-headed priests on Moche pottery, SO he knew that the Moche admired desert owls. They thought the warrior-priest must have been an important person, SO the archaeologists named him the "Lord of Sipán." The warrior-priest's bones weren't fractured, SO we know that he probably died a natural death. Looters were looking for gold to steal, SO they hacked many holes in the small pyramid. The excavators knew that the Moche usually lay their dead on their backs when they buried them, SO they knew that the crumpled skeleton with bent knees and arms had probably been sacrificed.

CHAPTER 19

Cast of Characters
Taycanamu: hero who led Chimú to Moche Valley
Allan Kolata: archaeologist who discovered three types of bricks in Chan Chan
Geoffrey Conrad: archaeologist who developed theory of split inheritance
Miguel Cabello: Spanish historian who wrote about the Chimú in 1586

What Happened When?
635 CE: flood destroys Cerro Blanco, capital of Moche Kingdom
900 CE: Chimú build city of Chan Chan
1465 CE: Chimú control 620 miles of farmland up and down Peruvian coast
1470 CE: Chimú become part of Inca Empire
1604 CE: Chimú storyteller recites origin myth to Spanish historian

Word Bank   1. anonymous   2. labyrinth   3. famine

Word Play   A *labyrinth* is a maze.

Critical Thinking   O; F; O; F; F; O; F; F
Split inheritance meant that each new king had to acquire enough tribute to build his own palace, because the palace of his predecessor was also a tomb.

Comprehension
1. Historians think that 10 kings ruled Chimor.
2. Visitors would be unsettled and intruders would be discouraged.
3. They have found droppings from the animals in those rooms.
4. They have found fine pottery, looms, fabric, and gold artwork.
5. They buried objects with the body so the person would have them in the afterlife.

All Over the Map   Check students' work against map on page 114.

CHAPTER 20

Cast of Characters
Pachacuti: Inca emperor who expanded the empire and rewrote its history
Topa Inca: son of Pachacuti; continued expansion of empire
Huayna Capac: son of Topa Inca; continued expansion of empire
Bernabé Cobo: Spanish priest who lived in Cuzco and wrote *History of the Inca Empire*

What Happened When?
1438 CE: Pachacuti defeats Chanca; becomes Inca emperor
1569 CE: Spanish writer records story of Pachacuti's victory
1460–1470 CE: Pachacuti builds Machu Picchu
1653 CE: Bernabé Cobo writes History of the Inca Empire
750 CE: khipu first used in coastal valleys of Peru
1471 CE: Pachacuti dies
1926 CE: khipu knot system deciphered

Word Bank   1. divind   2. slingshot   3. insignificant

Word Play   "Land of Four Quarters"

Critical Thinking   *Wari:* farming techniques and getting people to do labor in return for feasts   *Chavín and Tiwanaku:* claimed that Staff God was Inti   *ayllus:* the routes of the *ayllus,* improved by building roads and adding warehouses   *Chimú:* split inheritance and taking care of mummies   Students' outlines should include details from the chapter.

Comprehension   1. Pachacuti kept the sons of local rulers as hostages at Cuzco to make sure local rulers were honest.   2. The ancient Peruvians had no form of money.   3. Goods were moved quickly by runners along the Peruvian roads.

CHAPTER 21

Cast of Characters
Both men wrote about the details of life among the Inca people.

What Happened When?
1493: Huayna Capac becomes Inca emperor
1527: Huayna Capac dies

Word Bank   1. sibling   2. famished   3. pestilence

Critical Thinking   *Mama Kona:* spent four years away from their families, remained in the compound to teach young girls, cared for shrines, prepared festival foods, could never marry, could never speak to a man again   *Chosen Women:* lived in a compound with other girls and women, learned cooking, brewing chicha, spinning, weaving, and sewing, spent four years away from their families, after puberty, could be reclassified for sacrifice, became a Mama Kona after puberty   *Left-Out:* was expected to marry, at puberty, underwent a two-day fasting ritual followed by a feast, was given a grown-up name   If a Mama Kona was caught talking to a man, she was hung by her hair until she died.

Sequence of Events
The district commander placed the young men in a line facing the young women. A man pointed to his future bride, and she stood behind him. If two men wanted the same woman, the commander made the decision in the name of the emperor. The groom and his family visited the bride's home, where he placed a sandal on her foot. The bride gave the groom clothes and a gold or silver ornament. The bride's and groom's parents gave them gifts and advice. The wedding ended with a feast.

Group Together   When students have finished the activity, bring the class together for a large group discussion.

www.ingramcontent.com/pod-product-compliance
Lightning Source LLC
LaVergne TN
LVHW080116250326
834688LV00040B/1160